Four Queens

THE PROVENÇAL SISTERS
WHO RULED EUROPE

Nancy Goldstone

VIKING

VIKING
Published by the Penguin Group
Penguin Group (USA) Inc., 375 Hudson Street, New York, New York 10014, U.S.A.
Penguin Group (Canada), 90 Eglinton Avenue East, Suite 700, Toronto, Ontario,
Canada M4P 2Y3 (a division of Pearson Penguin Canada Inc.)
Penguin Books Ltd, 80 Strand, London WC2R 0RL, England
Penguin Ireland, 25 St. Stephen's Green, Dublin 2, Ireland (a division of Penguin Books Ltd)
Penguin Books Australia Ltd, 250 Camberwell Road, Camberwell, Victoria 3124, Australia
(a division of Pearson Australia Group Pty Ltd)
Penguin Books India Pvt Ltd, 11 Community Centre, Panchsheel Park,
New Delhi – 110 017, India
Penguin Group (NZ), 67 Apollo Drive, Mairangi Bay, Auckland 1311, New Zealand
(a division of Pearson New Zealand Ltd)
Penguin Books (South Africa) (Pty) Ltd, 24 Sturdee Avenue, Rosebank,
Johannesburg 2196, South Africa

Penguin Books Ltd, Registered Offices:
80 Strand, London WC2R 0RL, England

First published in 2007 by Viking Penguin,
a member of the Penguin Group (USA) Inc.

10 9 8 7 6 5 4 3 2 1

Copyright © Nancy Goldstone, 2007
All rights reserved

Illustration credits appear on page 323
Maps by Virginia Norey

ISBN 978-0-670-03843-5

Printed in the United States of America
Set in Bembo with Historical, Clairvaux, and Childs
Designed by Daniel Lagin

For Larry and Emily

CONTENTS

LIST OF MAPS

PREFACE

Paris, Christmas court, 1254 — Heralded by trumpeters
and the ringing of bells, a great procession, the most illustrious
of its day, made its way through the streets of the capital city.
At its head were not one but two kings—Louis IX, king of
France, and Henry III, king of England—accompanied by
their respective queens, Marguerite and Eleanor. All were on horseback, with stirrups and bridles of gold; the women's cloaks were
trimmed in ermine. Just behind rode Sanchia, countess of Cornwall,
wife of Richard, earl of Cornwall, perhaps the richest man in Europe. She was followed closely by the count of Provence, Charles of
Anjou, Louis's most powerful and ambitious vassal, and his wife,
Beatrice. A thousand knights, many from the countess of Cornwall's
retinue, "mounted on their best horses, with handsome trappings,
clad in rich clothes, that they might appear worthy of admiration in
the sight of the French," as one medieval chronicler marveled, trot-
ted smartly behind. Finally came the luggage carts bearing trunks
heaped with fine silks and ornaments of gold and silver, to be dispensed as Christmas gifts at the royal banquet that would crown the
festivities the following day.

The citizenry of Paris, also bedecked in its finest, was out in
force, jostling to get a glimpse of the luminaries, "the unusual novelty of the array causing great astonishment." Even the formidable
clerics at the University of Paris, the preeminent institution of learning in the thirteenth century, could not contain their curiosity and
had forsaken their disputations on Aristotle and Peter Lombard in

order to ogle the famous. A portion of the teaching masters' earnings had gone to purchase candles, holiday attire, and flowering branches to wave at Louis IX and his guests as they went by; they sang Christmas carols and strummed lutes as the nobility passed, mingling with the great mass of revelers lining the streets.

The cavalcade finally came to a halt at the Old Temple, a massive walled castle on the outskirts of the city, the only building large enough to accommodate a party of this magnitude—it "might well be considered a large army," the chronicler observed. The king of England, touched by the enthusiastic reception of the populace, let it be known that on the morrow he would feast not only the select company of invited nobility, but all the poor of Paris. He was taken at his word, and the hordes arrived the next morning at his doorstep. No one was turned away; there was roast meat and fish for all, and the wine was pronounced first-rate.

And then, finally, came the royal banquet itself, held in the great hall of the Old Temple. The floor had been freshly covered with braided rushes for the occasion and the walls hung with the shields and coats of arms of Europe's leading families, in keeping with the international motif. In addition to royalty, there were twenty-five dukes, eighteen countesses, twelve bishops, and countless knights of superior aristocratic lineage present: "Persons held in high reverence and respect, whose superiors it would be impossible, and whose equals even, it would be difficult to find in the world." No expense had been spared. The guests dined on fish and fowl, roast meat, and all manner of delicacies; the wine flowed freely.

The kings of England and France strove to outdo each other in graciousness. There was a small chivalric dispute over who should have the important center chair on the raised dais, with the king of England urging the distinguished seat on Louis IX, and Louis demurring in Henry III's favor; the king of France finally acceded to the honor reluctantly, murmuring as he took his place: "Would that everyone could obtain his right uninjured, but the pride of the French would not allow it." It was difficult to believe that the last time these two men had met had been ten years before on a battlefield.

In fact, this elite gathering represented a triumph of international diplomacy. Out of it would come the first face-to-face civilized conversation between the crowns of England and France. From this point on, until the death of both kings, distrust and uneasy truce would give way to sympathetic cooperation and a sturdy peace. Divisive issues of sovereignty, which had been used as excuses for invasion and armed conflict for over two hundred years, would now be settled by equitable negotiation. Neither kingdom would take advantage of civil unrest in the other to gain territory or influence. Indeed, the king and queen of England would find an ally—an ally!—in the crown of France when it was most needed.

The architects of this diplomatic coup were neither ambassadors nor statesmen. No king's counselor had a hand in it, no great knight nor influential baron. It was managed entirely by one family—a family of four sisters who had risen from near obscurity to become the most celebrated and powerful women of their time. Almost nothing of significance that occurred in western Europe during the period in which they lived was not influenced by the actions of this family. It is impossible to fully understand the underlying political motivations of the thirteenth century without them.

This is the story of four queens. Their names were Marguerite, Eleanor, Sanchia, and Beatrice of Provence.

A medieval chronicler at work.

Now will we . . . tell you of the King of France, who was now twenty years of age. And the queen had a mind that he should marry him; so he took to wife the eldest of the daughters of the Count of Provence, of whom there were four. And presently King Henry of England took the second; and Count Richard, his brother, who is now King of Germany, took the third; and the Count of Anjou, brother to the King of France, took the last, and he had the count-ship of Provence; for it is the custom of that country that the last child have all, and there be no male heir.

—Unnamed Chronicler of Reims,
1260

Four daughters had Count Raymond Berenger,
Each one of them a queen, thanks to Romeo,
This man of lowly birth, this pilgrim-soul.

—Dante Alighieri
The Divine Comedy: Paradise
Canto VI

CHAPTER I

THE LAND OF SONG

With my breath I draw toward me the air
that I feel coming from Provence;
everything that comes from there rejoices me,
so that when I hear good of it
I listen smiling,
and for every word demand a hundred:
so much it pleases me when I hear good of it.

For no one knows so sweet a country
as from the Rhône to Vence,
enclosed between the sea and the Durance,
and nowhere knows a joy so pure that it shines.

—Peire Vidal, troubadour, 1180–1206

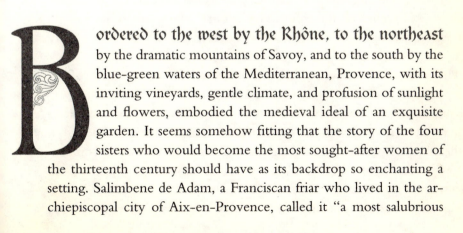

Bordered to the west by the Rhône, to the northeast by the dramatic mountains of Savoy, and to the south by the blue-green waters of the Mediterranean, Provence, with its inviting vineyards, gentle climate, and profusion of sunlight and flowers, embodied the medieval ideal of an exquisite garden. It seems somehow fitting that the story of the four sisters who would become the most sought-after women of the thirteenth century should have as its backdrop so enchanting a setting. Salimbene de Adam, a Franciscan friar who lived in the archiepiscopal city of Aix-en-Provence, called it "a most salubrious place with an abundance of grain." Its principal towns included Avignon and Arles, which bordered the Rhône and serviced the traders and travelers who flowed south with the current, for the river was the favored route to Marseille, which in turn served as a jumping-off point to the exotic and lucrative ports of Sicily, Cyprus, and Constantinople. Like much of the rest of Europe, the county of Provence—governed by a count, as a duchy was governed by a duke and a kingdom by a king—was sparsely populated and agrarian. Large tracts of countryside were still uninhabited, or dotted with small farms or the occasional château. The strongest of these was the castle at Tarascon, which stood large and reassuringly solid, its heavy stone towers dominating the landscape. The narrow, elongated windows of this citadel peered out like dark, mistrustful eyes, a trenchant reminder that, in the Middle Ages, even a garden needed protection.

The natural beauty of the landscape was of such potency that it inspired the voice of medieval culture—the troubadours, roving poets who set their words to music and played to the elegant audiences of the aristocracy. The troubadours were so ubiquitous to Provence, and so identified with its inhabitants and aesthetic, that the county was known throughout the rest of Europe as The Land of Song, and it was said by the chroniclers that Charlemagne himself had bequeathed Provence to the poets.

Marguerite, Eleanor, Sanchia, and Beatrice, as daughters of the count and countess of Provence, were steeped in the culture of the troubadours. It played as important a role in their upbringing as their lineage—indeed, it was their lineage. Their father, Raymond Berenger V, came from a long line of poets. His grandfather, Alfonso II, king of Aragon, was a highly respected troubadour whose verses were praised by Peire Vidal, the greatest poet of his day. Raymond Berenger V inherited his grandfather's talent and passion for literature, and embraced the troubadour culture. He wrote verses and his castle was always open to visiting poets and minstrels. His was a very literary court.

The troubadours were a cluster unto themselves, a microcosm of the society at large, and their poetry reflected the diversity of western European tastes and interests. They came from every class, career, and kingdom. Peers of the realm were troubadours, as were bakers' sons and serfs. Women, too, felt the allure of poetry and rambled around the south of France composing songs; they were called *trobairitz*. Although known today primarily as songwriters, they were also by turns journalists, political columnists, war correspondents, gossipmongers, actors, writers, directors; they were satirists, pageant artists, spin-doctors, and spies. For the savvy warrior, troubadours were as essential a part of his coterie as his lance bearers; how was the daring of one's exploits to be sung far and wide if there were no one present capable of composing a song? "It has been very justly remarked that Richard Coeur de Lion would never have had the brilliant reputation which he enjoyed in his time, if he had not patronized so many poets and minstrels," observed the French historian Fr. Funck-Brentano in his work *The National History of France in the Middle Ages*. Troubadours wrote the words and composed the music that other, lesser talents performed; they were higher on the social scale than the jongleurs, who were mimes and comics, or the minstrels with their red beards. A jongleur juggled or stood on his head, a minstrel could toss and catch apples with a pair of knives or make a dog walk on two legs, but a troubadour cast a spell over his audience, provoking laughter and tears at will, often by the sheer force of the music and the songwriter's charisma. Hundreds of troubadours roamed the south of France in the twelfth and thirteenth centuries, and 2,500 of their songs survive. From these we know what the people of the time thought and felt and saw, what they admired, what they despised, what they aspired to: in short, who they were.

The overwhelming predilection among the troubadours was for songs of love. These ranged from the prosaic—"I love her and cherish her so much," crooned Bernart De Ventadorn—to the practical: "God, let me live long enough to get my hands under her cloak!" exclaimed Gulhem de Peitieu. At the end of the twelfth century, a cleric named Andreas Capellanus, seeking to impress the Countess Marie of Champagne, the daughter of Eleanor of Aquitaine (who had herself raised promiscuity to an art form), had composed the definitive manual on the subject. Entitled *De Amore* (*On Love*), this treatise, written in a facetiously earnest tone, instructed the reader in every possible facet of lovemaking, including but not limited to medieval pickup lines ("When the divine Being fashioned you, he left himself no further tasks"); comebacks in the event of protestation ("Your objections to my bulging flabby legs and big feet are not securely grounded"); and chivalric delineation of what today would be called "rounding the bases": "Since ancient times, four separate stages of love have been distinguished. The first stage lies in allowing the suitor hope, the second in granting a kiss, the third in enjoyment of an embrace, and the fourth is consummated in the yielding of the whole person," Andreas wrote.

The whole concept of "courtly love," a highly idealized passion whereby the suitor suffers any degradation and performs any task demanded by a lady in order to win her affection, was the invention of a troubadour. The conceit had its genesis in the old King Arthur-Guinevere-Lancelot triangle. Courtly love was especially interesting because, according to the rules of chivalry, it could only take place between a married woman and someone other than her husband. Paradoxically, it was considered an ennobling passion. Knights were expected to be charming, courteous, gentle, and generous at court while under the spell of their one true love. (This last characteristic was especially important to the troubadours who relied entirely on their patron's hospitality for recompense for their efforts.) Moreover, courtly love was said to be responsible for augmenting a knight's physical strength and commitment. Just a glimpse of Guinevere could spur Lancelot on to feats of remarkable skill and bravery.

Despite the troubadours' influence, by all accounts, the sisters' mother, Beatrice of Savoy, countess of Provence, was very happy with her husband. Beatrice had married Raymond Berenger V in 1219, when he was fourteen and she twelve. Raymond Berenger V was the first count of Provence to actually live in Provence in more than a century—all his predecessors had preferred to stay in Aragon. During the summer months, when the weather was fine, he and Beatrice traveled around the county, meeting the barons and accepting their homage. The count was young and strong and athletic: he climbed the long eastern side of the Alps and visited villages unknown to his ancestors. In the winter months, he and Beatrice held court at their castle in Aix-en-Provence, or sometimes went south to Brignoles, which he had given to Beatrice as a wedding present.

Beatrice gave birth to twin sons in 1220, but they did not survive. Marguerite was born in 1221, when Beatrice was just fifteen years old. Eleanor came in 1223, followed by Sanchia in 1228, and finally the baby, Beatrice—four girls in ten years.

The children inherited their mother's loveliness. The renowned thirteenth-century English chronicler Matthew Paris, an eyewitness with no great love of foreigners, called Beatrice of Savoy "a woman of remarkable beauty." But she was also intelligent and capable. One of ten children, eight of whom were boys, Beatrice had learned at an early age to value strength and power. From her father, Thomas, a bellicose, domineering man who was happiest when making war on his neighbors, she had inherited a family ethos of solidarity at all cost. Thomas had ruled his large, unwieldy brood unconditionally and with an iron will. From their first breaths, Beatrice and all of her siblings had been taught to think first of the family's ambitions, and these were many.

The sisters' early education focused on learning to comport themselves as great ladies. They stood up straight while accompanying their parents to Mass and knew their prayers. For sport they went riding and hunting with falcons—falconry was very popular in the thirteenth century; the emperor had even written a book on it. They learned to dance and play chess. They listened to the stories of the troubadours and dreamed of Lancelot and Guinevere.

During this period, Marguerite and Eleanor, only two years apart, were each other's constant companion (Sanchia and Beatrice were too young to be interesting as playmates). Marguerite's temperament resembled her mother's. She was patient, capable, intelligent, and responsible, with a rigid and highly developed sense of fairness. Eleanor was more mercurial. As is often the case with second children, she both admired and competed with her accomplished older sister. The differences in their personalities were complementary, and the bonds these two established while growing up in Provence would survive into adulthood. Marguerite and Eleanor were always much closer to each other than they were to either Sanchia or Beatrice.

Theirs was a life of gaiety, affluence, and leisure. The court of Raymond Berenger V and Beatrice of Savoy was padded by elaborate manners and conspicuous expenditure. The count was an important man, and in the thirteenth century important men had a responsibility to live opulently. Plentiful food and gifts for guests were also the mark of true nobility. One troubadour outlined the menu of a meal that would do justice to his patron's status; the poet advised serving eighteen courses, including venison, wild boar, duck, capon, hens, fish, pastry, fruit, fritters, and spiced wine. Another troubadour reported that a viscount once used a shovel to dispense "priceless" pepper to a guest and built a bonfire of nuts rather than wood in order to prove that he was a real aristocrat and not a country bumpkin.

Raymond Berenger V and his family were very much a part of this culture of studied affluence. They entertained often and lavishly. "Count Raymond was a lord of gentle lineage . . . a wise and courteous lord was he, and of noble state and virtuous, and in his time did honorable deeds, and to this court came all gentle persons of Provence and of France and of Catalonia, by reason of his courtesy and noble estate," wrote the medieval chronicler Giovanni Villani. Among his many visitors were his wife's brothers.

The count kept a large retinue and rewarded his entourage with gifts of money and clothes. His daughters were dressed in gowns of rich red cloth, the sleeves long and tightly laced to their arms. Over this they might wear a jacket of green silk. White gloves protected their hands from the sun. Even as children, they had their hair, which they wore down around their shoulders (only married women put up their hair), dressed in jeweled combs.

They had no chores, they did no work. The nobility had by long custom set themselves as a class apart from and above the despised "villein" (peasantry), but Raymond Berenger of Provence took the notion a step further and established a series of laws institutionalizing the distance separating persons of quality from the rest of the county's inhabitants. Provençal knights were prohibited from farm work, including ploughing, digging, or carrying loads of wood or manure. A gentlewoman was defined by law as "one who went neither to the oven, nor to the wash-house, nor to the mill."

An excessive obsession with outward appearance, careless largesse, a disdain for physical labor—it was at precisely the time that Marguerite, Eleanor, Sanchia, and Beatrice were growing up that the nobility in France embarked consciously and deliberately on the path that six centuries later would lead directly to Robespierre and the guillotine.

If Raymond Berenger V's hospitality was prodigious, his income was not. The count was frequently in need of money to satisfy his household needs. Whenever his financial difficulties threatened to become embarrassing, Raymond Berenger turned to his most trusted adviser, Romeo de Villeneuve. Romeo was a judge of Catalonian descent whose father had been a loyal servant of Raymond Berenger's father. He was a shrewd administrator with an eye for undervalued assets and a knack for finance. One of Romeo's favorite borrowing techniques was to pledge one or more of the count's castles as security against future payments. The fact that he always pledged the same castles did not seem to bother anyone. "In a short time, by his industry and prudence, [Romeo] increased his master's revenue threefold," Villani observed.

There was an additional aspect of their childhood that set the sisters apart. The evidence is very strong that the daughters of the count and countess of Provence were literate. Customs in the south of France were different from those of the rest of Europe. There was precedence in France that, in the absence of a male heir, a woman could both inherit and administer her property. There were even women who acted as judges.

Raymond Berenger V had no male heir. He took seriously the Provençal tradition that allowed heads of households to will property to a daughter. Provence was a large county, the governing of which required literacy. As further evidence that all of the girls were trained in their native *langua d'oc* (vernacular southern French, the language of the troubadours) as children, there is the occasion much later, in 1256, when Beatrice of Savoy asked a doctor named Aldebrandino of Siena to compile all of the recent knowledge on pediatric medicine into a book so that she could take it to her daughters as a gift when she went to visit them in England and France.

But there was more to suggest that at least Marguerite and Eleanor knew their letters not only in the poet's *langua d'oc,* but in the scholar's Latin as well. Letters written in Latin when the sisters were older survive today. Matthew Paris would later sneer that Beatrice of Savoy referred to her daughters as "sons" in "a vulgar fashion"—but perhaps that was because she thought of them that way, had had them educated to rule as a son would rule, the way her brothers had been educated, and that would involve learning some Latin. Most telling of all is Marguerite's commissioning, when she was older, the composition of a children's book of simple first prayers in Latin, called a Psalter, specifically for girls. Psalters were the primers of the Middle Ages, the way young children learned to recognize letters and begin reading.

All of this, in combination with a father who penned verses, and a household steeped in the troubadour tradition, with regular concerts and performances and poets continually underfoot—the sisters from Provence could read and write.

Although their home was a contented one, the girls' situation was not without risk. The children themselves were too young to appreciate a growing danger of which their parents were only too aware. A war raged to the north and west, which threatened to spill over into Provence; it had its roots in a struggle between Church and state, king and count that would forever change the political landscape of southern France.

Thirteenth-century Europe inherited a world that was as stratified as it was unstable. There was a deep, universal respect, almost a reverence, for the past but this sentiment was paradoxically juxtaposed against a manifest and overwhelming opportunism that would shape the future. There were no lack of boundaries and laws and regulations in existence, but they only worked if they were enforced, and enforcement was by no means assured. Just the opposite. It often seemed as if the rules existed simply to be broken.

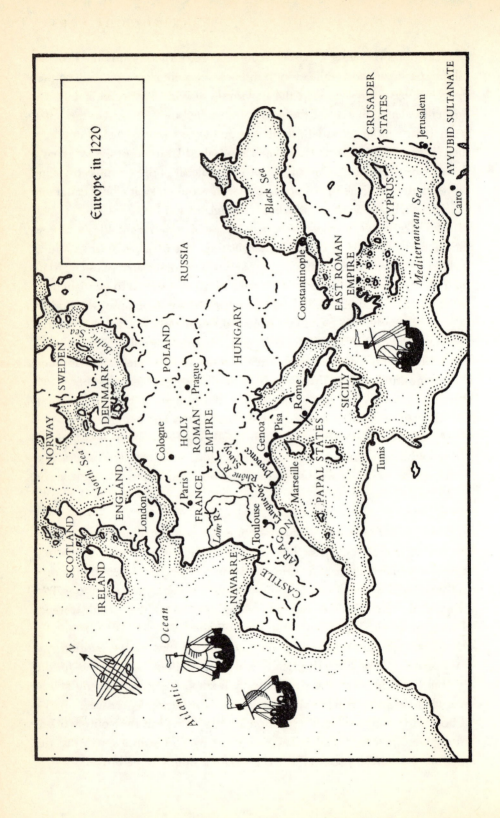

Europe in 1220

As might be expected under these conditions, power was a fluid and intensely personal concept. Each of the three great rulers of the time—the Holy Roman Emperor, the king of France, and the pope—were bent on enlarging their territory and authority at the expense of the other two. They were men who came to their positions with an inherited sense of imperial leadership and a devotion to an historic ideal. All of their efforts were focused on retrieving past glory. For the king of France, this meant a return to the ideal of Charlemagne, the greatest European king in memory, who four hundred years earlier had ruled an empire stretching from the Baltic to the Mediterranean. Similarly, the Holy Roman Emperor, whose dominions had so dwindled over the years that only Germany remained, aspired to be another Julius Caesar. The emperor (who also held the title of king of Sicily, a legacy from his family on his mother's side; his father had been German) was intent upon reclaiming the vast lands that had been Rome's a thousand years before, beginning with Italy. The pope's dreams were no less sweeping: he meant to hold not just spiritual but political sway over all of Christendom. In the Middle Ages, popes did not restrict their activities to the realm of religion but often engaged openly in territorial conquest, even going so far as to raise armies for this purpose. As the Church claimed authority over Rome and much of the surrounding area, the pope's ambitions came into direct conflict with the emperor's. The entire thirteenth century would be marked by their struggle.

Nobody in Europe questioned these goals. Great men were expected to have continental ambitions. Whether they would achieve those grandiose ambitions, or even come close to achieving them, depended on the political realities forged by the second order of stratification, the counts and marquis and dukes and other nobles who controlled the minor fiefdoms that nonetheless made up the real power base of Europe. This second tier of political aristocracy was driven by the desire for tangible, practical control of a specific region. Members of this group did not, as a rule, have great visions of world domination (although occasionally someone from the pack would try to organize a general revolt against the top tier, which would inevitably fail). What was important was to expand one's own territory at the expense of one's neighbors—or to foil a neighbor's plot to achieve the same against oneself. It was a game of relative numbers of households and knights, a town here, a castle there. This propensity for limited warfare was as much for pride, exercise, and a little excitement as it was for actual gain. Bertran de

Born, a troubadour who fought with Richard the Lion Heart, summed up this chivalric sensibility eloquently:

> *I tell you there is not so much savor*
> *in eating or drinking or sleeping,*
> *as when I hear them scream, "There they are! Let's get them!"*
> *on both sides, and I hear riderless*
> *horses in the shadows, neighing,*
> *and I hear them scream "Help! Help!"*
> *and I see them fall among the ditches,*
> *little men and great men on the grass,*
> *and I see fixed in the flanks of the corpses*
> *stumps of lances with silken streamers.*
> *Barons, pawn your castles,*
> *and your villages, and your cities*
> *before you stop making war on one another.*

The noblemen who controlled these fiefdoms operated in a netherworld of dependence and autonomy that today we would call spheres of influence. In theory, every count, duke, or marquis owed his land, position, and authority to the good offices of either a king or the emperor and as a result owed fealty to that sovereign.

For example, Provence was a fief of the Holy Roman Empire, which made the count of Provence a vassal of the emperor. Technically, this meant that if the emperor needed troops to conduct a war, he could call on Raymond Berenger V to provide him with a contingent of knights and foot soldiers, and Raymond Berenger would be obliged to either honor this request or pay a fine in lieu of supplying the actual regiment. It was also understood that the count of Provence would not act openly against the wishes or ambitions of the emperor, or join in a conspiracy against the Holy Roman Empire, or otherwise engage in activities that would damage his interests. In exchange, the emperor graciously allowed the count autonomous rule of Provence, which meant he did not meddle in its internal affairs or extract large cash tributes. Also, he was obliged to call upon the resources of the empire to defend Raymond Berenger V against attack if at all possible.

That was the theory. In practice, it worked a little differently. In Raymond Berenger V's case, Provence was so far from the emperor's base of operations in Sicily, and so tangential to his interests, that the emperor could neither enforce a demand on the count nor come to his aid. Also, as Raymond Berenger V was a pious man, the pope had influence over his decisions and policies. Since the pope's dictates were almost always in direct conflict with those of the emperor, Raymond Berenger was often forced to choose between the two. Lastly, there were the count's own territorial ambitions to consider and those of his extremely aggressive neighbor, the count of Toulouse.

Raymond VI of Toulouse (not to be confused with the sisters' father, Raymond Berenger V—Raymond was a very popular name in this part of the world) was an extremely powerful nobleman. During Raymond Berenger V's childhood, the county of Toulouse had dominated the south of France from the Pyrenees to the Rhône, a region that at the time was known, because of the regional dialect, *langua d'oc,* as Languedoc. By contrast, the kingdom of France was at the time confined to Paris and its immediate environs. Consequently, Raymond VI of Toulouse oversaw more territory than the king of France, owned more castles, commanded more knights. Although technically a vassal of the French king, Raymond was actually more of a rival, the monarch of a second, shadow kingdom to the south of Paris. But he was also reckless. Secure in his wealth and sovereignty, Raymond flouted the rules of polite society. He had married and buried four wives, and his womanizing was legendary. His court was a hodgepodge of suspicious characters whose tastes were none too particular and whose moral inclinations suited those of the count.

Worse, the count of Toulouse tolerated the heretical religion of Catharism. The Cathars were a peaceful Catholic sect whose members did not believe in worldly riches or ambition, and who did not recognize the pope's authority as head of the Church on earth. For years, the papacy had tried with conspicuous failure to curb Raymond VI's excesses and convert his citizens back to orthodoxy. The situation reached a crisis in 1208 when Raymond murdered a visiting papal legate who had refused to consider rescinding the count's latest excommunication ban.

It was an audacious move even for a shadow king, and it provoked an equally audacious reprisal from the pope. The pontiff called for a crusade against Toulouse, the first time in the history of the Church that Christian Europe was roused to fight against Christian Europeans. To encourage participation in what was admittedly a unique enterprise, the pope announced that any of Raymond's territory conquered by a true Catholic would henceforth become the property of that Catholic.

The pope's offer of land-for-heretics was a powerful inducement, and the call was answered. An army of French knights led by the seasoned crusader Simon de Montfort assembled and began the march south.

Simon de Montfort was one of the most renowned figures of his day, and a pivotal actor in the drama that would result in French hegemony in the region. Simon was austere, honest, pious, faithful to his wife, abstemious, uncomplaining, and relentless. His only flaw of character seems to have been the unbridled, exuberant brutality with which he slaughtered those whose religious beliefs did not conform to his own. Here was a man who loved his work.

Led by Simon, the crusaders marched to Carcossonne and Béziers. There, hundreds of Cathars were killed, including dozens of families who had sought sanctuary in a church and who were burned to death when the crusaders set fire to it. The viscount of Carcossonne, a relative of Raymond VI's, was thrown into prison and died of mysterious causes three months later. Simon de Montfort got all of his land.

From then on, the crusade pursued its deadly course in the name of the French. Heretic killing was a warm-weather sport, and every summer Simon de Montfort's army would swell with new recruits from the north and more towns would be destroyed and more land would change hands. Thousands of innocent people—farmers, peasants, shopkeepers, burghers, men, women, children—perished in the flames, still clinging to their faith like larks to a divine song.

Finally, Simon de Montfort, that battle-scarred warrior, avenger of the one true faith and slaughterer of an entire population, was himself killed by a large rock emanating from a siege-engine. The king of France, Louis VIII, impressed by his effort and the lucrative territories that were passed on to the French crown upon his death, pledged to continue the crusade. Every summer, Louis would come down from Paris with an army, kill a few heretics, take a castle here and there, and leave. But when it came to war, Louis was no Simon. And just at this time, Raymond VI's son, Raymond VII, took over Toulouse upon his father's death. Raymond VII was young, strong, and dedicated to recovering his family's former eminence. He began to fight back.

Events came to a head in 1226 when Louis made his annual appearance in Languedoc. It was a hot, hellish summer and taking the castle he wanted proved surprisingly difficult. The king of France caught a fever from the unhealthy conditions in the camp—they lived with the rotting garbage and sewage—and died on the way home, leaving his wife and twelve-year-old son to rule France.

The death of the king provoked a war of succession. History records the victor in this contest as Louis IX, the king's eldest son. He was to go on to become one of the most powerful and respected rulers of the thirteenth century. Under his administration, formerly independent fiefdoms would be absorbed one by one, with slow and relentless efficiency, making France the dominant force in Europe. This would in turn exert enormous influence on the fortunes of all four sisters from Provence.

Louis IX did become king. But it was not he who was responsible for the ascendancy of France. It was his mother, Blanche of Castile, the White Queen.

CHAPTER II

THE WHITE QUEEN

Anyone who argues that women did not really rule or wield power during the Middle Ages is obviously unfamiliar with the career of Blanche of Castile, queen of France, the widow of Louis VIII. For a quarter century, "The White Queen" dominated French politics. In an age when statesmanship was the sharp point of a sword and diplomacy a siege-engine, Blanche was nimble and discreet. She built alliances where others erected barriers, and brought peace to regions that had previously known only war. She weathered catastrophe, betrayal, prejudice; faced down enemies; and established a network of spies that any modern intelligence agency might have envied. When she died in 1252, the boundaries of France nearly stretched to present-day limits, and the foundation had been laid for the great nation that was to come. England, by contrast, was imploding in civil war.

Her husband, Louis VIII, seems to have appreciated his wife's political acumen, because when he died, he left the management of France not to his most trusted advisers, but expressly and specifically to his widow. She was not regent—someone appointed to govern for a specific time period—but ruler in her own right until her son, Louis IX, came into his majority. In the Middle Ages, the difference between regent and ruler was a subtle but telling distinction. Regents, as appointed officials, did not claim the same moral, political, or social authority as a ruler. Blanche had been crowned queen of France three years earlier, when her husband had been crowned king, in a ceremony conducted by the archbishop of Reims. This meant that she, as well as he, was formally recognized by the Church as a member of the royal line. It was from this investiture that she derived her legitimacy as ruler.

Still, royal deaths were frequently regarded as opportunities for advancement by ambitious noblemen. And a woman left in charge was perceived as weak. The threat of rebellion was real.

Blanche moved quickly to identify and isolate her enemies. Within three weeks of her husband's death she arranged for twelve-year-old Louis to be crowned at the cathedral at Reims. Even though it was clear that Louis was too young to actually rule, an early coronation would signal to the people Blanche's determination to ensure that the rightful line of succession remain unbroken, adding further validity to her administration. Even on such short notice, it was to be a theatrical affair, designed to impress. Fair-haired, delicate Louis would make his entrance to the church mounted on a great stallion and wearing the traditional golden spurs. His coronation robe was of purple silk, embroidered all over with fleur-de-lis, the symbol of France. His crown and scepter were gold. Three hundred knights, swords drawn, escorted the holy oil that would be used to anoint the new king from its usual accommodation at the abbey of St. Rémy to Reims for the ceremony. The old archbishop of Reims, whose job it was to officiate at coronations, had just died, so the bishop of Soissons was recruited to take his place. The count of Boulogne would raise the sword of Charlemagne and lead the young king to the altar where he would kneel to the strains of the *Te Deum*. Then Louis would be seated on a throne draped in silk to receive the homage of his barons.

But of which barons? Blanche was devoted to her son, but that was not the only reason she had for crowning him quickly. The ceremony was meant to inspire loyalty and confidence, to invest Louis with the power of God and the blessing of the Church, but it also served as a litmus test of fealty. Blanche knew she could trust those who came and knelt at Louis's feet and put their hands between his. But if there was a conspiracy afoot, there would be absences and excuses. So she sent out invitations to all who owned fiefs of France and waited to see which barons would show up and which would not.

Her instinct proved accurate. A rebellion was brewing. "Now we come back to the barons, who mediated nought but evil against the Queen of France. Oft held they parliaments together and saw that there was none in France could do them hurt; for they saw that the king was young, and his brethren also, and they held the mother of small account," reported the Chronicler of Reims. The leaders of the revolt were Hugh of Lusignan, count of La Marche, and Peter, count of Brittany. Both men had strong ties to England. Hugh had married Isabella, formerly queen of England and mother of the present King Henry III. Peter, known as Mauclerc or "bad clerk," also held land and a title in England, and was in the process of getting a dispensation from the pope so that he could marry his daughter to Henry III. Neither attended Louis IX's coronation. Instead, they recruited a group of barons to challenge Blanche. According to Sir John, lord of Joinville, a contemporary of Louis IX's, the barons claimed: "Queen Blanche ought not to govern so great a thing as the kingdom of France, as it did not pertain to a woman to do such a thing."

The situation quickly turned so ominous that Blanche and Louis, who after the coronation had gone to tour the countryside just outside Paris with a small band of loyal knights, had to seek refuge in the castle of Montlhéry. They were only twenty miles south of Paris, but were not sure they could make it back without armed intervention.

There wasn't time to raise a regular army. Many of the strongest barons still loyal to the crown lived several days' riding away. All that was available to Blanche were the people of Paris and its environs, and it was to them she turned—specifically, to the bourgeoisie, a group disdained, at least in terms of military alliances, by most medieval rulers. The citizens of Paris rose to her call and came en masse, armed and unarmed. They lined the streets for miles and rescued the boy-king. Neither Blanche nor Louis ever forgot.

The clustering of the rebels convinced Blanche to take action, and she summoned Mauclerc to appear at court. When he did not, she put together an army of her own and in 1229 brought the battle to the count's castle of Bellême. She did not wait for summer, the customary time of war, but caught Mauclerc by surprise in the middle of January. Both she and Louis accompanied the soldiers. Concerned about the bitter cold, she had trees felled and firewood brought from miles around so that huge bonfires could provide warmth to her forces. Mauclerc, undermanned and unable to summon reinforcements, sued for peace.

But the queen knew that she had gained only a respite and not a victory. Peter Mauclerc and his ally the count of La Marche were not yet vanquished. A peace treaty with England was due to expire later in the year, and sometime after that Blanche knew the rebellious barons would try again. When they did, they would come with more force, more organization, and more resolve. Ultimately, the threat would come from the west, from England. To be ready for it, there could be no other distractions.

So Blanche took a good look at the crusade against Languedoc, which had already gone on so long and claimed so many lives, and decided that she could not afford to fight a two-front war. In the spring of 1229, the White Queen reversed the policy of her late husband and forced terms on Raymond VII of Toulouse in exchange for calling off the crusade. Raymond, faced with a twenty-year drain on his family's resources, and uncertain how much longer he could afford to hold out against so strong an enemy, capitulated. The conditions of his surrender were sweeping. He gave up all of the land conquered by Simon de Montfort to the crown of France, promised to work with inquisitors sent by the pope to root out heretics in the future, and agreed to fund a new school for the education of the orthodox, the University of Toulouse, for ten years. He also pledged to pay a large sum in reparation to the Church and to go on crusade. To guarantee his continued cooperation, Blanche arranged for Raymond's only child, Jeanne, to marry Louis's younger brother Alphonse of Poitiers. Under the terms of their agreement, known as the Treaty of Paris, only a child of this union could inherit Toulouse; otherwise the county came to the French crown.

Immediately after the signing of the Treaty of Paris, Blanche made her presence known in Languedoc. A battery of French knights and foot soldiers descended on Toulouse to strip the city of its trappings of independence. Walls were torn down and many of Raymond VII's castles were destroyed. A French minister reporting directly to Blanche took control of Carcossonne. It was a signal from the White Queen that she intended to hold Raymond of Toulouse to every one of his commitments. Toulouse was now officially allied with Paris, and the political landscape of the south of France was changed forever.

As repugnant as the terms of the Treaty of Paris were for Raymond VII, the agreement at least left him the ability to try to recoup his family's former dominance by expanding his domain to the east. This ambition brought the count of Toulouse into direct conflict with the count of Provence. For centuries, Raymond Berenger V's family had been engaged with Raymond VII of Toulouse's family in an on-again, off-again struggle for control over certain contested areas of Provence, including the lucrative port of Marseille. While the count of Toulouse had been busy defending his territory from the French, his ancestral claims to these territories had necessarily lain dormant.

With the signing of the Treaty of Paris, however, Raymond VII was once again free to begin planning a strike against Provence.

Raymond VII's alliance with the French monarchy thus caused the count of Provence and his principal adviser, Romeo de Villeneuve, serious concern. The balance of power in the region had shifted. The presence of French soldiers and a French seneschal in Carcossonne was especially disturbing. Perhaps Queen Blanche would support Raymond VII's claim on Marseille against that of Raymond Berenger. Perhaps she would provide her new ally with funds, or even an army, which the count of Toulouse could then use to threaten Provence itself.

As always, Romeo was charged with finding a way to neutralize the situation. Accordingly, he formulated a plan. But before he could act on it, England invaded France.

The attack by England was again the work of Mauclerc. Blanche had been correct in assuming that she had bought time but not peace when she had besieged the count of Brittany the previous winter. By August 1229, Mauclerc was in England at the court of Henry III, assuring the English king that the barons of Brittany and Normandy would rise up against Louis IX and join forces with England if only Henry would cross the Channel with an army. Henry's mother, Isabella, and her husband, the count of La Marche would assist them, said Mauclerc, and he himself was willing to do homage to Henry for Brittany.

This was precisely what Henry III wanted to hear; the recovery of Normandy, lost by his father, King John, was one of his most cherished ambitions. Henry was twenty-three years old and had only just come into his majority two years before. He was chafing under the restrictions imposed by his counselors, who, familiar with the king's character and perhaps doubting his ability to inspire an insurrection against France, advised caution. Henry overruled them and ordered a fleet assembled at Portsmouth for an October launch, but his own barons stalled and it wasn't ready until the following Easter.

By that time, Blanche had made peace with Raymond of Toulouse and her southeastern flank was secure. Aware through spies of Mauclerc's visit to England and the rekindling of his ambitions, she offered generous terms to Hugh of La Marche and his wife, including a payment of ten thousand livres tournois and the promise of a marriage between the count and countess of

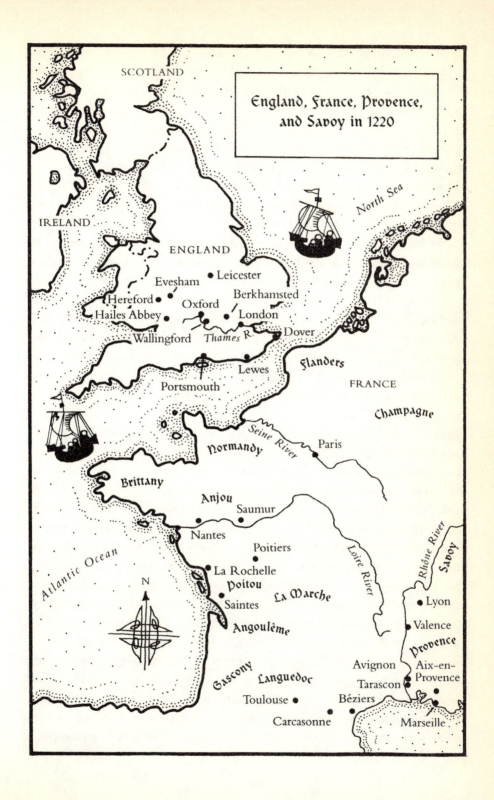

SCOTLAND

England, France, Provence, and Savoy in 1220

North Sea

IRELAND

ENGLAND

Evesham • Leicester

Hereford Berkhamsted
Oxford
Hailes Abbey London
Wallingford Thames R. Dover

Lewes Flanders

Portsmouth FRANCE

Champagne

Seine River Paris

Normandy

Brittany

Anjou
Saumur

Nantes

Poitiers

La Rochelle Loire River Rhône River Savoy
Poitou

Atlantic Ocean N Saintes La Marche

Angoulême Lyon

Valence

Provence

Avignon Aix-en-
Provence
Gascony Languedoc Tarascon

Toulouse Béziers

Carcasonne Marseille

La Marche's eldest son and one of her daughters. The result of these nego-
tiations was the defection of the count of La Marche from Mauclerc and the
English camp. The king of England could not hold his own mother against
Blanche.

Meanwhile, the English army had landed and Henry III, accompanied
by his brother Richard, Earl of Cornwall, made camp at Nantes, in the
southeast corner of Brittany. Here the king fully justified his advisers' opinion of his military capabilities. Henry and Richard stayed in Nantes through
July, doing nothing, wasting time, money, and resources. They might have
been on holiday. Finally, the English knights made a cautionary, circuitous
amble through Poitou, being very careful to avoid any encounter with Louis
and Blanche, who had raised an army of loyal barons, and were waiting to
fight. Instead, they captured a small castle that nobody else wanted, then
returned to Nantes. By that time, both Henry and Richard were ill from the
food and inactivity; in October they went back to England. Disgusted, even
Mauclerc gave up. In 1234, he allied himself firmly with Louis and Blanche,
and for the rest of his life remained loyal.

Blanche had won. She had saved the crown of France for her son.

Now she just needed an heir to succeed him.

Romeo de Villeneuve was an intensely practical man. The French queen's
victory over Mauclerc and the English king was impressive. She had become
too powerful to ignore. It was necessary for the count of Provence to find a
way to establish a tie with France separate and distinct from that negotiated
with Toulouse. It was too dangerous to have Raymond VII as Blanche's only
ally in the region. The difficulty was in arranging a concord that assured
Provençal independence of France. It wouldn't do to be swallowed up by
one's new sovereign as Raymond of Toulouse had been.

The answer, of course, was a royal marriage. A marriage with a prince
of France meant a uniting of equals; an alliance without fear of hegemony.
Here Romeo had hope. Jeanne of Toulouse, the daughter of Raymond VII,
had become engaged to a son of Blanche of Castile. Why should not the
daughter of Raymond Berenger V of Provence marry into the royal family
as well? It was true that the count of Toulouse was much wealthier and
more powerful than the count of Provence, but he was not regal in the strict
sense of kingship. Sons of queens had married daughters of counts before.
There was even the possibility that Blanche might consider one of Raymond Berenger's daughters a suitable wife for Louis IX himself. Graceful,

cultured Marguerite was almost twelve: just the right age for the nineteen-year-old French king. There would be the question of the dowry, of course—royal marriages did not come cheaply—but Romeo was sure that he could arrange the necessary financing.

There was no need to send a message to the effect that the count of Provence had four beautiful daughters, any one of whom might make an excellent bride for Louis IX. All that needed to be done was to encourage the troubadours, who were always around anyway, with a hint supplemented by gifts and fine dinners and flattery and wine. Very soon, songs of praise for the elegance and style of the court of the count and countess of Provence, and the gentle manners, superior breeding, and piety of their four lovely unmarried daughters, began to spread across France, but especially to the royal court at Paris.

The hook was baited, but would the fish bite?

Marguerite

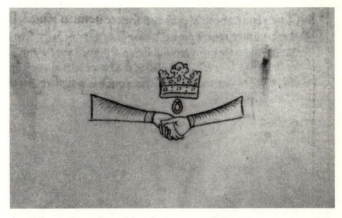

A royal marriage: clasped hands, crown, and ring.

CHAPTER III

A ROYAL WEDDING

I n the end, for all of Romeo's machinations, the count of
Provence owed the marriage of his eldest daughter, Marguerite,
not to the policies of his most trusted adviser, but to the actions of
his most reviled rival, Raymond VII, count of Toulouse.

By 1233, Raymond had come to regret his earlier treaty with
Blanche of Castile. The count discovered, once Toulouse was more
or less restored to him, and he was no longer in imminent danger
of being slaughtered by an opposing army, that he didn't really want
to yield authority to the inquisitors who flocked to Toulouse. Nor
did he care to listen to his bishop, nor to pay the Church the ten
thousand marks he'd promised in reparation, nor to go on crusade.
In short, the count found upon reflection that he did not wish to
adhere to *any* of the conditions of his surrender. Accordingly, he
began to protest both to Blanche and the pope, and to angle for advantage.

Blanche sent Giles of Flagy, a French knight and close confidante, to negotiate with Raymond and remind him of his responsibilities, but she knew even as she made the gesture that the count of
Toulouse was an unstable ally destined to cause her trouble in the
region. To secure Toulouse over the long term would require either
additional armed intervention tantamount to occupation (an expensive, not particularly attractive option), or the acquisition of a new,
reliable partner in the region as a counterweight to Toulouse. Blanche
discussed the matter at length with Giles before he left Paris, and the
result was that, just prior to his arrival in Toulouse, Giles made an

unexpected visit to Raymond Berenger V at his castle in Avignon for the purpose of personally inspecting the charms of his eldest daughter, Marguerite.

The Provençals knew why he had come, of course, and the entire household threw itself into the task of delighting the French queen's emissary. Giles was fêted nightly; troubadours composed new works for his entertainment; the jongleurs clowned; wine flowed (fully 80 percent of the inhabitants of Provence owned vineyards); and Provence lived up to its reputation as the garden of Europe. The count discussed politics and religion with his guest while the countess stressed the family's emphasis on personal piety. Twelve-year-old Marguerite, grand in her finest silks, was produced for Giles's inspection.

Giles left Provence for Toulouse, where Raymond VII, unaware of the diplomat's earlier visit and oblivious to the contrast made by the count of Provence's happy domestic circumstances as compared to his own, proceeded to lay out his grievances for arbitration. Raymond had been struggling with the Church for the right to control his legitimate inheritance and to reclaim his family's lost honor and status for over twenty years, and the long conflict had left its mark on him. An air of desperation hung about Raymond VII, desperation tinged with bravado. It was not an attractive combination. Giles listened but made no promises.

Upon his return to Paris, Giles was once again closeted with Blanche. His firsthand observations confirmed her suspicions. Most disturbing was Giles's disclosure that the count of Toulouse was applying to the pope for an annulment of his current marriage. It was an indication that Raymond VII wished to remarry and produce heirs. This would violate the clause in the treaty of 1229 which expressly stipulated that upon his death Toulouse would come to the French crown through his son-in-law Alphonse of Poitiers. Blanche had succeeded in wresting Toulouse from the count's family; she had no intention of giving it back.

The discussion then turned to Provence. Louis IX was already nineteen—late to be married. France needed an heir to the throne and Blanche needed a new ally. It was true that Raymond Berenger V had close ties to the Holy Roman Emperor Frederick II, but that could work to France's advantage. It was tempting to make an inroad into imperial territory. Also, the count of Provence would naturally resist any effort on the part of the count of Toulouse to expand his influence in the region. Blanche would gain a partner willing, even eager, to fight if necessary. There was the issue of the Provençal's inferior rank, of course, but there were ways around that.

But what of the prospective bride herself? What was she like? Giles had known the White Queen a long time and understood what she wanted to hear. Consequently, he did not speak of troubadours or gracious living, of pleasing manners or rich jewels or aristocratic style. He said, "A girl of pretty face but prettier faith."

The decision was made. Louis IX would wed Marguerite of Provence. The difference in rank would be redressed by a dowry of ten thousand silver marks. If the count of Provence was to have the opportunity to ally himself and his heirs with the royal family of France, the least he could do was to pay for the privilege.

The news of the French crown's proposal of marriage was greeted with great joy in Provence, followed almost immediately by acute consternation. A dowry of ten thousand silver marks! The sum was enormous. Raymond Berenger V did not have one thousand silver marks in ready cash, let alone ten. Moreover, the messengers indicated that Blanche was unyielding on this point. It looked as if the Provençals would have to regretfully decline the offer.

By this time, the entire family was involved, including two of the countess's elder brothers, Guillaume and Thomas of Savoy. The Savoyards were extremely conscious of the advantages of an alliance with the French crown and argued in favor of the match. Both men were rising forces within the Church and ambitious for power. They used their influence in favor of their niece. A strong suggestion was made to the archbishop of Aix to the effect that he might want to participate in the transaction. The archbishop agreed to front two thousand marks in silver in return for unspecified future favors.

With eight thousand marks still hanging in the balance, Romeo de Villeneuve came through with his customary creative solution. "Leave it to me, and do not grudge the cost, for if thou marryest the first well, thou wilt marry all the others the better for the sake of her kinship, and at less cost," he said. Through emissaries, Romeo arranged for the count to pledge the usual castles, including the fortress of Tarascon, in lieu of funds. Blanche found this compromise acceptable, and papers were drawn to legitimize the match.

The double ceremony—for Marguerite was to be married and crowned queen of France on consecutive days—took place in Sens in 1234. It was an affair of imposing dimensions. The archbishop of Sens himself, accompanied by a senior French ambassador, was dispatched to Provence to escort the bride to the altar. He and his entourage arrived in Aix in May and were treated as honored guests, the count bestowing costly gifts and presiding once again over nightly entertainments. Marguerite eventually left Provence on horseback in the company of a retinue that included the French envoys, her parents, her Savoyard uncles Guillaume and Thomas, her childhood nurse, some ladies-in-waiting, the archbishop of Aix (no doubt protecting his investment), and a host of courtiers and influential clergymen, the whole proceeded by six trumpeters and the family's favorite minstrel. They stopped first in Lyon on May 17 to sign the marriage contract. Here the count and countess of Provence made their farewells and turned back, leaving the future queen of France in the care of her worldly and ambitious uncles. The rest of the company journeyed on, arriving in Sens on May 26.

Preparations for the wedding had been progressing for weeks. Couriers bearing royal invitations had traversed the kingdom, delivering personal messages from Blanche to the most important families in France. Dignitaries from as far away as Castile and Flanders were invited. The streets of the quiet little cathedral town were clogged with richly dressed visitors and their luggage. Armed guards protected wagons and barges full of money and jewels. The lodging situation was so tight that the archbishop had to give up his own quarters to the royal family. Blanche and Louis, accompanied by Louis's younger brothers Alphonse and Robert, senior members of the court, personal servants, and a military escort consisting of two dozen crossbow men and twenty knights, were already ensconced in their apartments when Marguerite's entourage appeared on the horizon.

Louis and a small party of French nobles, including his brothers, rode out to meet her. He was now twenty to her thirteen. The Franciscan chronicler Salimbene de Adam, who knew Louis, described him as "slender and delicate, tall . . . [with] a very pleasing face and an angelic expression." His blond hair fell to his shoulders, as was the style in France. He was so resplendent in the decorative gold mail of the new knight's costume his mother had given him for the occasion—even his horse's bridle and stirrups were of gold—that the crowds in the street drew back in awe to let him pass.

He arrived bearing gifts, anticipated, organized, and purchased by Blanche. There were new saddles for Marguerite's horse (complete with her own golden bridle), as well as a heavy golden goblet to be used during the wedding ceremony. There was also a golden tiara, diamond-and-ruby studded jewelry, and, most magnificent, a sable cloak adorned with fifteen gold buttons.

The prince, lithe and athletic, surrounded by minions waving banners and flags embroidered with the traditional fleur-de-lis of France, bowed and presented Marguerite with this treasure trove of furs, gold, and jewels. It was the first time Marguerite met the man who would be her husband. He made a very good first impression.

Marguerite was married on May 27 and the next day crowned queen in St. Stephen's Cathedral, which was bedecked with magnificent tapestries for the occasion. She wore a robe trimmed with ermine over a dusty pink dress; on her head was a golden crown handwrought by the most accomplished jeweler in Paris. Afterward, she sat on a silken throne, beside her husband's, to receive the homage of the barons. One by one, all of the most important men in France—the counts of La Marche, Poitiers, Artois, Champagne, even her father's sworn enemy, the count of Toulouse—knelt before her and pledged their allegiance to the king of France and his new queen.

Three full days of feasting and merrymaking had been allotted to the festivities. Marguerite watched knights joust, jongleurs juggle, troubadours sing, and minstrels clown, all from the exclusive vantage point of a special seat built into a convenient garden. She shared her first sip of wine with her husband from her new marriage cup, and ate sumptuously at a banquet table. Trumpeters heralded each new course, and she was served by the first knights of the realm. Marguerite danced with her new husband and laughed at the minstrels, her own included.

And in the background, the figure of a woman, erect, forbidding, always watching, never smiling, holding secret meetings, giving orders in an undertone—Marguerite's new mother-in-law, Blanche of Castile.

Marguerite's first suspicion that, despite the flattering homage of the barons, her prerogatives as queen of France were decidedly limited, came as soon as the ceremonies were over. Her polished Savoyard uncles, who had fully expected to accompany their niece to the Parisian court, were summarily dismissed by her mother-in-law at Fontainebleau with polite expressions of appreciation and the gift of a draft for 236 livres drawn on the royal bankers for their trouble. The same thing happened to Marguerite's Provençal ladies-in-waiting and her nurse. Even her minstrel got ten livres to go home.

The abrupt decampment of her friends and relatives at Fontainebleau, while unusual, was not remarkable, and Marguerite consoled herself with the intoxication of her new position and the excitement of the journey to Paris. All along the route, people lined the roads to get a glimpse of the king and his bride, and to ask for favors and blessings. When the royal party reached the capital on June 9, nearly all of the populace turned out to welcome her. As she was aristocratic, lovely, and exceedingly well dressed, "the young queen" was immediately admired by her new subjects.

Louis, too, approved of his new wife. Marguerite had been warned while still in Provence that the king of France was very religious, so she was prepared when he took her aside soon after the wedding ceremony to explain to her that the marriage could not be consummated until each of them had spent three full nights in devotions and prayer. In fact, Louis spent his wedding night worshipping alone in his bedroom and on the succeeding nights he and Marguerite recited their prayers together. She went with him to Mass every morning, heard the Hours recited daily, and was assigned her own confessor, William of Saint Pathus, in whom she confided the details of her life. Louis was evidently impressed with the sincerity of her devotion and warmed to her quickly. It was charming to have so young and eager a companion. A stranger in Paris, Marguerite was completely reliant upon her husband's company. She looked up to and deferred to him, but she also amused and enchanted him. Marguerite came from a much more refined household than did Louis. The presence of four daughters and no sons meant that a decidedly feminine influence prevailed at the court in Provence. Although Louis had a sister, Isabella, she was only nine at the time of Marguerite's marriage, and the atmosphere at the Parisian court was dominated by Louis and his three brothers, two of whom, Robert and Alphonse, were teenagers. Their manners were much rougher than those to which the young queen was accustomed. No one at Marguerite's mother's court would ever have thought of expressing displeasure by having his valet pour a bucket of curdled milk on a visitor, as had Louis's brother Robert of Artois when the grossly overweight dandy Count Thibaud of Champagne, resplendent in a richly ornate and expensive new court costume, came to pay his respects to Louis and Blanche. Marguerite had been drilled in the graceful arts since infancy, and consequently knew how to please. Captivated, Louis began to spend more and more time with her.

For her part, Marguerite adored her handsome new husband, who spoke so beautifully and treated her with such gentleness and kindness. They toured Paris together and Louis pointed out all of the improvements begun during the reign of his grandfather, Philip Augustus, which he and his mother were in the act of completing. With justifiable pride, he explained all of the Crown's advancements in the city's security, directing his wife's attention to the great wall surrounding Paris. This first line of defense had been envisioned by Philip Augustus but the undertaking was so immense that the work was still progressing. At least the Louvre, the great stone fortress at the edge of the Seine, easily distinguished by its formidable square center tower, which housed an impregnable dungeon, was finished. In accordance with the traditional architecture of the period, the Louvre was flanked on either end by crenellated towers, resembling two hulking rooks standing guard in a chess game. It was from behind the crownlike top floors of these towers that the royal archers would crouch and shoot in case of attack. Louis and Marguerite did not live in the Louvre; that castle was for protection only. They and the rest of the royal family much preferred the comfortable Palais du Roi (today the Cité), which was located nearer to the center of thirteenth-century Paris.

These martial improvements were precautions against unknown future threats; luckily, it had been a long time since Paris had trembled at the approach of a siege-engine. The years of peace had produced a vibrant and thriving metropolis. Marguerite and her servants could inspect the goods and produce at the renowned open-air market at Les Halles, where the finest linen from Normandy and Reims was delivered each Saturday strapped to the backs of horses. These could then be made into sheets and other household items by drapers living near the Palais du Roi in the Ile de la Cité. Louis and Marguerite rode easily through the narrow streets, especially the main boulevards, which Philip Augustus, disgusted one rainy day in 1185 by the mud and the stink (people dumped all of their refuse and sewage in the streets), had had the foresight to begin paving. There was such an immediate and obvious improvement in travel and cleaning that Blanche and Louis were persevering in this modernity despite the expense. They had also issued a proclamation requiring that Parisian throughways be wide enough to allow two carts to cross in opposite directions. This edict was difficult to enforce because of the many two-story white plaster-and-timber houses lining the streets, and some roads were still only wide enough for a single rider to traverse.

Louis also introduced the young queen to the grand new cathedral, Notre Dame, parts of which were still under construction, and to some of the masters at the city's celebrated university, where the best minds in Europe were instructed in philosophy and theology. Louis was very interested in religious theory, sometimes listening to disputations on questions of scriptural ambiguity, sometimes seeking private counsel as to strict interpretation of Church doctrine. He was also drawn to the wave of asceticism sweeping over Europe, as personified by two new religious orders, the Dominicans and the Franciscans. These men, called friars, eschewed material wealth in favor of a life of pious poverty. Barefoot in all weather, dressed only in coarse robes of black or gray or brown, the Dominicans and Franciscans sought to emulate the simple life of Christ by walking the streets begging for sustenance. A reaction to the excesses of a Church whose cardinals, bishops, and priests lived grandly at the expense of their flocks, the friars' influence was on the rise; already two of the coveted twelve chairs in theology at the University of Paris were held by members of the new orders.

The austerity of the friars' life style appealed to Louis, whose own religious training mirrored the harsh, joyless, inflexible Catholicism of his Castilian mother. "Child as he was, she [Blanche] made him recite all the Hours, and listen to sermons on days of high festival. He always remembered how she would sometimes tell him that she would rather he were dead than guilty of committing a mortal sin," observed Joinville. Now in his twenties, this guilt-inducing early indoctrination was having its effect upon the king; Louis's piety was veering peculiarly toward the masochistic. He often did penance by washing the feet of the poor, and submitted to scourging on a regular basis.

Her husband's excessive piety did not bother Marguerite much in the beginning—after all, everybody was pious and the seriousness with which Louis took his devotion to God was rather a point in his favor. Besides, he wasn't like that when he was with her. With Marguerite, Louis was attentive and caring. Marguerite's principal complaint was that she did not get to see her husband often enough. They did not live together—her rooms were on the ground floor, near the public chambers, while he had the whole north wing of the Palais du Roi—but they could meet in the enclosed courtyard in the center of the palace, or take a walk through the surrounding rose gardens and orchards. She was happiest when they went riding together, or listened to music, or when Louis, who loved books, helped her with her Latin. (All of Blanche's children were trained in Latin from an early age. Isabella showed such a facility for the language that she used to correct her chaplains when they misspoke during Church service.) Whenever she could, Marguerite coaxed Louis away from what he was doing to be with her, and Louis frequently allowed himself to be persuaded.

Blanche observed Marguerite's pretty ways and her eldest son's growing attachment to his wife with steadily increasing resentment. For over thirty years, since she had first come to Paris as a girl in 1200 to marry Louis VIII,

Blanche's had been the prevailing feminine influence at the French court, the focus of masculine attention, the lily around which hummed the drones of chivalry. As recently as 1230 she had still been attractive enough to provoke the spiteful rumor that she was pregnant by the papal legate and had been required to show herself at court wearing only her shift to dispel the insinuation. Fat Thibaud, count of Champagne, who wrote romantic poetry and had been hopelessly in love with her for years, called her his "Lady" and sent her love songs:

> I know full well that my lady is loved by a hundred
> And more still . . . it provokes me to anger,
> But I love her more than any living man:
> Would to God I might clasp her lovely body . . .

> (To which a wit replied:

> Sir, you have done well
> To gaze on your beloved;
> Your fat and puffy belly
> Would prevent you reaching her.)

Blanche tolerated and even encouraged her overweight suitor's attentions since a besotted Thibaud could be relied upon to send a sizeable contingent of knights to buttress the White Queen's forces whenever she needed them. Also, Blanche found the count of Champagne's passion and devotion rather flattering, although after the curdled milk incident the volume of his poetic output dwindled significantly.

The presence of a magnetic ingénue, who showed every promise of developing into a glamorous sophisticate, changed this equation. No one looked at the queen mother when the charming *jeune fille* was around. From the day Marguerite set foot in Paris, Blanche's tenure as a sexual being ended. It was a consequence of her son's marriage that the older woman, who had prided herself on a rigorous evaluation of the match from every angle, had not considered, and she did not like it.

Even so, it might have been all right were it not for her eldest son's growing preference for his wife's company. Blanche could accept the diminution of her physical attractions to the world at large, but she could not bear the thought of a rival for her son's affection. She had procured Marguerite for him as one would a pedigreed mare—for breeding purposes only, not to ride. When it became clear that Louis's concept of wedlock was more comprehensive, and that she was in danger of having to share her son's attention, or, worse, be supplanted altogether, Blanche was moved to action.

And so began a carefully planned, long-term campaign against the young queen. Marguerite was to be watched carefully. She was not to be left alone with the king for any extended length of time. She was not to distract him from his responsibilities. A king should be attending to business, not spending his time walking in a garden with a girl. Blanche made a point of knowing where Marguerite was at all times, in order to separate her from her husband whenever possible. The queen mother's feelings in this matter were no secret. "Queen Blanche had treated Queen Marguerite so harshly that, in so far as she could help it, she had not allowed her son to be in his wife's company except when he went to sleep with her at night," Joinville wrote.

What was obvious to everyone at the French court was not lost on Marguerite. At first she found it difficult to believe that Louis would choose his mother over his wife. She knew that he wanted to be with her. Together, she and Louis searched for little ways to circumvent Blanche. They contrived to meet secretly, enlisting the aid of sympathetic courtiers and servants. This was easier to do when the court traveled, as it did frequently. Marguerite once confided to Joinville:

> The palace in which the young king and his wife had most liked to live was at Pontoise, because there the king's room was on an upper floor and the queen's room just below it. They had so arranged matters that they had managed to meet and talk together on a spiral staircase that led from one room to the other. They had also arranged that whenever the ushers saw Queen Blanche approaching her son's room they would knock on the door with their rods, and the king would run quickly up to his room so that his mother might find him there. Queen Marguerite's gentlemen of the bedchamber did the same when Queen Blanche was going to her daughter-in-law's room, so that she might find the young queen safely installed within.

But a king who hides from his mother makes an unlikely champion. Although Louis came into his majority with his marriage, he did not establish his own rule, or challenge his mother's authority in any way. The king, Joinville explained, acted "on the advice of the good mother at his side, whose counsels he always followed." Blanche continued to run the government, to make policy, answer correspondence, and receive reports from spies and field agents. Marguerite soon understood that Louis, however much he cared for her, could never bring himself to confront his mother, and consequently could offer no protection.

Her one defense against her mother-in-law's onslaught lay in fecundity. She had been brought to Paris to provide an heir to the throne. If she could conceive a son, Louis might be hers again. Marguerite could even hope that the responsibilities of fatherhood would produce that awakening of independence from his own parent that marriage to herself had failed to provoke. As mother of the heir to France, Marguerite's influence could no longer be swept aside; power would tilt away from Blanche, and the White Queen's loss would be the new queen's gain.

But it is difficult to conceive if you have to sneak around corners to see your husband. A year passed, then two, then three, and still the royal couple remained childless. There were rumors, as there always are in such cases, that Marguerite was barren, and that the marriage should be annulled.

It must have been terrible for a girl who was raised in the warmth of a happy, loving household to endure the loneliness and shame of her new situation. Later, looking back, Marguerite recounted a story to Joinville that offers a glimpse into her early despair:

> The King was once by his wife's side, at a time when she was in great danger of dying . . . Queen Blanche had come to her room, and taking the king by the hand, had said to him: "Come away; you're doing no good here." Queen Marguerite, seeing that the Queen Mother was taking the king away, had cried out: "Alas! Whether I live or die, you will not let me see my husband!" Then she had fainted, and they had all thought she was dead. The king, convinced that she was dying, had turned back; and with great difficulty they had brought her around.

Marguerite did not die, but she was forced to acquiesce. Her husband's passivity toward his mother ensured his wife's good behavior. She learned to observe and even anticipate her mother-in-law. Everyone reacts to adversity differently; Marguerite grew up.

Soon, however, the focus of the royal household was diverted from petty rivalries by the advent of a genuine crisis. Blanche's spies reported the conclusion of a secret alliance between rebellious barons to the west and a powerful outside enemy. Invasion plans had been drawn up and an army was being readied against the kingdom of France—and Marguerite's sister Eleanor was right in the thick of it.

Eleanor

The coronation of King Henry III.

CHAPTER IV

ROYAL RIVALS

The wisdom of Romeo de Villeneuve's observation that Marguerite's marriage to Louis IX was worth the expense because it would increase the desirability of the count of Provence's remaining daughters was appreciated by the girls' uncle Guillaume of Savoy. Third sons like Guillaume, who did not inherit fortunes from their fathers, were always on the lookout for advantageous situations. Being bishop-elect of Valence was adequate employment but Guillaume was convinced that he could do better. All he lacked was a powerful patron capable of dispensing largesse in return for sage advice and discreet service. Guillaume had hoped that the young and impressionable Louis IX could be cajoled into accepting this role, but he had been anticipated and prevented in this by the ever-watchful Blanche, who had a keen eye for aspiring parasites. But Marguerite was only one of four, and Guillaume, riding home from Fontainebleau with the White Queen's draft in his purse, reflected suddenly that his sprightly little niece Eleanor had just reached the interesting age of ten.

It is not clear exactly how Guillaume initiated the negotiation for Eleanor's marriage, but initiate it he did, as the majority of the correspondence concerning this matter was addressed to him. Probably he used his connections within the Church. It is testament to the bishop-elect of Valence's diplomatic skills that Marguerite had been married less than a year when a new envoy arrived in Provence, this time for the purpose of inspecting Eleanor. The envoy's name was

Richard le Gras. He came bearing greetings and protestations of respect and affection from Henry III, king of England.

Henry III was twenty-eight years old and very publicly engaged to another woman when he sent Richard le Gras to Provence to assess Eleanor's suitability. He had already been king of England for nearly twenty years, ever since his father, the reviled King John, had gorged himself on unripe peaches in a fit of pique and died from the resulting dysentery. In 1216, Henry had inherited an England in the midst of a civil war, and his side was losing. Crown Prince Louis of France (later Louis VIII, Blanche's husband) had invaded at the request of some rebellious barons and had succeeded in taking London and most of southeast England. Henry was knighted and crowned, not at Westminster as was his right, but at the abbey church in out-of-the-way Gloucester. The ceremony was a makeshift affair, attended by a handful of influential loyalists; there wasn't even a proper crown, his father having lost it along with the rest of the royal jewels when he tried to ford a river at the wrong spot and ended up drowning the luggage. The boy knelt, his mother provided a diadem from her own collection, and England had a new king. He was nine years old.

Rarely has a sovereign been as burdened by his parentage as was Henry III. His father's reign had been a nightmare. King John's talents ranged from ineptitude to outright malfeasance. He lost the extremely wealthy province of Normandy to the French early in his reign, which was a source of much unhappiness to those prominent English barons who had built expensive country houses there and were subsequently forced to give them up without compensation. Vindictive, suspicious to the point of paranoia, and unscrupulous, John murdered his teenaged nephew and political rival Arthur, had the body dumped into the river by some henchmen, and then covered up the crime by taking hostage the children of those who could betray his secret.

John's administration was so feckless that toward the end of his reign he suffered the ultimate indignity of having Magna Carta, a list of grievances and redresses, forced on him by his barons. He had fallen into the habit of helping himself to castles and legacies that were not his, so the majority of the more than sixty aristocratic privileges enunciated in Magna Carta dealt with property rights. The document spelled out an understanding between the crown and the baronage over correct procedure in the event of various cases of inheritance, marriage, indebtedness, fines, levies, fees, and other issues involving a transfer of assets. Some of the clauses were quite specific: "Neither we nor our bailiffs will take other people's timber for castles or other works of ours except with the agreement of him whose timber it is," read item number thirty-one. There was also some effort made to weed out governmental corruption and the more egregious examples of administrative incompetence. "We will not make justices, constables, sheriffs, or bailiffs save of such as know the law of the kingdom and mean to observe it well," the barons stated in item number forty-five. By far the most controversial of the remedies forwarded in this remarkable document was number sixty-one, a requirement that the king be guided in all matters by an advisory counsel composed of twenty-five of his most outspoken barons. John signed under duress and then, characteristically, reneged the following morning. Civil war ensued; the French were invited in, and John died ignominiously from his peaches.

Henry's mother, Isabella of Angoulême, was no better. She had married John in 1200, when she was twelve and John was thirty-four. He had stolen her away from one of his own vassals, Hugh of Lusignan, count of La Marche, to whom she had been legally betrothed, and Hugh did not appreciate the gesture. The count of La Marche retaliated by appealing to the French crown for assistance and instigating an armed revolt against his English overlord. The result was that John gained a pretty young wife but lost more of his territory to the French.

Isabella proceeded to give John five children, two boys and three girls; Henry was the eldest. Thinking perhaps to regain by diplomacy territory lost through romantic impetuosity, John tried to make amends to the count of La Marche by affiancing his eldest daughter, Joan, to Hugh's son, also called Hugh of Lusignan. But before the marriage could take place, John died and Henry became king.

The grim old men surrounding Henry, whose job it was to win a civil war and reinstate the monarchy, made it clear from the outset that there was no place in English politics for a foreign-born queen mother, so soon after Henry's coronation Isabella volunteered to escort six-year-old Joan to her intended. When mother and daughter arrived in Lusignan, however, Isabella decided that her former fiancé's son was too good a catch to waste on a child, so she married him herself. She was thirty-three, he twenty-five. Then she and her new husband held Joan hostage in Lusignan as security against Joan's dowry, which Isabella now claimed for herself. Joan was finally released and shipped home to marry Alexander II of Scotland, but only

after the pope wrote to Isabella upbraiding her for abusing her son by trying
to extort money from him. Isabella and Hugh went on to play off English
interests against those of the French for their own advantage; it was Isabella
who had helped lure Henry into his unsuccessful invasion of France in 1230
by promising support and then switching sides. Even by medieval standards,
mothers like Isabella were rare indeed.

So Henry was raised by his father's advisers—seasoned older men (one
might even say elderly; William the Marshal, earl of Pembroke, who essentially assumed the position of regent during Henry's minority, was already in
his seventies when King John died). The first order of business, naturally,
was to secure Henry's kingdom for him. This was accomplished by a deft
political move. William reissued a revised Magna Carta, called "The Charter
of Liberties," and had Henry publicly pledge to uphold it so long as he was
king. The Charter of Liberties redressed almost all of the grievances raised in
the original document, minus that clause about the twenty-five-baron advisory counsel—William didn't want twenty-five barons telling him what to
do, either. Henry's pledging to uphold the Charter of Liberties eliminated
the reason the barons had rebelled in the first place, and gave them a chance
to reflect on whether they really wanted to give up their sovereignty as an
independent kingdom in order to become vassals of the French. A large
percentage of them decided they didn't, and defected to the royalists. After
that, Henry's side had a number of victories, further reducing Louis's forces
and resources. In the end, William bribed Louis to leave, Louis accepted,
and Henry had his kingdom back.

Or at least that part of his kingdom that the French gave back, and this
did not include Normandy. It is impossible to overestimate the importance
Henry III set on restoring Normandy to England. It constituted his entire
foreign policy, at least for the first half of his reign. And there was good
reason for Henry's commitment to this goal. Normandy was one of the richest duchies in Europe. In 1238, for example, fully half of the French crown's
total revenues came from Normandy. That kind of money was worth fighting for.

It was also worth marrying for. In 1226, Henry had agreed to wed
Yolanda, the daughter of Peter Mauclerc, the count of Brittany, so that he
could use his future father-in-law's county, which was immediately south of
Normandy, to launch an attack against the French. He was prevented in this
by Blanche, who, discovering the scheme, threatened Mauclerc with force,
and, when he surrendered, arranged to have Yolanda marry Louis's younger

brother John instead. (John only lived until 1232, just long enough to thwart Henry's matrimonial prospects in Brittany.)

Having been frustrated to the south, Henry and his advisers looked north, and settled on Joan of Ponthieu, an heiress of some consequence, and as such a highly desirable match. Ponthieu would have made an ideal base of attack against Normandy, and his wife's wealth would have ensured money for adequate troops. Unfortunately, what was obvious to Henry was also obvious to Blanche. This time, Henry got as far as actually pledging himself to Joan, and she to him, which ought to have been enough to secure the marriage, had not Blanche intervened again. The French formally complained to the pope that the marriage was outside canon law, as Henry and his intended were closely related, and the Church forbade the union of cousins related within certain degrees. (In fact, Henry had applied—and paid—for a papal dispensation allowing him to marry his cousin, which would certainly have been granted but for Blanche's vigorous opposition.) Not content to rely on diplomacy in Rome, Blanche and Louis also put considerable pressure on the bride-to-be, threatening to invade Ponthieu with an army if the marriage went through. This was where matters stood when Guillaume of Savoy entered the picture.

Guillaume, born and raised on the continent, in a county sandwiched in between warring factions in Toulouse, Provence, and northern Italy, had a much more international approach to the problem. The Savoyards, as gate-keepers to the only reliable pass through the Alps, had learned the art of geopolitics early. The best way to contain Blanche of Castile, Guillaume counseled, was for England to ally itself with the only other great power in Europe, the Holy Roman Emperor Frederick II. Both Provence and Savoy were fiefs of the empire, and a marriage with his niece Eleanor, Guillaume hinted, would go far toward establishing that intimate relationship with the emperor, which might yield future fruit in the form of tangible military aid. In fact, Frederick II was planning on knighting Raymond Berenger V in December 1235, and Guillaume, who would be attending the ceremony, was prepared to do his best to personally promote Henry's cause with both his brother-in-law and his suzerain.

As it happened, Henry and his advisers had already thought of promoting an alliance with Frederick II. To this end, Henry was in the process of arranging his sister Isabella's marriage to the emperor. It was a matter of some discord in England. An imperial alliance, while prestigious, was also alarmingly expensive. The emperor, whose traveling court included a harem

and Arab dancing girls, and so did not need (or particularly want) a wife for
romantic purposes, set a great store by hard cash, which could be converted
into military victories and territorial gain. Frederick was at the time waging
war against northern Italy and wanted to sell his nuptial prerogative to the
highest bidder. Henry was forced to tax the English populace to come up
with his sister's marriage portion. "The king received a hidage," Matthew
Paris reported, "namely, two marks on every hide, for the marriage of his
sister Isabella; at whose marriage the king paid out to the emperor, within a
short space of time, thirty thousand marks, besides the ornaments of the
empress, and a crown of immense value." Just what, precisely, Henry hoped
to gain by this sacrifice of his sister from a man whose interests were very
specifically tied to Sicily, Italy, and Germany, and who had never even visited England, is unclear. (And it *was* a sacrifice; Isabella spent just enough
time with the emperor to get pregnant before being forced into his harem—
she died six years later, without ever having worn her crown in public.) But
Henry was the sort of man who leapt at comforting abstracts, however fanciful, and this particular invention—that an alliance with the empire would
materially strengthen England—was in vogue at the moment.

The strategic advantage a wedding with Eleanor of Provence would
provide toward this goal was even more doubtful. Henry was already negotiating to become Frederick's brother-in-law—how much closer could marriage with the daughter of one of the emperor's many vassals bring the king
of England to his prey? And then there was the awkward question of the
dowry. Henry had just taxed his own people heavily in order to secure his
sister's match. It was naturally assumed that the future queen of England
would bring a comparable sum to her husband's treasury. Yet it was common knowledge that the count of Provence was a man of straitened means.
Why take a poor girl when one could have a rich one?

It wasn't that Henry wasn't aware of these issues. But he was possessed
by a more fundamental impulse. The king of England was locked socially,
geographically, culturally, and personally in a great struggle for dominance
with the crown of France. So far in the game Henry and his unfortunate
parent had been bested at every turn first by Louis IX's grandfather, then by
his father, and now by Blanche of Castile and Louis IX himself. The fact that
the White Queen had selected a daughter of the count of Provence to be the
wife of her eldest son carried weight with Henry, just as Romeo had predicted. There must be something to it. The French were seeking to expand
their influence in the south? Very well, Henry would, too. It made no dif-

ference that French and English interests were not identical; that France, by virtue of its geographic placement, was much more involved in continental affairs than was isolated England. To Henry, the issue was simple. Blanche had moved a chess piece. It was his job to counter.

Guillaume of Savoy's proposition touched this chord. When Richard le Gras returned from Provence and reported Eleanor to be "of handsome appearance," Henry sent back a new set of emissaries empowered to begin negotiations for Eleanor's hand in marriage.

By the time this second delegation from England arrived in Provence in October 1235, everyone at Raymond Berenger V's court was aware that the king of England wanted to marry Eleanor. Henry had admitted as much in a letter to Guillaume dated June 22. The king had acknowledged at that time that there was still pending the issue of his other, binding engagement to Joan of Ponthieu, but Henry assured Guillaume that he was working on it. What he did was to order his ambassadors in Rome to stop trying to acquire a papal dispensation so that he could marry Joan, and start trying to acquire a papal dispensation to let him out of his vows so that he would not have to marry her. Both Guillaume and Raymond Berenger were highly sympathetic to Henry's predicament, and assured him of their support and goodwill.

Once again, the court of the count and countess of Provence received a party of distinguished foreign visitors. By this time, no family in Europe could organize a tableau of charming domesticity to match that of Raymond Berenger and his wife. There were, again, the nightly entertainments, the sumptuous banquets, the lavish gifts, the adorable daughters, devout mother, and vibrant father. Even Matthew Paris was impressed. "This said count [Raymond Berenger V] was a man of illustrious race and brave in battle," he wrote. "He had married . . . a woman of remarkable beauty . . . [Henry III's] messengers were received by the count on their arrival in Provence with the greatest honor and respect."

To settle the matter of the dowry as tactfully and conveniently as possible, Henry had provided his ambassadors with no fewer than six written versions of the engagement agreement, all of them inscribed with a different figure for the dowry, beginning with the handsome sum of twenty thousand marks and descending by increments to a skimpy three thousand marks. Then, fearing to lose such a desirable bride if he haggled over money, the king completely undercut his own negotiating position by ordering his envoys to agree to the match even if the count of Provence could provide no dowry at all. With its hands thus tied, the English delegation was forced to accept Raymond Berenger V's assertion that, regretfully, he was not liquid enough at this time to dower Eleanor with cash, although he assured them that he intended to leave her the tidy sum of ten thousand marks on his death.

It was done. On November 23, 1235, in a brief ceremony at the Provençal castle at Tarascon (promised to France, as per Marguerite's dowry) Eleanor publicly pledged herself to the king of England. One of the English ambassadors, standing in for his sovereign, then publicly pledged the king of England to Eleanor.

Henry III was now officially engaged to two women.

A prior royal dalliance was not the only obstacle to the marriage. To become Henry's wife, Eleanor had to make the long, arduous journey from Provence to England. This involved traveling through France. But if Blanche of Castile and Louis IX proved hostile to the engagement, Eleanor faced dangers more significant than a rough Channel crossing. The wedding party could be surrounded and delayed indefinitely. She and her relatives might even find themselves held hostage under armed guard. It was essential to try to ascertain French reaction before starting out. Guillaume of Savoy threw the dice and applied to Louis IX for a safe passage through the kingdom.

There was much sentiment among Blanche's counselors against the union. It was such a poor match on its face that it could only be explained in Paris as one step in a larger imperial conspiracy. Henry III was either a great fool or a cunning adversary. If the latter, the threat could be significant. It was whispered that Frederick II intended to outfit Henry III with supplies and troops for the purpose of wresting the western fiefs away from French control. The emperor could be a powerful enemy, if he chose to be.

On the other hand, it was clear that Henry III, who was already twenty-eight, was going to have to be married to someone, and soon. The vital point was to keep him from getting a strong military base in western France from which to launch an offensive against Normandy. The White Queen would worry about phantom imperial troops when they arrived—if, in fact, they ever did. On the whole, Blanche decided that if Henry had to marry someone, it was better that he should marry Eleanor, the second daughter of an impecunious count, than an heiress like Joan of Pontheiu. She and Louis could always apply pressure to Raymond Berenger V if the need arose, and if compelled, could occupy the fortified castle at Tarascon. If she opposed the marriage, and Henry was denied both Joan and Eleanor, he might end up making an even stronger match, with a princess from the kingdom of Aragon, for example. Of course, with her younger sister married to the king of England, Marguerite's loyalty to her husband's country would come under suspicion. She would have to be watched even more closely.

The decision was made. The king of England would marry the sister of the queen of France. An official safe passage, issued in the name of Louis, Marguerite, and Blanche, was graciously authorized.

The wedding procession left Provence immediately, and the marriage contract was signed in Vienne in December. (When a girl is affianced to an already betrothed man, it doesn't do to tarry.) Eleanor's retinue was even more impressive than Marguerite's had been. Good-natured Count Thibaud of Champagne, ever the convivial host, "went joyfully to meet them, and accompanied them as a guide through his dominions during a journey of five days and more; he also, from his natural generosity, paid all their expenses, both for horses and attendants. Their retinue consisted of more than three hundred horsemen, not including the people who followed them in great numbers." There was a slight delay while her father and uncle went on to meet the emperor, but the two returned quickly. Then her father turned back to Provence, leaving Guillaume of Savoy to accompany Eleanor to her wedding, just as he had Marguerite two years before.

They had a long trip together, uncle and niece. There is no record of their conversation, but from their subsequent actions it would appear that Guillaume drilled the family ethos of solidarity into Eleanor. She was a cog in the larger machine of Savoyard and Provençal interests. Her duty was as much to her blood relatives as to her new husband. Guillaume was there to help her. But he could not protect and advise Eleanor if he was sent home as before with Marguerite. Eleanor must do all she could to bring her new husband and her uncle together.

Eleanor, a bright girl of thirteen, listened. She was an unusual mixture of the fanciful and the determined. She had observed the preparations for Marguerite's wedding with envy. Of all her sisters, Eleanor was the most drawn to the songs of the troubadours. Later, as queen of England, when she had the resources, she would buy romances and histories that recounted the thrilling adventures of classical heroes, chivalrous knights, and seductive ladies. (In 1252 she bought two, one right after the other, and books were expensive.) She knew the drama of long-ago Caesar, Alexander, and exotic Cleopatra, and the much more recent, but equally sensational, twelfth-century true life saga of tragic Abélard, a Parisian scholar who had fallen deeply in love with his beautiful young pupil Héloïse, married her in secret, and was subsequently castrated by her relatives as punishment.

But of all the favorite tales of the period, the one that Eleanor knew best, as indeed no one in Europe, from the most aristocratic gentlewoman to the most impoverished *villein* could have failed to have known, so popular was the story, so widespread, so readily available in every language, was the romantic triangle of England's King Arthur, Queen Guinevere, and Sir Lancelot. The yearning of the lady, the miraculous feats executed by her lover in her name, the secret meetings, the nobility of Arthur, in short, the whole tangled mess, had been brought brilliantly to life by the most famous troubadour of the age, Chrétien de Troyes, artist-in-residence at the court of Marie of Champagne half a century earlier, in his definitive work, *Le Chevalier en la Charrette* (*The Knight in the Cart*).

And now here was Eleanor en route to this enchanted place, England, to become queen as Guinevere had once been queen. It must have seemed like fate to the girl. And Henry, in true chivalric fashion, had taken her without a dowry. She would have her own King Arthur, and perhaps even a Lancelot—who could tell?

The weather proving auspicious for a Channel crossing, the wedding party arrived in Dover ahead of schedule in January 1236. Henry III, who had been waiting impatiently for this moment since Christmas, having been informed of their safe passage, hurried to meet them.

CHAPTER V

QUEEN ELEANOR

Eleanor's first sight of her future husband came at Canterbury, where, in his excitement, the king of England "rushed into the arms of his messengers, and, having seen the lady . . . received possession of her." Had King Arthur been an older man of twenty-eight, possessed of a drooping eye, as disappointing physically to Guinevere as Henry was to Eleanor? If so, the troubadours had neglected to mention the fact. Happily for Eleanor, the bridegroom made up for any deficiencies in his personal appearance by his generosity and enthusiasm. He insisted on marrying her immediately, and the ceremony was performed in Canterbury on January 14, 1236. It was a relatively private affair— Henry was saving the big public spectacle for Eleanor's coronation at Westminster the following week. He still hadn't received a papal dispensation releasing him from his engagement to Joan of Ponthieu, but this seems to have been ignored, as the ceremony was performed by the archbishop of Canterbury, the highest-ranking Church official in England. In fact, the legitimacy of Henry's marriage to Eleanor was open to question for the next fifteen years, until he was finally able to obtain an officially favorable ruling on the matter from the pope.

By all accounts, Henry was ecstatic with his delicate young bride. There was no three-day waiting-and-praying period for thirteen-year-old Eleanor. The newlyweds went right from the church to the blessing of the nuptial bed. Then it was on to Westminster five days later for the coronation.

It had been a long time since England had anything to celebrate, and the kingdom relished the diversion. Henry's various marital transactions had dragged on so long that many of his subjects must have despaired of his ever getting married. They were as thrilled to finally have acquired a queen as Henry was, and, although they were probably a little bit disappointed that Eleanor did not herself come from either royalty or wealth, they were willing to give her the benefit of the doubt, and especially to toast her health and happiness at their sovereign's expense. "There were assembled at the king's nuptial festivities such a host of nobles of both sexes, such numbers of religious men, such crowds of the populace, and such a variety of actors, that London, with its capacious bosom, could scarcely contain them," Matthew Paris observed. The hordes came expecting a good party, and they were not disappointed. Henry might be capricious in foreign policy and somewhat wanting in military prowess, but he had a positive gift for extravaganza. The festivities surrounding Eleanor's installment as queen were as opulent and magnificent as a keen eye for detail and unlimited access to the royal treasury could provide. London (where the dark, narrow streets were definitely *not* paved) was cleaned up and bedecked with rich tapestries and silken hangings. Everywhere lanterns and candles flickered, dispelling the winter gloom. The great day began with the multitudes following a parade of London's most affluent citizenry, mounted in orderly rows and dressed in their finest, bearing the 360 gold and silver cups to be used by the English aristocracy at the gala banquet, the whole led by the royal trumpeters tooting the way to the palace at Westminster, "so that such a wonderful novelty struck all who beheld it with astonishment." They arrived in time to view the procession of their king and future queen as they walked the short distance from the castle to the abbey church along a formal blue carpet that had been laid on the street. It was a very dignified proceeding. First came the earls brandishing the ceremonial swords of state; then the treasurer and chancellor with the sacramental bowl and cup, then two knights of the realm with the royal scepters. Henry, shielded from the weather by lengths of violet silk tied to four silver lances, his ermine-trimmed coronation robe flowing, came next, followed closely by Eleanor, who had her own silk canopy, a copy of the king's. The queen-to-be, as dictated by tradition, was flanked by two bishops, a consideration that had evolved either out of respect for the bride's piety or perhaps, in older days, to keep her from bolting.

The ceremony, which involved Eleanor's kneeling before the archbishop, having her brow anointed with holy oil, and, finally, the placing of

King Henry III meets assembled prelates at Westminster.

the great gold crown embossed with lilies on her head, was followed, as was customary, by a magnificent banquet. Eleanor and her guests were served at table by all of her husband's leading barons—the grand marshal, the earl of Leicester, the earl of Warren; the chancellor, the chamberlain, the constable took their appointed seats. There was music, dancing, singing, performing. It was everything a celebration should be. "Why describe the abundance of meats and dishes on the table?" Matthew Paris demanded. "The quantity of venison, the variety of fish, the joyous sounds of the glee-men, and the gaiety of the waiters? Whatever the world could afford to create pleasure and magnificence was there brought together from every quarter."

And while England reveled, the White Queen quietly arranged for Joan of Ponthieu to marry her nephew Ferdinand III of Castile, thus securing France's western border.

Out of the hundreds of noblemen who attended Eleanor's coronation, who knelt at her feet in homage and drank her health at the feast, two would have an enormous impact on the life of the new queen and of the kingdom she now ruled. The first of these men was Henry's younger brother, Richard of Cornwall.

Richard was born in 1209, which made him a little less than a year and a half younger than Henry. Despite the closeness in age, they lacked intimacy in their youth, having been raised separately after their mother, Isabella, decamped to Lusignan. Henry went to court under the care of William the Marshal, the justiciar (the English term for regent). Richard was sent to Corfe Castle in Dorset, to be raised by a tutor. He and Henry didn't see much of each other until Richard was sixteen, when Henry knighted him and gave him Cornwall as a birthday present.

Richard's relationship with his older brother was turbulent, teetering as it did on a seesaw of ambiguity. On the one hand, Henry was his brother and the king, and Richard owed him allegiance on both counts. On the other hand, it was only by an accident of birth that he, Richard, the more able, intelligent, and sensible of the two (an opinion shared by many of his peers) was not king and Henry the earl of Cornwall. Hence frustration, envy, condescension—trouble.

It began early, when Richard was eighteen and Henry nineteen. Richard, who had not as yet come completely into his inheritance (another source of friction with Henry, who controlled Richard's finances when he was younger), tried to take a castle that belonged to somebody else. When Henry told him in no uncertain terms to give it back, Richard refused and instead invoked the Charter of Liberties, demanding to have the matter judged by a jury of his peers. Henry, furious at the presumption, told Richard to give it back or leave the kingdom. When Richard did neither, Henry put out a warrant for his arrest. Richard escaped into the countryside and complained to some of his friends who were also earls that Henry was up there in London trampling all over the Charter of Liberties and generally running amok. His friends were outraged, and they got some of their friends together, along with all of the knights who owed them service, and pretty soon Henry was facing an armed insurrection involving some of England's most distinguished noblemen, including William Marshal II, the late justiciar's eldest son. The king was only able to restore the peace by buying his own brother off with a gift of the lands of Brittany and Boulogne, as well as some property originally belonging to their mother.

It was a poor precedent to set, particularly as Richard was beginning to show a marked appreciation for the coin of the realm. He was quite adroit at capitalizing on profitable investments, and his relations with the king soon fell into that category. When Henry wanted Richard's support for his imprudent invasion of Poitou in 1230, he had to give his brother one thousand marks before Richard would agree to accompany Henry on his short-lived offensive. This period of forced intimacy served to aggravate Richard's disdain for his brother's abilities, as it allowed him to scrutinize firsthand the flaws in the king's leadership and decision making.

Richard's next big coup was his marriage in 1231 to Isabella Marshal, daughter of William the Marshal. Isabella had been an heiress even before she married her first husband, the wealthy earl of Gloucester. The earl had not been dead six months when Richard, who did not bother to inform Henry of his intentions, wed Isabella in an abbey church in out-of-the-way Buckinghamshire. Isabella was nine years older than Richard, with six children by her previous marriage, but she brought him substantial fees and holdings and allied his interests even more closely with those of her family.

Henry was angry with Richard when he heard about the marriage. He was afraid of the Marshal family, and with good reason: they were rich, influential, and often opposed him. When William Marshal II, Isabella's brother, died soon after Richard's marriage, another Marshal inherited his position of leadership and asserted himself against the crown, threatening the king once again with civil war. Henry, fearing that Richard would side with his wife's family, bought his brother's loyalty a third time with a gift of more lands and estates. In 1233, when the conflict with the Marshal family reached crisis proportions, Henry handed Richard a truly royal bribe: he was to receive all of the penalties imposed by the traveling judicial court when it came to Cornwall. Since these were the first royal justices to appear in that part of the country in more than thirty years, this represented an unprecedented windfall. In fact, the arrival of this circuit court so panicked the local citizenry that many of them ran and hid in the forest to escape prosecution. The sheriff had to flush them out. "Richard never quarreled with Henry without coming away a richer man," Richard's biographer, Oxford scholar N. Denholm-Young, noted.

As a result, by the time of Henry's marriage to Eleanor, Richard was an extremely wealthy man. That kind of money carries its own authority, making Richard a favorite among the barons who saw in him a counterweight to the king, so much so that Henry usually made sure to consult his brother whenever an issue of policy materialized.

The other notable man at the wedding was Simon de Montfort, the third son of the warrior-crusader Simon de Montfort, who had had such success against the helpless heretics of Toulouse and Languedoc. Warrior, athlete, statesman, scholar, intelligent, cultured, charming when he wanted to be, ferocious in battle, determined in policy—the younger Simon was all of this and more.

As a younger son, Simon had known from an early age that to succeed in the world he would have to follow the chivalric model of winning capital or perhaps a rich wife by employing his wits, skill in battle, and daring. He seemed to relish the opportunity. Simon had inherited his father's brains, drive, courage, and physical prowess. He threw himself into his education, mastering Latin and the important subjects of the day, and spent grueling hours practicing martial arts. By the time he was twenty-one he could trade witticisms in Latin and French and was expert in the saddle and with a lance. Thus equipped for life, he set off in 1230 to make his fortune.

Through his grandfather, the Montforts nursed a faint claim on the earldom of Leicester, one of England's most prestigious properties. The elder Simon had been too preoccupied with Languedoc to aggressively pursue this English inheritance, so the title had reverted to the crown and had subsequently been reassigned to Ranulf, the earl of Chester. Ranulf, one of the most powerful barons in England, had already held the earldom for a full decade when Simon decided to claim it for himself. It is testament to the improbable success of this venture that Simon had no trouble extracting a document from his older brother relinquishing all rights to this legacy. It is easy to give away that which you never expect to have.

So Simon, a man in his twenties, the younger son of a family very publicly committed to the French king, rode off and presented himself to the earl of Chester, one of the most venerated, hardened, experienced patriarchs in all of England, to ask him to voluntarily surrender a large portion of his holdings. It was an astoundingly presumptuous move, and astoundingly it worked. "And I went to the earl," Simon de Montfort later recalled, ". . . and prayed him that I could . . . have my inheritance, and he, graciously, agreed and in the following August took me with him to England, and asked the king to receive my homage for the inheritance of my father, to which, as he said, I had greater right than he, and all the gift which the king had given him in this he renounced, and so he received my homage."

There can be no greater affirmation of Simon de Montfort's uniqueness than this event, which overnight lifted him from the obscurity of the minor nobility to the ranks of the most elite powerbrokers in the kingdom. Ranulf, it is true, had no direct heirs, but there were plenty of cousins who were closer to him than this Frenchman who had no resources to speak of beyond his father's reputation for fierceness. Either the earl of Chester was a scrupulously just and fair-minded individual, or he looked at Simon and saw himself as a younger man, or perhaps a vision of the man he had always wanted to be.

With the sponsorship of the earl of Chester, Simon came to the attention of his new sovereign, Henry III, to whom he did homage for Leicester in 1231. Henry took to Simon immediately. The king had a way of dropping old advisers in favor of new ones the way a child leaps on a fresh toy at the expense of a formerly treasured stuffed bear. He made much of Simon, granting him gifts of lands in addition to those he had inherited, and including him in his circle of close friends. By the time of Eleanor's marriage, Simon de Montfort, at twenty-eight, was one of the most influential barons in England.

Eleanor would have noticed him at her wedding, because in his position as earl of Leicester, he was responsible for making sure that all went smoothly in the kitchen during the banquet, and he was singled out, according to Matthew Paris, to "supply the king with water in basins to wash before his meal," a symbolic act of servitude for which he wore his official robe of office. It was the first time Simon had had the chance to discharge his ceremonial responsibilities, and he made sure that his position was not slighted in any way. He even took on small tasks that technically belonged to the earl of Norfolk, and did not back down when challenged. Ambition is in the details.

London, with its labyrinth of dirty, crooked streets, jostling markets, and perennially overcast skies, represented a distinct change of atmosphere for a thirteen-year-old girl raised in the pastoral charm of sunny Provence. The city's 40,000 inhabitants were all crammed in as close to the Thames as possible, which inevitably led to congestion, and, in the frequent bad weather, muck. The houses, half-timbered like their Parisian counterparts, were covered with lime, and jammed so closely together that the risk of fire was a deadly and ever-present reality. A new law addressing this concern had just been passed prohibiting the traditional thatched roof in favor of slate, but the old ways persisted despite the regulation. The native language, at least, would not have presented Eleanor with a problem as she would never have to learn it; vernacular English was disdained as vulgar by the indigenous aristocracy, who spoke instead the northern French of Paris, *langue d'oil*.

Like its population, London's principal buildings hugged the north bank of the river. The city was sandwiched at either end by royal residences, the palace at Westminster to the west and the fortified castle known as the Tower of London to the east. The Tower of London would become notorious in later centuries as a fearful prison but in Eleanor's day it was used by the royal family as living quarters and as a place of refuge during times of civic unrest. Criminals were housed instead at the prison at Newgate, in the center of the city, well back from the river. To the east of Westminster was the Strand, one of London's most exclusive areas, where Henry's barons built opulent residences for those periods when they were called to town, and conveniently near the Strand stood the Temple, the stone edifice that functioned as the city's vault, and within whose walls the royal family, nobility, and rich merchants kept their money, jewelry, and other valuables. Between the Temple and the Tower lay London Bridge, the longest, most solidly built stone bridge in England. The masterwork of the kingdom, London Bridge had taken thirty years to build; construction had not been completed until the start of Henry's reign. Like everything else in the city, the bridge's passageway was cramped and so frequently clogged with traffic—carts and such—that it was quicker to cross the Thames by rowboat.

London was an unabashed center of commerce, with whole neighborhoods given over to specific trades. The fishmongers peddled their wares on Old Fish Street, the bakers had taken over Bread Street, the drapers congregated near Candlewick, and fresh milk was always available from the cows tethered patiently on Milk Street. Merchants and bankers from Flanders, Germany, and even as far away as Italy were drawn to London by the high quality of Lincolnshire wool and by the furs from Russia transported south across the Baltic and North seas. London burst with energy and activity, and its citizens were the most prosperous in the kingdom.

Despite the cultural differences, Eleanor's first years of marriage were gratifyingly agreeable. She had a husband who adored her, and who liked nothing better than to surprise her with a furred robe, an elegant gold ring, or a jeweled pin. Henry's artistic sensibilities were highly developed and refined—he would eventually rebuild and magnificently refurbish Westminster Abbey—and he lavished attention on her surroundings, taking an active hand in the decoration of her rooms at each of the nine separate castles owned by the monarchy. At the royal residence at Westminster, for example, Eleanor's boudoir was warmly luxurious as a refuge against the bitter cold of winter; at the Tower of London it was airily delicate and evocative of a garden, the walls covered by a field of exquisitely painted roses. Henry, like Louis IX, was a deeply religious man, but his piety was neither cold nor guilt-ridden; he found inspiration and generosity in worship, an attitude shared by his wife. It was a marriage of compatibility, despite the difference in their ages; both loved sociality, gracious living, laughter, dancing, and fine clothes. Henry even shared Eleanor's infatuation with chivalric stories. One of their first excursions together after they were married was to Glastonbury, to see where King Arthur was supposed to have been buried, and the year after that he had the cover of his copy of *The Great Book of Romances* mended.

Even more agreeable was the respectful atmosphere at court. Eleanor was afforded her own "household"—servants, administrators, ladies-in-waiting, and a generous expense account over which she exercised authority. Her position as queen and the dominant feminine influence in England was unchallenged, even though Henry's younger sister (also named Eleanor) lived with them in the beginning. Henry's sister was twenty-one to Eleanor of Provence's twelve. She had been married in 1224, at the tender age of nine, to thirty-three year old William Marshal II. It had been another attempt by Henry and his advisers to keep the powerful Marshal family loyal to the crown.

Eleanor Marshal was only sixteen and childless when her husband died in 1231, leaving her England's youngest, most attractive, most affluent widow, although her brother controlled her inheritance, a source of much acrimony between them. Soon after her husband's death, she had taken a very public vow of chastity, witnessed by the archbishop of Canterbury, with the intention of later becoming a nun. This step is usually attributed to the influence of her governess, an extremely pious older woman who took the vow with her, but perhaps Eleanor, whose only experience with conjugal relations was with a man twenty-four years her senior, hadn't considered that she was giving up much. After the vow, Eleanor resolutely put away her beautiful gowns and jewels, and dressed in the sort of homespun worn by paupers and peasants. She had been doing this for almost five years when her brother got married.

Nine months after his wedding, Henry gave his sister her own castle. It has been hypothesized that Eleanor Marshal moved out because she did not get along with her new sister-in-law, but this seems unlikely in the light of later events. Eleanor of Provence, happy in her new surroundings, beloved and petted by her husband, would not have seen an older woman of twenty-one who dressed poorly as a threat. It is far more likely that Henry's sister, observing her brother's happy marriage, felt uncomfortable with the newlyweds' intimacy, and asked to leave. Also, she may have been struggling a bit with her earlier decision to renounce love and the possibility of motherhood, and felt the need for more privacy. Henry, for his part, obviously preferred to live alone with his wife. There were still some nagging details about his sister's inheritance that he had yet to clear up to her satisfaction and he did not enjoy her continual reminders that he owed her money. Giving Eleanor Marshal her own establishment was a way to show favor without having to pay her in full. He even threw in hunting rights and a new horse somebody else had given him in the bargain.

All in all, it did not take Eleanor of Provence long to establish that aura of affectionate closeness, of caring interdependency, which are the mark of a successful marriage. She had been raised in a supportive, loving environment; it required no artifice on Eleanor's part to evoke the attitude of a happy home. And Henry was an easy husband in this respect. He yearned for domesticity. In his happiness with his new life, Henry became expansive. At last he had a family, and in his conception of that family, Eleanor made sure that Henry included *her* family, and very specifically her uncle Guillaume. Consequently, this time Guillaume of Savoy was not sent home.

The king of England had not often had a chance to meet a man like the bishop elect of Valence. For all his dreams of an imperial alliance, Henry's outlook was very parochial. He was nearly thirty years old and the only time he had been out of the kingdom was his abortive sally across the Channel to the banks of western France six years earlier. Guillaume of Savoy, on the other hand, had spent his life visiting places Henry knew only through hearsay. Suave, international, erudite, and sophisticated, Guillaume stood out at the provincial English court. He was personally acquainted with the pope, the emperor, and the king of France, and was in the confidence of at least two of the three. He was a rising force in the Church, a man of letters, and a seasoned diplomat whose counsel was apparently much in demand. His political vision swept far beyond the narrow confines of Normandy into the great wide world. He was a player and a maker of players; his very presence evoked opportunity.

And he was present very often during the first months of the king's marriage. Guillaume was a daily guest at court where he spoke of both international and domestic affairs with the assurance of one who is kept informed as a matter of course.

The result of all of this eloquence was that when Henry decided in April 1236, just four months after his marriage, to organize an advisory council of twelve barons to help him manage the kingdom's affairs, he put Guillaume in charge of it. "It was a cause of astonishment to many that the king followed the advice of the bishop elect of Valentia more than he ought, despising, as it appeared to them, his own natural subjects," Matthew Paris wrote. "At this they were annoyed, and accused the king of fickleness . . . And they were highly indignant." The barons were so indignant, in fact, that Henry had to hide in the Tower of London, and finally sent an urgent message to the pope, asking for support and a papal legate to help control them. The pope, who was in private communication with Guillaume, did what he was asked, and more: he arranged for Guillaume to remain in England for an extended period of time without having to renounce his bishopric. Evidently, the pope felt that the people of Valence did not require a bishop who lived in the vicinity.

For the next year and a half, it would not be an overstatement to say that Guillaume of Savoy ruled England. "He was virtually Prime Minister," medieval historian N. Denholm-Young asserted flatly. This led to very uneasy relations with the English aristocracy, a segment of the population that Henry could not afford to alienate, as was made clear in January 1237, when the king had to ask his barons to help him raise money to cover the cost of his wedding and the remainder of his sister Isabella's dowry. The resentment against Guillaume, the fear that the Savoyard was committing England to policies about which they, the king's barons, were uninformed but would be required to pay for anyway, made the peerage truculent. They refused Henry's request for a new tax unless a committee of barons oversaw its collection and disbursement (a condition Henry agreed to and then ignored). Presciently, they feared that Henry had asked the pope to release him from his obligations under the Charter of Liberties, an accusation the king fiercely denied. In the end, Henry renewed his commitment to the Charter under oath and got his money. But the seeds of baronial discontent—and doubt—were planted.

From her privileged position at court, Eleanor observed her uncle's startling ascent, and the subsequent hostility addressed to her husband and herself because of it. Eleanor was anything but stupid, and she had a formidable tutor in her uncle. She recognized that, unless something was done to diffuse their power, her husband's barons would pose a growing impediment to the royal prerogative.

The policy she and her uncle chose to address this difficulty was time-honored and practical. An opposition movement requires leaders. Separate the leaders from the pack, ally their interests more closely to those of the crown, and the pack falls apart. There wasn't any question about who the two most influential barons in England were in 1237. They were Richard of Cornwall and Simon de Montfort. Co-opt these men, and the king could do as he pleased.

It was simply a matter of recognizing opportunity when it appeared, and it appeared very quickly. They began with Simon de Montfort.

CHAPTER VI

FAMILY AFFAIRS

imon de Montfort's acquisition of the earldom of Leicester had only whetted his appetite. The next stage in any aspiring chivalric program was to marry well, and so Simon looked around for a wealthy wife. Being Simon de Montfort, he felt no inhibition about aiming high. He launched his first attempt at Mahaut, the widow of the count of Boulogne, and then, when that fell through, he sought the hand of Joan, the countess of Flanders.

Flanders, on the western coast of France just north of Ponthieu, was one of those strategically placed counties on which Blanche of Castile kept a close watch. The count had died in 1233, leaving the county outright to his wife, Joan. Joan was in her thirties, rich and susceptible to male attention. By early 1237, Simon was making considerable headway.

It is not clear how Blanche found out. She had her own spies, of course, but it is also possible that Guillaume of Savoy informed her of Simon de Montfort's intentions. Perhaps he worried lest one of Henry's barons become too strong. Perhaps he sensed an opening. Guillaume was adept at playing both ends against the middle.

A marriage between Joan of Flanders and Simon de Montfort was out of the question for Blanche. Simon was committed to Henry III and could very well use his position as count of Flanders to help the English launch an invasion of Normandy. Henry III might not have much martial ability, but Simon de Montfort had it to spare. Put the resources of Flanders behind that man and the kingdom of

France could lose more than Normandy. Blanche applied pressure to the prospective bride. If she married Simon, Joan could count on the enmity of the White Queen and possibly an invasion. Joan reconsidered.

The only way to assure Joan's complete compliance, however, was to substitute an attractive alternative for the earl of Leicester, someone Blanche of Castile could trust to keep well out of England's sphere of influence, who understood that he owed a debt of gratitude to the French crown. This was not going to be a difficult task, as whoever got to be the next count of Flanders was going to be extremely rich. The White Queen looked around and settled on Thomas of Savoy, younger brother to Guillaume and uncle to Marguerite and Eleanor.

By this time, Guillaume must have been involved. Thomas, formerly *prévôt* of Valence (a secondary Church position in Guillaume's bishopric), had resigned his post the year before. His nieces' marriages may have prompted this decision. He was one of those younger brothers who had been forced into the Church by his father, and he had never been happy there. Thomas was in his thirties and vibrant. Why should not an uncle to the queens of France and England be married, and married well? Thomas was very close to Guillaume and would have discussed this option with his older brother, and asked for his help.

Blanche of Castile's reasoning is more complex. Thomas was the right age and possessed enough charisma to have made a suitable candidate for Joan. Although he was in line to inherit Savoy on the death of his eldest brother, he did not have property of his own; this was also in his favor as he would recognize, and be grateful for, Blanche's generosity in allowing him this marriage. But Blanche's thinking went further than this. Guillaume's powerful new position in England may have troubled her. She could not allow Savoy to go uncontested to the English. Giving Thomas of Savoy the county of Flanders guaranteed his allegiance and split the family, limiting Henry III's influence.

The irony is that Guillaume might have himself suggested it through Church channels as a way of ingratiating himself to the French. By the autumn of 1237, when Thomas's marriage to Joan took place, Guillaume had gotten to know the king of England quite well. He may have hesitated to ally himself so completely with a monarch of Henry's indecisive temperament and questionable leadership skills.

But his younger brother's good fortune was only the first phase in a larger, subtler, more intricate intrigue engineered by the bishop-elect of

Valence. The marriage of Thomas of Savoy and Joan of Flanders ought to have aroused the ire of Simon de Montfort. After all, the earl of Leicester had been stripped of a particularly valuable prize by this agile bit of double-dealing. People like Simon, when they are outmaneuvered, tend to get angry and Simon would certainly have suspected that Guillaume was behind it. He could have caused Guillaume—and Henry—a great deal of trouble because of it. Yet, he did nothing.

He did nothing because there was a second stage to this transaction, and it involved the king's sister, Eleanor Marshal.

By 1237, it was clear that Eleanor Marshal was in love with Simon de Montfort. It was not a difficult scenario to predict. Young men like Simon, who are capable, by sheer personal magnetism, of persuading older, seasoned men to part with extensive holdings voluntarily, generally do not have a great deal of trouble seducing sheltered young women, even (or especially) those who have taken a vow of celibacy. Eleanor Marshal was in Simon de Montfort's company regularly after he did homage to her brother in 1231. She saw him at court, Christmas, and at all the usual holidays. Against this backdrop, her prior commitment to the Church was weighed and found sadly wanting on all counts. It may well have been the reason for the separate castle.

Simon was more than willing. The king's sister was as rich as Joan, and of a higher social standing. Marriage to Eleanor Marshal was a more than satisfactory alternative to marriage to the countess of Flanders.

The problem was that, under ordinary circumstances, an Eleanor Marshal would not have been available to a Simon de Montfort. Aside from that prominent and very public promise of celibacy, she was royalty and Simon was not. Her children would have a claim to the throne of England, and, as such, she was an asset to the kingdom. If she were to remarry at all, it should have been in order to further English interests at home or abroad. Henry could have used her to make a grand alliance as he had her older sister Isabella, the empress. Eleanor's marriage should have been the subject of debate among the larger body of royal advisers. Her brother would not have promised her even to another king without first vetting the prospect thoroughly with his barons. It had taken years for the nobility to agree to Eleanor's first marriage, and that had been to William Marshal II, son of the most revered man in England.

But these were not ordinary circumstances. A marriage between Eleanor Marshal and Simon de Montfort served Savoyard and Provençal interests in England. It separated a potential opponent from the pack, and allied his interests thoroughly with those of the king and queen (and the queen's family). It was a great favor to bestow, and the recipient would appreciate it as such, and be grateful in proportion, thus ensuring loyalty. To coax Simon de Montfort in this way meant the acquisition of a valuable accomplice.

That year, Henry held his Christmas court at Westminster. All of the players in this drama were present. It was a joyful time for Henry. He loved Christmas, and giving presents, and having the support and love of his family. It is not at all surprising that Simon de Montfort and Eleanor Marshal chose the holiday period to approach Henry and ask him to allow them to wed.

It is possible, of course, that Henry decided completely on his own to approve this marriage. He might have been moved by his sister's evident preference for this man, and her desire to replicate the domestic happiness that he himself now enjoyed. It is possible that Simon de Montfort managed to convince Henry to do him this incredible favor, as he had convinced Ranulf, the earl of Chester, six years before. It is also possible, as has been suggested by many, that this was just another in a series of Henry's capricious decisions, that he did not breathe a word of it to his endearingly vivacious young wife, with whom he was so enchanted, or her uncle, who was right there with them, even though Henry hadn't turned around for the past eighteen months without consulting Guillaume first.

Whatever the correct interpretation of events, the end product cannot be denied. On January 6, 1238, the day after the Christmas court disbanded, Eleanor Marshal and Simon de Montfort were married in a secret ceremony conducted in the king's private chapel. The king himself gave his sister away.

The one member of the family whom Henry clearly did not consult before agreeing to the marriage of his sister was his brother, Richard of Cornwall. Richard's reaction was recorded for posterity by Matthew Paris. The earl of Cornwall was "provoked to anger; for having heard that this marriage was confirmed clandestinely, that is, without his knowledge, or the consent of the nobles being obtained, he was justly much enraged, especially as the king had often broken his oath, that he would do nothing of importance without the advice of his natural subjects, and especially of himself. He therefore assailed the king with warnings and threats, and gave vent to great complaints and disaffection against him, because he had rashly managed important business of the kingdom, taking the advice of those foreigners."

Richard, who was extremely conscious of his rank and dignity, felt that his sister had been demeaned by this alliance, and that the insult tarnished the entire family. Disgusted with Henry's cowardice in not consulting either his council or himself before approving the match, he turned once again to his in-laws, the Marshal family, for support. The Marshals were only too happy to take the earl of Cornwall's side. Richard and Gilbert Marshal, the third son (the other two having died), called together a number of other high-ranking earls and barons to protest the marriage. They, in turn, brought their knights along, and this time Henry, fearing foreign intervention, was forced to warn those nobles still loyal to the crown, who watched over the ports, that Richard was not to be trusted. "Receive no orders from my brother who has risen against me because I have married our sister to Simon de Montfort," he wrote early in February 1238.

The rebellion took hold. Guillaume of Savoy and a representative of the papacy tried to mediate but their efforts were not fruitful. Henry was on the verge of capitulating to the demand that in the future he submit all questions of state to a council of opposing barons who would essentially run the kingdom for him, when Richard of Cornwall suddenly defected to the side of the monarchy. The explanation for this may lie with the 6,000 marks that Henry forwarded to an account in Richard's name in Paris. Within a week, Richard was reconciled to Henry, and the next month to Simon de Montfort. With the earl of Cornwall no longer in a leadership position, the other barons' resolve faltered, the revolt fizzled, and everybody went home.

Guillaume of Savoy judged this a good time to leave England. The crisis was over, and he did not expect a recurrence of hostilities. Richard of Cornwall had taken the cross and was preoccupied with the myriad of administrative details necessary to conduct a successful crusade. Simon de Montfort, after "extorting an immense sum of money from every quarter he could," had hurried to Rome to apply personally for a papal dispensation releasing his now pregnant new wife from her previous vow of chastity. Guillaume used as his excuse a call for aid from the emperor, who was engaged in expanding his holdings into northern Italy. He left in April 1238, taking with him a contingent of English troops handsomely equipped at Henry's expense. So upset was Henry at this loss of his wife's uncle that he tried to lure him back almost immediately by nominating him as the bishop of Winchester when the old bishop died in June. This caused considerable controversy as Winchester was a particularly wealthy and important see, and the monks responsible for nominating and electing the bishop objected to naming a foreigner to the position. The dispute was settled by the untimely death of Guillaume in November 1239, rumored to have been from poisoning. It seems that he had recently left the emperor's service in favor of the pope, and the emperor had not appreciated the move.

Guillaume had stayed in England long enough to leave his niece with a strong grasp of politics, and to instill within her a desire for influence beyond the borders of her adopted kingdom. In fact, Eleanor was ambitious for both herself and her husband. Already, she understood Henry's flaws, but felt that her strengths could compensate for his deficiencies. He may have been indecisive, but she was not. He may have lacked vision, but she saw. Already, she had learned that opponents could be cajoled into capitulation through mutual interests, or, failing that, bribed outright, although between these two methods, she much preferred gentle persuasion. Bribery was expensive and Eleanor liked money. She saw the way to power but was still a stranger in England; her uncle's policies, while ultimately successful, had marred the opening of her reign with suspicion. She moved slowly, consolidating her resources.

Then, on June 16, 1239, at the age of fifteen, Eleanor gave birth to a son.

There was wild rejoicing in England. A kingdom could ask no more from a queen than that her firstborn child be a healthy son. "At this event all the nobles of the kingdom offered their congratulations, and especially the citizens of London, because the child was born at London," Matthew Paris wrote. "And they assembled bands of dancers, with drums and tambourines, and at night illuminated the streets with large lanterns." Eleanor's position was immediately solidified. She was no longer a foreign woman married to the king; she was the mother to the heir to the throne of England. Henry was beside himself with joy. Nothing was too good for Eleanor or the child, whom they named Edward. He inspected all of the gifts bestowed on the infant with care, and if a present did not meet the royal standards, he demanded another, causing a wit to observe, "God gave us this child, but the king sells him to us."

The disquietude between the barons and their sovereign over the preference given to the queen and her relatives lulled. In July, Edward was christened at Westminster by the archbishop of Canterbury. His two uncles, Richard of Cornwall and Simon de Montfort, both participated in the ceremony. The royal family presented a united front.

Then Thomas of Savoy, the new count of Flanders, came to London to visit his niece and admire his new great-nephew. He planned to stay to attend Eleanor's purification on August 9, a grandly solemn occasion celebrating her motherhood. Henry was thrilled to have another member of Eleanor's family in town. Although he had never met Thomas, he had heard all about him from Eleanor and Guillaume. As a mark of respect he had the streets of London purged of refuse and swept clean; the citizens were required to wear their best clothes on the day of Thomas's arrival.

Henry was not disappointed in this new uncle. Thomas, like Guillaume, was an exceedingly impressive man, who wore his exalted new position—the count of Flanders was also a peer of France—easily and well. He was as worldly as Guillaume, and shared his sweeping political views. Uncle Thomas was very close to the French court, but this only raised him in his nephew's estimation, for Henry was jealous of his rival.

The count of Flanders did homage to Henry in return for a customary yearly income of five hundred marks, and then got right down to business. The French crown had recently assigned Thomas, as Joan's husband, several outstanding liabilities that were currently in arrears and required immediate payment, the most serious of which was a debt of two thousand marks owed by Simon de Montfort. Thomas had been in communication with Simon about this problem, and Simon had named his new brother-in-law, Henry, as surety for the loan; if it wasn't too inconvenient, would Henry mind paying up now?

Henry did mind. Simon had not bothered to inform him that he had named him as guarantor for a large debt to a member of the family. Being caught by surprise in front of Thomas embarrassed Henry greatly. It made him look provincial and ineffectual. Moreover, this was not the first time that Simon had used Henry's name to secure a debt that the earl could not pay. Henry had only recently discovered that Simon had put forward the king of England as security against loans granted in Rome to pay for his wife's papal dispensation from her vow of chastity. The archbishop of Canterbury had told Henry in confidence that Simon had been excommunicated in Rome for nonpayment. Henry had not married his sister to the earl of Leicester to bail him out of his many debts. With Guillaume away in Rome getting ready to be poisoned, and so not available to provide immediately soothing urbane advice, Henry forgot all of the good reasons he had originally been given for acceding to the marriage.

The result was a scene at Eleanor's purification ceremony. Five hundred candles had been lit, and a large company of noblewomen, dressed as elaborately as their individual estates could afford, had assembled to escort Queen Eleanor to the church, when Simon and Eleanor de Montfort, who had been invited to witness the ceremony, appeared and Henry let fly. In front of the assembled guests, in front of the archbishop of Canterbury, in front of his stunned wife, he confronted the earl of Leicester. All of the gossip and innuendo of the previous nine months, prompted by his sister's obviously rushed and clandestine wedding ceremony, which had been followed immediately by her pregnancy, rose in Henry's breast and hurled from his lips. The Montforts left hastily, but returned later, "begging his pardon with tears and lamentations," according to Matthew Paris. But "they could not appease his anger; for, said he, 'you seduced my sister before marriage, and when I found it out, I gave her to you in marriage, although against my will, in order to avoid scandal; and that her vow might not impede the marriage, you went to Rome . . . and on your failing to pay the money you promised, you were excommunicated; and to increase the mass of your wickedness, you, by false evidence, named me as your security, without consulting me, and when I knew nothing at all of the matter.' " Simon and his wife were forced to flee to France to escape Henry's anger; it was only by Richard of Cornwall's sensible politicking that the earl of Leicester was not arrested.

As for Eleanor, her grand day was completely spoiled by Henry's tantrum. She had not really seen him behave like this before, and the contrast between the king's childish outburst and Richard of Cornwall's mature mediation was apparent to Eleanor, her uncle, and her many guests. It likely prompted the reflection that molding her husband into a universally respected, cosmopolitan statesman was perhaps going to take a little more work than she had initially anticipated.

Thomas of Savoy thought so, too. He came back to England in the spring of 1240 to collect on the Montfort debt. Henry gave him 500 marks from the royal accounts and stripped the earl of Leicester of some of his English possessions for the remaining 1,500 without bothering to consult him, an action that infuriated Simon when he found out.

It was a period of relative tranquillity in England. Both Simon de Montfort and Richard of Cornwall were away on crusade. Eleanor was already pregnant again and the family had retired to the castle at Windsor for Thomas's visit. She and the count of Flanders and Henry had the time and privacy to discuss the future of the kingdom.

This was not an idle conversation. Henry and Eleanor were now parents of one child, with another on the way. They would have to provide for each new member of the family in addition to safeguarding the realm for Edward so that it was not diminished during their tenure. Guillaume's death the previous November had come as a shock. Henry had rent his robes at the news and given in to loud expressions of grief; Eleanor was still in mourning. They had expected Guillaume to accept the bishopric of Winchester, and to live in England so that they could avail themselves of his advice. They would love to have Thomas nearby, but Thomas was a busy man, with his own county to run. What were they to do?

The result of this conclave was that, when Thomas left England, he carried a private message from Henry and Eleanor to his younger brothers in Savoy: whosoever of the family was willing to reside in England could rely upon the grateful favor of the king, and be more than generously compensated for the gesture.

The first to take Henry up on this interesting offer was Peter of Savoy. Peter was the sixth brother, just after Thomas. He was the same age as Henry, but he had managed to pack quite a bit of helpful international experience into his life. Like Guillaume and Thomas, he had started in the Church, but tired of it even faster than Thomas, and Guillaume had arranged for him to marry a wealthy local girl, Agnes of Faucigny, whose father held property near Geneva. Peter married Agnes and promptly made war on the count of Geneva; of all the brothers, Peter seemed to have taken his father's aggressive military policies most to heart. He was both ferocious and successful; he was once ambushed in the mountains by enemies and fought so valiantly despite his wounds that his attackers were deeply regretful that they had initiated the confrontation. Called a "second Charlemagne" by contemporaries, he expanded the family holdings significantly: "If the inhabitants of western Switzerland today speak French instead of German, it is partly because French was the language of its thirteenth-century conqueror, Pierre de Savoie [Peter of Savoy]," observed Savoyard historian Eugene L. Cox.

Peter arrived in London in December 1240, "as he perceived it was such a profitable country," Matthew Paris noted drily, and Henry was so thrilled to have him, that, determined not to lose him the way he had Guillaume, he immediately granted him the earldom of Richmond, one of England's most illustrious (and affluent) honors. He also knighted him, and threw a grand ball in his honor, complete, as usual, with a "rich and costly banquet," attended by numerous socialites. Londoners "were compelled, under penalty of a fine of a hundred shillings, to come there dressed out for a feast, or as if to celebrate a marriage," reported the chronicler. Peter was instantly made chief counselor, privy to all of the king's business, and the longer he stayed the more he got. In less than a year he had Sussex and Surrey in addition to Richmond, the castle of Lewes, the castle of Rochester, and the Cinque Ports. His astonishingly swift rise dwarfed even Guillaume's; there was so much it was embarrassing, not to mention dangerous, and Peter, no fool, tried to give some of it back. But Henry wouldn't hear of it.

Even more astonishing to the inhabitants of England was Henry's insistence (guided by Eleanor and Peter) that the seventh brother, Eleanor's uncle Boniface of Savoy, be elected to the archbishopric of Canterbury, the highest Church position in the land, after the old archbishop, Edmund Rich, died at the end of 1240. No one in the kingdom had ever laid eyes on Boniface—not even Henry. Yet archbishop of Canterbury he became on February 1, 1241, although England was without its principal spiritual adviser for the three years it took Boniface to relocate.

To many of his contemporaries, the king's sudden overwhelming preference for the queen's relatives was inexplicable except as the work of an infatuated fool who was being manipulated by his pretty young wife. Historians, too, have deemed Henry capricious and incompetent for this policy, since clearly the extravagant rewarding of these outsiders drove a wedge between the king and the English aristocracy, which so festered over time that the result was civil unrest.

Yet Henry's actions were neither foolish nor whimsical; they were modern. The kingdom was entering a critical period, particularly in its relations with France. The French crown, under Blanche's direction, was seeking to expand and consolidate its influence in Europe, with the aim of becoming a great power. If this were allowed to occur, England would be left diminished.

To contain this threat, Henry was going to need advisers who appreciated the seriousness of the situation and who could bring effective counsel and allies to the struggle. The uncles from Savoy were the medieval equivalent of a world-renowned firm of international consultants or investment bankers. In luring them to England, Henry was not only acquiring the kind of diplomatic experience he required, he was keeping that same experience away from the French, so it could not be used against him. That kind of talent doesn't come cheap, and Henry knew it; hence the uncles' munificent remuneration.

Eleanor also understood and approved her husband's strategy; indeed, it was she who urged its adoption. By 1241, the year of Peter's and Boniface's ascension, she was the mother of two children (the second, a girl, named Margaret after Eleanor's older sister, Marguerite, had been born in September of the previous year). No longer a child herself, Eleanor was an assured young woman, interested and active in the stewardship of the kingdom. Confident in her position, she and Henry worked as a team to promote their vision of the future. She was seventeen years old and poised on the very brink of greatness.

And, as events would very shortly attest, the Savoyard view of the world was correct. England did stand at a crucial crossroads in regards to its relationship with France. Henry and Eleanor would have their chance at glory.

Sanchia

The Municipal Band of Cremona, mounted on an elephant.

CHAPTER VII

AMBITION AND OBEDIENCE

Richard, earl of Cornwall, left England to go on crusade to the Holy Land on June 10, 1240. Although he was a pious man, and sincere in his desire to aid those struggling to hold Jerusalem and the surrounding area for the Church, there were other factors that influenced the earl in this impulse. A successful crusade represented a tangible demonstration of courage and character. Additionally, the journey to the Holy Land offered the chance to acquire invaluable firsthand diplomatic experience, as crusaders of high rank were often invited to confer with the pope and other important foreign princes along the way. All of this greatly increased a man's stature in the eyes of the world.

The seriousness with which Richard took his crusade can be measured by the extent of his preparations; he applied the same keen eye for detail and ruthless efficiency that he generally reserved for transactions of a more obviously commercial nature. Over the course of the preceding two years, he obtained no fewer than nineteen separate bulls from the pope, anticipating every possible development, including his death, capture, imprisonment, ransom, or excommunication, and outlining the appropriate disbursement of his effects in the event of each contingency. He received Henry's official promise to protect his lands and income from pilferage during his absence, and to look after his interests. As a crusader, Richard was entitled to a blanket forgiveness of all debt, a privilege of which he availed himself with alacrity. Nor did he neglect to solicit all necessary information as to prevailing conditions in Jerusalem and the surrounding area in advance of the actual excursion. He communicated extensively by mail with the Holy Roman Emperor and met personally with Baldwin II, the emperor of Constantinople, who had lost his empire and was shuttling around Europe begging for funds. He even interviewed a Saracen courier whom Henry had locked up in Canterbury castle as a spy.

His departure was marred by the death of Isabella, his wife of nine years, in January 1240. Although she was considerably older than he, she and Richard had grown up together, and it had been a marriage of equals. He loved her deeply, and Matthew Paris reported that Richard "broke out into the most sorrowful lamentations, and mourned inconsolably," when he heard the news. Isabella had given Richard four children, but all but one, a son, Henry, had died in childhood; and this son Richard prized above all. It must have been a wrench to leave the boy with his uncle and aunt, the king and queen, so soon after his mother's death, but Richard was not a man who allowed sentiment to interfere with his plans.

He embarked from Dover in the company of a force of some fifty knights and their corresponding men-at-arms. His first stop was Paris. Richard intended to cross the Mediterranean from the port at Marseille, and as this meant traveling through the heart of France, he needed a safe passage from the king for himself and his men. Also, Henry had instructed him to renew the truce between the two kingdoms that had been in existence since their ill-fated expedition through Brittany in 1230, and which was due to expire shortly.

Louis and Blanche, who knew that the earl of Cornwall was held in high regard by both the pope and the emperor, went out of their way to treat Richard with deference. They did not wait for him to reach Paris, but had the whole court ride out to meet him. The feasts were more sumptuous, the exchange of gifts especially lavish. According to Matthew Paris, Richard, by virtue of his relationship to Marguerite through her sister Eleanor, was greeted "as a beloved relation."

Marguerite was eighteen by this time. Her position at court had been strengthened by the ascension of her uncle, Thomas of Savoy, to the countship of Flanders, for Blanche needed Thomas and could not openly abuse or insult his niece, with whom she knew he was in contact. Similarly, repressive French policies to the south were causing unrest in the region, and the White Queen could not afford to alienate Marguerite's father, Raymond Berenger V. Consequently, Blanche had begun to confine her ill-treatment of her daughter-in-law to petty torments, under a mask of concern about her infertility. Marguerite had been forced to endure a very public, humiliating pilgrimage to the shrine of Saint Thibaut, a twelfth-century monk reputed to have the power to overcome barrenness, taken at the insistence of (and, worse, in the company of) her mother-in-law. It was even more difficult for her to watch her sister Eleanor give birth so quickly to a son.

Then, at the end of 1239, Marguerite was rewarded with a pregnancy, much to the joy of herself and her husband. She and Louis both prayed devoutly for a son and heir, but apparently Saint Thibaut's influence only went so far, and she gave birth to a daughter just at the time of Richard's visit. It was a terrible disappointment. A son, she knew, would have cemented her position at court, as it had her sister's; she could have held her head high at last and silenced her mother-in-law for good. She cried when she knew the baby was a girl, and, fearful of Louis's reaction, begged the bishop of Paris to intercede with her husband on behalf of herself and the child. The bishop soon reconciled the king to his daughter's existence by reminding him that a girl could further the interests of France through marriage. They named the baby Blanche.

But Marguerite had proved, at the very least, that she was not barren, and that was not insignificant. There would be no more talk of annulment at the court. Moreover, with the birth of this first child, Blanche finally moved out of her son's home. This gave Louis and Marguerite more privacy, which in turn led to greater intimacy and more pregnancies. She had another daughter, Isabelle, in 1242, and then, finally, a son, Louis, in 1244.

She had survived the cruelty, jealousy, and hate of the early years of her reign; she had learned to wait and watch. Life at court became easier for her. Although she did not know it, power had begun to shift ever so slightly away from Blanche and toward her.

And she had reason to hope that the birth of this first child—even if it was only a girl—would prompt her husband, now in his mid-twenties, to assume his responsibilities as an adult, assert himself more forcefully in the day-to-day administration of the kingdom, and, most important, separate himself from his own parent, although in truth there did not seem to be much evidence that Louis was willing or even capable of doing this. By now, Marguerite understood that her husband's temperament was much more suited to a life in the Church than one at court. Religion was the only area in which he demonstrated a definite interest, and that interest was all-consuming. At the time of Richard's visit, the king of France was aglow over having successfully negotiated the purchase of an important relic, the Crown of Thorns, from Baldwin II, the emperor of Constantinople. Baldwin, who was desperate for money, had already pawned the Crown of Thorns to the Venetians, but Louis had it redeemed and brought to France. He and his younger brother Robert had then gone down to meet this precious parcel at the small town of Villeneuve-l'Archevêque in Burgundy, and from there, dressed as penitents, Louis in front, Robert behind, they escorted the treasure all the way to Paris. It took more than two weeks. Encouraged by the king's interest, Baldwin had recently shared the information that a shard of the True Cross, which he had unfortunately pledged to the Knights Templar against some outstanding loans, might also be available at the right price, and Louis was busy trying to buy that, too. Such important antiquities could not be stowed just anywhere, so Louis was also engaged in designing a won-

King Louis IX, with cross and Crown of Thorns.

derful new chapel for them, to be built in 1242. This would be the magnificent Sainte-Chapelle.

Louis's piety went beyond ceremony and architecture. The one area in which he took an active leadership role was in the suppression of heresy. Although he preferred to encourage conversion, Louis recognized that there were many people who could not be reasoned into accepting Christianity, and for these people he advocated torture and death. He especially hated Jews. He once told Joinville the story of the abbot of Cluny, who held a great religious symposium at his monastery and invited the surrounding Jewish population to participate, with the idea of converting as many as possible. At this meeting were a number of educated clergymen, but also a poor knight who was nonetheless a man of action. As soon as the Jews had assembled, this knight took over, asking the head rabbi if he believed that Mary was a virgin at the time of Jesus's birth. When the rabbi replied that he didn't, the knight beat him, and the Jews fled.

The abbot scolded the knight for ruining his conference, but King Louis disagreed, siding with the knight, "because there were many good Christians there who, before the discussion ended, would have gone away with doubts about their own religion through not fully understanding the Jews. 'So I tell you,' said the king, 'that . . . a layman, whenever he hears the Christian religion abused, should not attempt to defend its tenets, except with his sword, and that he should thrust into the scoundrel's belly, and as far as it will enter.'"

Accordingly, Louis was very interested in Richard's crusade, and readily renewed the truce and issued the order for safe passage. The French, too, had sent an army to retake Jerusalem only the year before, led by the duke of Burgundy and Blanche's old suitor, Count Thibaud of Champagne. The crusading force had consisted of many important French knights, including Simon de Montfort's older brother Amaury.

Both Richard and Louis knew, however, that Thibaud's crusade had been a disaster. A letter had arrived from a survivor in Damascus before Richard had left England that indicated that the crusaders had been routed by the Egyptians. Hundreds of French soldiers had died and many of their leaders, including Amaury de Montfort, had been captured. King Louis hoped that the earl of Cornwall would make contact with the remains of this crusade and continue their good work.

Although there is no record of Richard's meeting with Marguerite, it is highly unlikely that Richard would have come all the way to Paris and not brought greetings to Marguerite from Eleanor, as well as news of her health and well-being. Similarly, Marguerite would have wanted to see Richard, since he would be traveling through Provence on his way to Marseille and intended to see her father. Marguerite was very concerned about her parents and younger sisters. Her husband's and mother-in-law's repressive policies in Toulouse were prompting her father's old rival, Raymond VII, to act aggressively against Provence. War raged intermittently in Provence, and Raymond Berenger was struggling against the superior numbers brought against his forces by the enemy. Marguerite would have encouraged Richard to meet her family, assuring him of their goodwill and hospitality, and asking him to do what he could to ease political and military tensions.

And so Richard, a grieving widower on a mission that he feared could very well end in suffering or death, took time out of his grim journey south to call at the gracious home of the count of Provence, his delightful wife, and their two youngest, unmarried daughters, one of whom, Sanchia, had just turned thirteen.

Sanchia was a child of war.

For most of her life, or as much of it as she could remember, her father had fought with Raymond VII, the count of Toulouse. When she was smaller, these hostilities were sporadic and restricted to skirmishes over castles, but as she grew older the battles were larger, more frequent, and menacingly closer to home. The count of Toulouse, in his forties and still without a son to inherit a land under siege from Louis and Blanche's inquisitors, had become increasingly desperate with each passing year. In 1235 Raymond VII had tried to reassert his authority by throwing the pope's Dominican inquisitors out of Toulouse, but they had only hurried to the safety of the French fortress at Carcassonne and had him excommunicated and the city placed under interdict. When Raymond VII relented the following year, the interdict was lifted, and the inquisitors returned to Toulouse, this time with a brigade of French knights to protect them. They conducted long, repetitive, sinister interviews with every man over the age of fourteen and every woman over twelve. These interrogations were designed to elicit names, any names. The names went on a list and never came off, until the accused had been punished in proportion to the crime. The lucky ones were arrested and had all of their possessions confiscated. The unlucky ones were burned—but not before, in a futile attempt to please the inquisitors, they had given more names for the terrible list. Not even the dead were safe: if it was determined by an inquisitor that a person had died a heretic, his or her body was exhumed, carried through the streets, and thrown into a bonfire with other rotting heretical bodies, accompanied to the chant of *"Qui aytal fara, aytal pendra"* (Whoso does the like, will suffer a like fate).

Frustrated by his inability to resist the French, Raymond of Toulouse turned to an easier target. If he could not recover Languedoc, at least he could take Marseille and Provence, which he also considered to be his by birthright. He was encouraged in this scheme by Frederick II, the Holy Roman Emperor, who was having his own quarrel with the pope, even though it meant betraying Raymond Berenger V, count of Provence, whom Frederick had recently knighted as a loyal servant of the empire. Perhaps the emperor thought that Raymond Berenger, through the marriages of Marguerite and Thomas of Savoy, was leaning a little too closely toward the French point of view, which rigidly favored the pope. It was about this time, after all, that Frederick had had Guillaume of Savoy poisoned. In any event, when Raymond VII assembled a sizable army in 1240 to march against Provence, he knew he could rely upon the emperor for support.

The extent of the threat by the count of Toulouse against Provence can be measured by Raymond Berenger V's panicked reaction to it. The count of Provence wrote letters to both of his sons-in-law begging for help. Louis and Blanche sent troops but the emperor supplied the count of Toulouse and they were initially overmatched. (Henry, "at the pressing instance of his queen," wrote a letter to the emperor, asking him, as a family favor, to stop supporting the count of Toulouse; the emperor wrote back protesting his innocence and denying all participation in the matter.) Matthew Paris reported: "There were at Avignon, and especially in the provinces lying near the Rhône, some French nobles . . . These men, when they heard that the father of the queen was getting the worst of the struggle, and was begging for assistance . . . assembled and flew to arms to assist the count of Provence. The count of Toulouse, however, being aware of their plans, laid an ambuscade for them, and meeting them in great strength, slew numbers of them at the sword's point . . . and in a short space of time he took about twenty castles from the French and the count of Provence."

Yet what Raymond VII really wanted was not territory but a son. Under the terms of the Treaty of Paris, if he died without leaving a son and heir, the entire county went to the French crown through Raymond VII's son-in-law, Louis's younger brother Alphonse of Poitiers. The idea of letting the once proudly independent, powerful mini-kingdom of Toulouse fall into the hands of the now-hated French was anathema. Raymond's wife was past the age of childbearing, and, at any rate, she had given him only one daughter, Jeanne, in their twenty years together. It was this daughter whom he had agreed to marry to Alphonse of Poitiers as part of the 1229 treaty with the White Queen. His wife's barrenness had been another source of frustration for the count, and he and the countess had separated in 1230; since that time Raymond VII had been applying for an annulment. Confident that after ten years the pope would finally accede to his suit (or perhaps past caring whether he did or not), by 1240 Raymond was actively seeking a new, young bride to bear him children.

Louis IX promised Raymond Berenger V more troops after the first defeat, but the count of Provence was unsure of the French commitment. Raymond VII, encouraged by his initial victory, was positioning himself for an invasion. Raymond Berenger felt an urgent need to come to terms with his adversary. But what did he have of value to barter?

He had Sanchia, of course, by all accounts the most beautiful of his daughters. She promised to be fruitful; both of her elder sisters had already proved the family fecundity by giving birth. But Sanchia was very timid. (She alone, of all the sisters, would be escorted on her wedding journey by her mother, to whom she clung, and not given into the care of an ambitious uncle.) Her parents, understanding their third daughter's temperament, had originally promised her to a neighborhood boy, Guigues, the dauphin of Vienne. This engagement was now broken off and thirteen-year-old Sanchia was promised to forty-three-year-old Raymond VII of Toulouse.

Sanchia could not have been happy with this arrangement. Guigues, her first intended, had been only eleven at the time of their betrothal, much more suitable to a shy girl's taste. Sanchia was now to marry someone three decades her senior, the very man who had terrorized her family for the past ten years.

It was just at this moment that Richard of Cornwall arrived in Provence on his way to Marseille. He was not in a good humor. The trip from Paris had been vexing. He'd had his ships stolen in Vienne and, even though the property was later returned, Richard and his men had lost valuable time traveling by land instead of sailing down the Rhône as originally planned. The theft had occurred in a part of the country under the control of the count of Toulouse, which made it his fault, although very likely he had nothing to do with it. Still, this did not endear Raymond VII to the earl of Cornwall.

Raymond Berenger V, on the other hand, had hurried to meet Richard "with joy and gladness, ready to serve him, and to do him any kindness," as Matthew Paris put it. The earl of Cornwall was escorted safely to the fortified castle at Tarascon, the most secure military facility in Provence. Here Richard rested, and met the countess, Beatrice of Savoy, and her two youngest daughters. The family did their best to soothe this influential visitor from England. Richard listened to the count's complaints against Raymond VII with a sympathetic ear, but it was to the women that he was most receptive. Even in a fortress like Tarascon, Beatrice of Savoy was able to create an environment that was both refreshing and captivating, a domestic oasis that transcended the woes of war. It was precisely the kind of charming family portrait destined to stay with a troubled man. No one could replace Isabella, but there was much to be said for youth and beauty. And Sanchia was the definition of youth and beauty.

As for Sanchia, it is unlikely that she felt romantic stirrings toward the earl of Cornwall, even when he began to show her marked attention. Her fate had been sealed. Sanchia had not Marguerite's strength of character nor Eleanor's bright ambition. She was sweet and retiring. The years of conflict and fear had made her fragile. She would not have looked at Richard and envisaged a life of splendor, as had her sister Eleanor when thinking of his brother. Besides, the earl of Cornwall was thirty-one, and to a thirteen-year-old there is very little difference between thirty-one and forty-three.

Richard left Provence sometime in early September and arrived at Acre, on the Mediterranean, about eighty miles north of Jerusalem, on October 8, 1240. He found a mess. Thibaud had organized the beginnings of a truce with the sultan of Kerak, who had jurisdiction over Palestine, as well as the sultan of Egypt, before decamping for Champagne with that part of his army that hadn't already been captured. But it was a poor truce, as he had left many of his men prisoners in Palestine, with no hope of rescue. Richard, who wrote a long letter home about his activities in the Holy Land, was scathing about Thibaud: "Behold the king of Navarre, the then head and chief of the army, and the count of Brittany, although aware of our approach for fifteen days before we arrived at Acre, took their departure with an immense host. Before they left, however, in order that they might appear to have done something, they made a kind of truce with Nazir, the lord of Kerak . . . fixing on a term of forty days for fulfilling the terms of the truce. Before that period, however, had elapsed, the said king and count departed, paying no heed to the time agreed on, or to the terms of the truce."

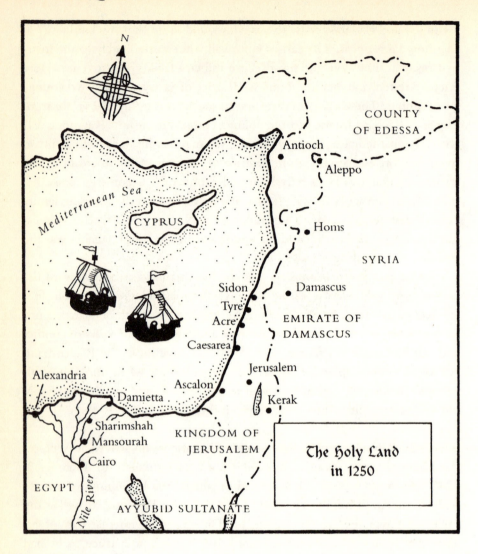

The Holy Land in 1250

What was needed was not military prowess but a seasoned diplomat, and Richard excelled at negotiation. He spent some time assessing the situation and listening to the advice of various parties, and then he concluded the truce that Thibaud had initiated with both sultans, bargaining for much better terms than had the count of Champagne. (Richard had taken the precaution of bringing quite a bit of money with him on crusade, and was thus able to make a persuasive case to his Arab opponents.) All the French prisoners, including Simon de Montfort's older brother Amaury, were released into

French prisoners released by the Saracens.

Richard's custody, "nor did it appear to us, on looking at the melancholy condition of surrounding events, that we could then employ ourselves more advantageously than in releasing the wretched prisoners from captivity," the earl of Cornwall's letter concluded. Richard also had the old kingdom of Jerusalem, which included Bethlehem, returned to the Knights Templar, who had been the occupying Christian force before Thibaud's unhappy intervention. He helped the duke of Burgundy to rebuild French defenses at Ascalon, about thirty miles east of Jerusalem, and had the corpses of all the French nobles slain at Gaza, which had been left to rot in the desert, removed to the newly fortified castle at Ascalon for proper Christian burial. This accomplished, he embarked for home at the end of June 1241, taking dozens of grateful French soldiers with him. His remarkably successful interlude in the Holy Land had lasted all of four months, during which time he never led an attack, or even brandished his sword.

The trip north to England was as lighthearted as the trip south had been sober. Richard took his time, stopping first in Italy to pay a courtesy visit to Frederick II, the Holy Roman Emperor, under whose jurisdiction Jerusalem technically fell, and in whose name Richard had conducted his negotiations.

Frederick II, who had been crowned emperor by an earlier pope (only the pope could crown an emperor), was titular ruler of what remained of the Roman empire, which was why he was called "Holy" and "Roman," although he was in fact neither. The principal components of his empire were the kingdom of Germany, whose monarch was called king of the Romans (even though it was nowhere near Rome), and the kingdom of Sicily, which Frederick had inherited from his Sicilian mother. Technically, Sicily was not a part of the Holy Roman Empire at all but this did not make any difference as Frederick had no intention of giving it up. As emperor, Frederick II therefore also claimed the title of king of the Romans (although later he passed this honor on to his eldest son) and king of Sicily. Just to add to the confusion, Frederick was also recognized as the monarch of Jerusalem, a designation he had acquired while on crusade some ten years earlier, although he had not been back since and had no control over events in the Holy Land.

It was Frederick's avowed intention to unite the disparate units of his far-flung empire. Since Germany and Sicily were inconveniently separated by Italy, this meant not only conquering independent city states like Genoa and Pisa, but Rome and the Papal States—the area around Rome over which the Church claimed jurisdiction—as well. (Frederick's coronation as emperor

Seal of Emperor Frederick II, king of Jerusalem and Sicily. He holds a sceptre and orb.

had taken place while he was still quite young, before his ambition had revealed itself; since that time the Church had come to regret deeply its role in the evolution of this particular prince.) By the time of Richard's visit, the emperor was making excellent progress in subduing much of northern Italy.

Frederick's was the most arresting personality of the century. He was called *Stupor Mundi,* the Wonder of the World. Certainly, he was the most educated ruler in Europe. He read widely, spoke seven languages, and had even written a book (on falconry). He was interested in everything: science, alchemy, history, law, architecture, medicine, mathematics. He started the first university in Europe where the teachers were paid not by the students but the state, and then recruited the most respected scholars in his empire to teach at it. All sorts of seers flocked to his court; Fibonacci himself had solved complex equations in a public square for the emperor's amusement. The celebrated astrologer/alchemist/philosopher Michael Scot, who had made a name for himself translating Aristotelian manuscripts recovered from the Arabs, was retained at the imperial court specifically to answer Frederick's many scientific queries, among which, according to his biographer, Ernst Kantorowicz, were the following:

How is the earth fastened above the abyss of space?
And how is this abyss fastened beneath the earth?
Is there aught else that bears the earth save air and water?
Or does the earth stand fast of itself?
Or does it rest on the heavens below it?
And how many heavens are there? . . .

Frederick's wit was impressive. When a descendant of Ghengis Khan, who was wreaking havoc in the Muslim world, wrote threateningly that the Holy Roman Emperor should surrender his lands and come to his court to become one of his vassals, Frederick replied that he'd think about it and to please hold open the position of falconer.

The imperial court was as outsized and exotic as its ruler. Sicily's proximity to the Arab empire had greatly influenced Frederick. Unlike other European sovereigns, the Holy Roman Emperor was personally acquainted with several of his Arab counterparts, including the sultan of Damascus, to whom he sent such complicated geometry problems that that gentleman was obliged to hand them on to his most advanced mathematicians for solution. Frederick loved the grandeur and opulence of the Byzantine world, the jewels, the spices, the manners, the art of living. He traveled with musicians, players, athletes, and dancing girls, as well as a menagerie of rare beasts; and his personal bodyguard consisted of Saracen archers who were reputed to be the most lethal assassins in the world, "an extraordinarily dangerous troop, obeying the emperor alone," Kantorowicz observed.

Frederick was in a very good mood when Richard arrived, having just subdued the Italian city of Faenza, and he treated the earl of Cornwall like a visiting potentate. Imperial slaves soaked Richard in hot tubs and the emperor entertained him with athletic spectacles during the day and the Arab dancing girls under silken tents at night. The women performed by undulating rhythmically to music while balancing on large balls that rolled across the mosaic floors, a dance movement decidedly superior to those practiced by their northern European counterparts. The emperor introduced Richard to exotic spices and foods, and showed off his menagerie of wild animals, including leopards, lions, bears, apes, peacocks, a giraffe, and the crowning triumph, an elephant with a tower strapped to its back, on which the emperor rode when decorum demanded. Richard had the opportunity for a long visit with his sister Isabella, the empress, the last time a member of her family would see her alive. In the end, Frederick heaped costly gifts on Richard and made much of him, and said he hoped that Richard would put in a good word for him with the pope, with whom Frederick was feuding, and Richard promised he would. It was altogether a heady experience for an Englishman, and Richard spent a long time savoring his triumph at this novel and fascinating court.

Between the elephant and the dancing girls, Richard did not get back to England until January 7, 1242. By that time, his reputation exceeded that of his brother, the king. He was a hero to the rescued French nobility, and a man of the world to the emperor; he had secured Jerusalem for the Church, dined with Louis IX, eaten dates from the hand of a Saracen slave, seen Paris, Toulouse, the Mediterranean, Egypt, and Rome. Whatever thoughts he might have had in the way of matrimony, and the beautiful young girl in Provence, had surely been forgotten, or given way to ambition.

It didn't matter anyway, as Sanchia had been married by proxy to her father's mortal enemy, Raymond VII of Toulouse, on August 11, 1241.

CHAPTER VIII

A WAR AND A WEDDING

On June 24, 1241, just as Richard of Cornwall and his horde of recovered French prisoners were embarking from the Holy Land on their way to visit the emperor, the entire French court was at Saumur, in Anjou, about fifty miles northwest of Poitiers. The reason for this unusual visit was to celebrate the knighting of Louis IX's younger brother Alphonse and his investiture as count of Poitou.

It was a very grand occasion. Blanche had gone out of her way to emphasize the legitimacy of the ceremony by throwing an extremely expensive party. Joinville, an eyewitness, put the number of knights in attendance at three thousand. Louis's shirt was of blue silk, and his red coat was lined with ermine, even though the weather was warm. The king of France sat on a high dais at the front. Seated with him were his brother Alphonse and the important French noblemen of the surrounding area, including Hugh of Lusignan, the count of La Marche. Marguerite was present, but the chroniclers do not tell us where she sat, although it is likely she was with her husband. Blanche had her own table, where she entertained other distinguished guests. The White Queen faced her son, so that she could observe the expressions on the countenances of those noblemen who had formerly been Louis's retainers, but who would now pay homage to Alphonse instead.

The investiture of Alphonse with Poitou was a gamble, a play for power. The White Queen was attempting to consolidate French influence in the west, in effect to legitimize, once and for all, French control over the area. To do this, it was necessary to force the fiercely independent local baronage, of which Hugh de La Marche was the acknowledged leader, to accept Alphonse as overlord.

There was only one problem with this: everyone on both sides of the Channel knew that England claimed jurisdiction over Poitou. Poitou had been one of those counties lost to France by Henry III's father, King John, and subsequently claimed as a fief by both England and France. Up until Alphonse's investiture, the count of La Marche and his fellow barons had essentially paid homage to both kingdoms. They hadn't minded being fiefs of Louis IX—he was a king, and it was prestigious to kneel directly to a king. But now Louis and Blanche, by requiring them to pay homage to a count rather than a king, had added a layer of bureaucracy between the aristocrats of Poitou and the crown of France. It was a demotion of social status.

Further complicating the situation was the additional wrinkle that Poitou already had a count: Richard of Cornwall. Henry had granted the title to his brother back in 1225. The local aristocracy had not minded having Richard as overlord. He made no demands on them; he was never there. Besides, his mother, Isabella, was married to Hugh de La Marche. The Poitevin lords were rather proud of having a former queen of England as the wife of one of their own. It was what gave Hugh his influence in the area, that and the fact that he was easily roused to violence.

But the new count and countess of Poitou, Alphonse and his wife, Jeanne of Toulouse (Raymond VII's daughter), were different. Alphonse's investiture was a signal that France was intending to have a much more hands-on approach to the governing of the area. Alphonse and Jeanne were already planning on spending Christmas at Poitiers.

It was no accident that Louis and Blanche decided to raise Alphonse to this position while the earl of Cornwall was away on crusade. It was a flagrant violation of the truce that Louis had concluded with Richard in Paris the year before. However, since it was Richard's countship, Henry would have to wait for his brother's return before challenging the gesture. By that time, Alphonse should be securely in control, England would be marginalized, and France would assume ascendancy as the most powerful kingdom in Europe. It all depended, Blanche thought, on Hugh of Lusignan.

Actually, as it turned out, that was not quite right. It all depended on Hugh of Lusignan's wife, Isabella of Lusignan, formerly queen of England and mother of Henry III.

★ ★ ★

If chivalry could be said to have one inviolate rule, it was this: queens do not kneel, even symbolically through their husbands, to counts. It didn't matter what your present circumstances were; once a queen, always a queen: that was Isabella of Lusignan's motto.

Richard of Cornwall was a different matter, of course. Richard was Isabella's son, and having her husband kneel to her son was in itself an acknowledgment of Isabella's superiority. It was, after all, only Isabella's legitimacy as the former queen of England that gave the earl of Cornwall (and count of Poitou) his legitimacy.

It appeared that when the French court first arrived in Saumur, Isabella was prepared to be gracious. If the king of France wanted to make his younger brother count of Poitou, well, that was his business. It wasn't going to affect her. She was a queen. She would sit on the dais with Louis, Blanche, and Marguerite and preside over the occasion. It might be rather fun. Isabella loved a good party. *She* wasn't going to have to kneel to the new count.

It therefore came as something of a shock when the former queen of England discovered that Louis and Blanche *did* expect her to give way, not only to Marguerite, but also to the new count and countess. That put Isabella's official public social standing below that of Jeanne of Toulouse. More than that, when she went to pay her respects to the French court, Louis, Blanche, and Marguerite kept her waiting. It is difficult to believe that this treatment was not a deliberate provocation on the part of the French royal family. A report from one of Blanche's spies, an unnamed burgher from La Rochelle, who sent handwritten reports on parchment addressed only to the White Queen, still survives, and makes Isabella's feelings on the matter, as she explained them to her husband, plain. "Wretch! Did you not see, at Poitiers, how they kept me waiting for three days, to the delight of the King and Queen! How, when I was at last received by them, in the chamber where the King sat, he did not call me to his side, did not bid me sit next to him? It was done by spite, to disgrace me before our own people! There I was, kept standing like a kitchen-wench! They rose for me neither when I came nor when I departed! Did you not see their scorn? I forbear to say more—the shame and despair are stifling me, even more than their forwardness in stealing my lands! I shall die of it—of rage!—if God does not make them suffer for it! They shall lose their lands, or else I shall lose all I have and die of it to boot!"

As soon as the feast was over and the guests had gone home, to make her point, Isabella took every household item that had been used by or for the

French court during their visit—every furnishing, down to the last kitchen pot—and threw it out the window. When her husband protested, she threw some of the stuff at him, too. Then she locked him out of her castle in Angoulême for the better part of a week. He had to go sleep at the local branch of the Knights Templar.

The outcome of this marital tiff, according to the spy, was that the count of La Marche decided that he could not, in fact, lower himself to pay homage to Alphonse, and would instead mount a conspiracy against the French and rise up in armed rebellion with the aim of ousting them from Poitou forever.

Very shortly after being reconciled to his wife, Hugh of Lusignan called a secret meeting of other like-minded barons for the purpose of organizing a full-fledged insurrection. Present at this conclave were the most important noblemen of Poitou. The spy must have been one of them, or supplied the provisions, for he was able to report to Blanche that Hugh had no trouble convincing his fellows to take up arms. "Above all, as one of them said, as the French have always hated us Poitevins, they wish to seize from us all our goods, in order to array us by right of conquest in their domain, and they would treat us worse than the Normans and the men of the Albigeois" [Albigensians, a reference to the Inquisition in Toulouse]. Having come to an agreement, the conspirators sent out feelers to the lords of Gascony, Bordeaux, and Bayonne, to see if anyone to the south might want to join the intrigue. Fearing that French aspirations for dominance would not end with Poitou, and that it would be best to confront this issue before it reached their own doorstep, the lords of Gascony agreed to participate. The Gascon barons then went east and approached Raymond VII of Toulouse, who joined without hesitation; he had been trying to dislodge the French for more than two decades. The count of Toulouse informed Frederick II, who approved, while Isabella of Lusignan and the seneschal of Gascony (a sort of resident governor) apprised Henry III of the plan; and there it was, suddenly, that which the king of England, encouraged by his queen and her relatives, had most hoped for and the advisers to Blanche of Castile had most feared: an alliance stretching from England to the empire, bent on displacing the French, reducing their territory, and curtailing their influence.

The plan went as follows: Hugh and Isabella would use the occasion of Alphonse's Christmas court to express defiance; Henry would use the investiture of Alphonse as count of Poitou as an excuse to break the truce with France; the English would raise a large army and cross the Channel around

Easter (except for Blanche of Castile, nobody fought in the winter); the Englishmen would join the armies of the rebellious barons of Poitou, Gascony, and Toulouse; there would be a great battle where the French would be annihilated. Afterward, everyone would get just what they wanted, which was in effect to turn back the clock. England would recover the lands, prestige, and influence lost by Henry's father, King John; the count of Toulouse would reign once again over a mighty and independent Languedoc, free from the pernicious tyranny of the French and the Inquisition; Gascony and Poitou would remain quasi-independent fiefs of faraway, permissive England; Hugh of Lusignan would effectively rule as England's stand-in; and Isabella would be revenged for Blanche's unspeakable discourtesy.

When Alphonse and Jeanne held their first Christmas court as the count and countess of Poitiers in 1241, Isabella and Hugh were ready. Isabella, her head held high, flounced into the royal salon and called Alphonse a usurper. Hugh refused to do homage, saying, according to Matthew Paris: "I declare and swear to you that I will never make nor observe any bond of allegiance to you, injurious man that you are, who have shamelessly taken away his county from my son-in-law Earl Richard, while he was faithfully fighting for God in the Holy Land, and compassionately liberating our imprisoned countrymen, thus returning evil for good." Then, in a gesture that served the dual purpose of underscoring his commitment and satisfying his wife's cravings for the dramatic, "while the Poitevin cross-bowmen bent their bows, he [Hugh] boldly burst through the midst of them," set fire to the house he and Isabella kept in Poitiers to perform their duties as vassals of the crown of France, and then galloped back to Lusignan under cover of night.

Alphonse sent out an urgent plea for reinforcements to Louis and Blanche. The insurrection had begun.

Henry and Eleanor did not wait for Christmas. On December 14, 1241, the king ordered a meeting of all of his barons, called the Great Council, to be held on January 29, 1242. He had to wait because he needed the approval of his brother Richard, the real count of Poitou, before breaking the truce. Richard finally returned from his crusade on January 28, landing in Dover, and Henry and Eleanor hurried there to meet him.

Richard's support was critical to the plans of the king and queen of England. In recognition of his success abroad Henry and Eleanor had organized a splendid banquet and had the streets of London hung with lanterns and tapestries, as though awaiting the arrival of a foreign dignitary. And, in a way, that was what Richard was, an important international statesman, more important than Henry in the eyes of many. If Richard chose to contest his brother's leadership, everything that Eleanor and the Savoyard uncles had worked to achieve would be lost. Something had to be done to secure Richard's goodwill and enthusiastic participation, not just for the immediate Poitou project, but for all future royal undertakings.

Richard had barely time to unpack before they brought up the idea of a marriage with Eleanor's sister Sanchia.

This was clearly part of an orchestrated effort between England, Provence, and Savoy. Richard's reaction to Sanchia before he embarked from Marseille must have been duly noted and considered in his absence. A marriage between these two suited everyone's purposes. No one in Provence had been happy about Sanchia's marriage to Raymond VII. If Richard married Sanchia, she would be saved from a forlorn alliance and he would be tethered firmly to the Provençal–Savoyard orbit. Savoyard ambitions, which were fueling Henry and Eleanor's policies, would become his ambitions; the king of England would in the future have nothing to fear from his younger brother. It was, once again, the way the family always worked.

And there was still time. Sanchia had been wedded to Raymond VII by proxy; their union had not yet been consummated. The pope had died before issuing the count of Toulouse the long-awaited annulment from his previous marriage, and no pope had yet been elected in his place. Nor was there much hope that the papacy would be filled quickly. Frederick II was waiting with a large army just outside the gates of Rome, ready to overrun the city if a pontiff unsympathetic to the empire was chosen. Since the majority of the candidates for the position were clearly opposed to Frederick's ambitions in Italy, nobody really wanted to be pope just yet. Consequently, Raymond VII's annulment was on hold for the foreseeable future. He hadn't even met his bride—he'd been too busy conspiring against the French. If another girl acceptable to the count of Toulouse could be found as a substitute for Sanchia, the alliance could be broken.

An acceptable bride was found. Hugh of La Marche was happy to offer Raymond VII one of his own daughters, if it meant securing Toulouse's support for the insurrection. The count of Toulouse was a formidable warrior who could bring experienced troops with him into any fight. Raymond VII was also willing to yield to the earl of Cornwall in this matter if it guaranteed the enthusiastic participation of the English royal family in the conspiracy.

That Richard, who had sufficient prestige to attract an heiress or even royalty as a spouse, would consider marrying the third daughter of an impoverished count, no matter what her connections, proves that he was, in fact, in love with Sanchia. It was the one occasion of his life when he did not consult his ambition, but took a leap of passion. She must have been beautiful indeed.

Not that the earl of Cornwall was so besotted that he was willing to forego a dowry. Even Henry knew better than to suggest that Richard accept castles in lieu of cash, or a bequest upon the death of the count of Provence, as he himself had done. Richard demanded coin of the realm, and that is what he got: three thousand marks, paid by Henry, with Eleanor's encouragement, out of the royal accounts. The king of England threw in four manor houses as well, so the young couple could have someplace to call home in addition to Richard's estate at Cornwall and all of the other property he owned from Henry's previous bribes. Thus satisfied, Richard agreed to support the Poitou campaign (which was in his interest anyway), even presenting the case in its favor at the Grand Council the day after his return from crusade.

As persuasive an advocate as Richard could be, this time it wasn't enough. The English barons assembled at the Great Council refused the request for funds to equip an army to fight against the French in Poitou. The lords of England saw not a bold international presence but a foolish king bent on wasting time and money on a flight of fancy. "When, therefore, the king made known to them [his barons] the irrevocable determination of his heart, namely, to cross to the continent in accordance with the summons of the count de La Marche, and with various arguments demanded pecuniary assistance from them, the nobles replied with great bitterness of spirit, that he had conceived this design without consulting them; that he was void of shame, to make such a demand; that he had so frequently harassed and impoverished his faithful subjects, . . . and had so often extorted large sums of money from them, which was expended with no advantage; they therefore now opposed him to his face, and refused any more to be despoiled of their money to no purpose," wrote Matthew Paris.

Parliament went on to point out that, just a few years before, they had been pressured to supply the king with monies for the purpose of attacking France and restoring Normandy, an expensive undertaking that had failed miserably. Finally, they warned Henry that the count of La Marche and the other Poitevin lords were not to be trusted: "You have also, to your peril, put too much faith in, and have promised your presence in person to those notorious continental nobles who are raising their heels against their lord, the French king; on which very account they ought not to be trusted, as they are noted for manifold treachery." If Henry broke the previously nego-tiated truce with the French, parliament warned, it would not be to his credit. They advised him instead to negotiate. It was all very well for a Peter of Savoy to counsel war; Peter of Savoy had singlehandedly fought off an ambush and subdued the majority of his neighbors. But the English barons knew Henry. Henry had heretofore shown very little talent for warfare.

There was no denying that these were very good arguments, and a far more levelheaded approach to the problem. Naturally, Henry did not think so. Instead, he flew into a rage, vowing to raise the money on his own so that he could cross the Channel by Easter. Then he dissolved the council.

Henry managed to raise quite a tidy sum without Parliament's help by levying fines, demanding scutage (payment in lieu of military service from his nobles), wheedling loans from the clergy, and, mostly, by plundering the wealth of the Jewish population—a full twenty thousand marks, one-third of the cost of the entire expedition, was secured in this way. He made plans to sail in May, which was a little later than Easter, but was the best he could do under the circumstances. He understood the need for haste. By April he had begun to receive letters from Hugh of La Marche, urging Henry to hurry up and bring a lot of money with him; the war was going well, he needn't bother about soldiers, really, Hugh had a force all ready, but funds were in short supply. "As though the king of England were a banker, ex-changer, or huckster, rather than a king and a noble leader and commander of knights," Matthew Paris sniffed.

Even though Eleanor was six months' pregnant with their third child, she was determined to sail to Gascony with her husband. Richard was com-ing as well, although he was less enthusiastic about the project. Henry and Eleanor considered the earl of Cornwall's wedding to Sanchia so necessary to the maintenance of his cooperation that they decided to forego Uncle Peter's military prowess in favor of his diplomatic skills and sent the Savo-yard off to Provence ahead of schedule in April in order to arrange the de-tails of the marriage.

The English force sailed from Portsmouth on May 9, landing on May 13 at Royan in Gascony. There they were joined by more knights and foot soldiers, as well as some Welsh mercenaries lured by the prospect of pay-ment. There had been a prior arrangement to meet with French ambassadors at Pons on May 25 in a halfhearted attempt at negotiation, but when the diplomats failed to show, Henry unilaterally broke the truce. On June 8 he wrote to Louis that: "You have twice failed in your engagement to meet our commissioners on the subject of infractions of the truce. We are no longer bound to observe it."

The war was on.

Unfortunately for Henry and Eleanor, however, in actuality the war was already over.

Louis and Blanche had acted swiftly upon receiving Alphonse's call for help. The matter had been referred to a council of French barons known to be loyal to the crown, who not surprisingly decided that the count of La Marche and his wife were in the wrong and officially dispossessed them of their fiefs. Louis did not need to plead with his barons for money, as did Henry, in order to fund a military enterprise. The royal treasury had ample funds available, having been swelled over the past years by the Inquisition's appropriation of all of that heretical property in Languedoc. Louis thus had a large army in Poitou by April. By May he had penetrated deeply into enemy territory. Hugh's company was reduced and the spirit of the rebellion broken before Henry had even crossed the Channel.

Unaware of this, Henry sent Eleanor, hugely pregnant, to Bordeaux to have the baby while he took the army to Taillebourg, at the southern end of Poitou, to rendezvous with Hugh of La Marche on July 23, 1242. But Louis was already there; the gates of the town had been thrown open by a defector. The English were so outnumbered that Henry was in danger of being taken hostage. He turned on Hugh of La Marche in a fury, accusing the count of deception: "When we were in England, you promised us many times, by several messengers, and certified to us by your letters patent, that you would, when necessary, prepare such a force for us as to be able, without any fear, to oppose the French king, and you told us only to trouble ourselves about money." Hugh retorted that it was Henry's mother, Isabella, not he, who had sent the letters.

It was Richard who saved Henry from capture and ransom. The earl of Cornwall recognized many of the barons in the French army across the river as those whom he had just rescued while on crusade. Ironically, they had come home just in time to fight against him. Richard put down his sword in order to indicate neutrality, and crossed to the bridge to negotiate for clemency. The French knights, remembering that but for the earl of Cornwall they would still be languishing in Arab prisons, agreed to let Henry go on condition that he leave as quickly as possible, before Louis found out. ("When the French king heard this report he could scarcely credit it," wrote Matthew Paris.) Henry wasted no time. The English army retreated so fast that they left their equipment, supplies, and luggage behind. In gratitude, Henry granted Richard the entire duchy of Gascony.

Hugh rallied his forces one last time and joined Henry at Saintes, just south of Taillebourg. Simon de Montfort, too, joined Henry's army at this time. He had gone to the Holy Land after Richard, and stayed until a summons from England asking for his assistance in the Poitou campaign obliged him to return. He offered the king his help, but at a price: Henry must forgive the debt of two thousand marks that Simon owed Thomas of Savoy. It was a very good time to strike a deal with Henry, who agreed to the condition. The king and his brother-in-law were thereby reconciled. The enemy was engaged, and Simon de Montfort distinguished himself in battle. But it would have taken a Ghengis Khan to rout the French at that point. The English lost.

As a last resort, Isabella, true to character, attempted to have Blanche, Louis, and Marguerite poisoned by sending her own chefs to prepare the food at the enemy camp, but the scheme was thwarted, and the unhappy cooks summarily executed. She next tried to commit suicide but was prevented by loyal servants; when she had fully recovered she turned on them in a rage. Finally, she was forced to submit, and on July 26 she and Hugh and their two youngest children humiliated themselves by surrendering with bowed heads, on their knees, Hugh in tears, before Louis and Blanche. Hugh forfeited all of the castles and territories he'd lost to the French, and henceforth was required to bow to Alphonse. Isabella, broken and disgraced, went into the nunnery at Fontevrault, where Eleanor of Aquitaine had also taken refuge at the end of her life. "Even there, in her secret cell, under the religious habit, she was scarcely safe, for many of the French, and of the Poitevins, pursued her with inexorable hatred, saying that she ought to be called a wicked Jezebel, rather than Isabel, for having sowed the seeds of many crimes." She died at Fontevrault in 1246.

The surrender of the count and countess of La Marche signaled the defeat of the rebels; by August it was all over. Henry had to flee all the way back to Gascony with Louis and his army in hot pursuit. Only an outbreak of fever and dysentery amongst the French saved Henry from Louis's taking Gascony in addition to Poitou. The king of France himself fell ill, and the army retreated to French territory.

Her husband's military failure meant that Eleanor was also in danger. Bordeaux, where she had given birth to a daughter, Beatrice, on June 25, was on the northern border of Gascony. Although officially allied with England, the barons of Gascony feared a French invasion and were unwilling to protect her. Several Gascon towns went over to the French side even after Louis had retreated, and the queen of England's incapacity made her an easy target for those threatening to defect. "They did not have mercy on you [Henry] when you were fleeing from the treachery and persecution of the French king, nor on the queen in her pregnancy, when she was lying ill at La Réole and when she was delivered at Bordeaux," Simon de Montfort later reminded Henry.

Eventually, Henry, Richard, Simon de Montfort, and the remaining English forces joined Eleanor at Bordeaux. Henry tried to regroup with the count of Toulouse, but Louis's victories had brought in new recruits and the king of France sent that portion of the army that was not ill to fight Raymond VII. The French were again victorious, and Raymond VII sued for peace on October 20. Henry was forced to come to terms with Louis and in April 1243, a formal five-year truce was arranged between England and France. All of Poitou went to the French, and some of the towns of Gascony. "Every conquest which the king of France had made in that expedition was to remain to him," said Matthew Paris of this treaty. Additionally, Henry was required to pay Louis a thousand pounds every year that the truce remained in effect.

As unfavorable as this settlement was to the king of England, it might have been much worse. Louis was so much stronger than Henry at the end of this escapade than at the beginning that he could have tried to force the king of England to renounce his interests in Gascony altogether. The fact that he did not is credited to Marguerite's interference. Louis gave as one of his reasons for not pressing for harsher terms that his wife and the king of England's wife were sisters and that he hoped for better relations between the two families. "And," Louis added, when his advisers protested that he had given too much away, "it seems to me that what I give I employ well, for he [Henry] was not my man and now has done me homage."

In fact, Louis could afford to be gracious. The western and southern boundaries of France had been secured. Both Hugh of Lusignan and Raymond VII were broken men. Never again would Toulouse or Poitou rival the crown of France as a source of power. The rich lands of Normandy were also safe; Henry of England had been exposed as a colossal bungler. Simon de Montfort, in his exasperation, told the king of England to his face that he ought to be "shut up like Charles the Simple," an insult that lived long in Henry's memory. The troubadours were even more merciless, composing verses ridiculing the English:

> They did not stop to spin a tale,
> The English with their barley-ale;
> For all of France did dance and dine,
> For barley-ale is not worth wine.

From autumn of 1242, then, France was assured its place as the richest and most powerful kingdom in Europe. It was Marguerite, and not Eleanor, who was married to the most respected king in the Christian world.

With England's influence abroad shrinking daily, Eleanor, a much more practical individual than her husband, acted at once to limit her losses. Specifically, she told Henry that she didn't care what he had promised; under the circumstances he could not afford to give Gascony to Richard. Gascony should be reserved for the crown, so that it could eventually go to their son Edward, heir to the throne. It did not take too much convincing to get Henry to agree to rescind the award.

Richard was furious. He, Henry, and Eleanor, stuck in Bordeaux in the heat of August, had a vehement quarrel that degenerated into unproductive behavior. Richard threatened to leave the army without the king's permission. The king bribed some unsavory characters to throw Richard into a dungeon. Richard escaped by hiding in a church. There was a reconciliation of sorts in early September, and the earl of Cornwall hung around another month before sailing back to England, but their relationship was damaged. Eleanor felt more urgently than ever the need to harness Richard's rebellious spirit to the royal interests through marriage to Sanchia.

This, at least, she had been able to accomplish through the intercession of her uncle Peter. In July, while Henry and Richard were fighting their one battle at Saintes, Peter of Savoy was in Provence negotiating the final details of Sanchia's marriage contract with the earl of Cornwall. The agreement was formalized as usual at a ceremony at the castle of Tarascon but there was still the problem of getting the bride to her prospective husband—a dangerous undertaking during a time of war. Peter, who could not resist the temptation, since he was in the neighborhood anyway, of waging war on the count of Geneva, entrusted this task to his younger brother Philippe, the new bishop-elect of Valence. Philippe was the one member of the family who had not yet been to England (although he had already been the beneficiary of Henry's munificence, having been awarded three livings in absentia). Sanchia's mother, Beatrice of Savoy, also accompanied her daughter on the wedding journey. They had to wait until the truce between England and France was concluded in the spring of 1243 before starting out, but by May they had reached Bordeaux, where Henry and Eleanor, who were reluctant to return home to face the English baronage, were hiding out. Simon de Montfort was still with them, helping to hold and administer Gascony for the English. Richard, of course, was already home, having left the previous October.

Henry and Eleanor were buoyed by the arrival of their Provençal relatives. Eleanor hadn't seen her mother or sister in seven years. It must have been wonderful to have so sympathetic an audience after the turmoil and shame of the previous months. Henry was so relieved to see them that he granted Philippe another living on the spot.

It was decided that the wedding should be particularly grand, in part to soothe Richard's feelings, but mostly to distract the English populace from their king's recent military fiasco. Henry, who was never happier than when planning a party, brightened considerably at the prospect, and sailed home in September with Simon and the remains of his army in order to see to the arrangements. He landed at Portsmouth and immediately "he gave orders that the city should be adorned at his entry with hangings and curtains, with garlands and lighted tapers; that the citizens should meet him in their holiday dresses, and that all the bells of the place should resound with joy." Eleanor, Sanchia, and Beatrice of Savoy stayed on in Bordeaux before making a similarly grand entrance at the port of Dover on November 14.

They were met by a large party of noblemen including Richard. If he had in mind the shy child of thirteen whom he had met on his way to the Holy Land, he must have been surprised. More than three years had passed since he had first been introduced to Sanchia at Tarascon, and three years makes a great deal of difference when one is a teenager. She was nearly seventeen, much older than either of her sisters had been when they had married. But she had the same quiet, retiring manner that he remembered, a little fearful, a little reserved. The months at Bordeaux with her mother and sister had been a relief to her, but now she was in a new country, a cold country, and expected to become a great lady. She knew it was her job to influence the important man she was marrying, to keep him allied to her family's interests, but she lacked self-confidence.

Beatrice of Savoy was aware of her daughter's limitations and sought to camouflage them; as a result, it was the mother and not the bride who shone at the subsequent festivities. She was "a woman of gracious mien, prudent and civil," who conducted herself with great diplomacy and much ostentation (paid for by Henry). The wedding was held within the week at Westminster, where "worldly pomp, and every kind of vanity and glory, was displayed in the different bodies of gleemen, the variety of their garments, the number of dishes and the multitude of feasters." It was a large and impressively noble gathering—Matthew Paris put the number of place settings at three thousand—and the presence of the Savoyards added a distinctly international and cosmopolitan atmosphere. Thomas of Savoy, the count of Flanders, was invited and presented Sanchia, Beatrice, and Eleanor with a gift of rich ruby fabric, which Henry had made into gowns.

Richard reciprocated at Christmas with a marvelous feast of his own, to which Henry and Eleanor were invited, and at which Beatrice of Savoy and Sanchia (whom the English called Cynthia) were the guests of honor. Matthew Paris reported that the bride was "of pleasant looks" and that Henry did all he could to ingratiate himself with her. "Of pleasant looks" was an oddly restrained term for a chronicler to employ about a woman who was supposed to be beautiful beyond compare. It is likely that Matthew Paris was unwilling to give Sanchia's good looks their due because the chronicler disapproved of Richard's marriage. "The whole community in England was much excited, and began to fear that the whole business of the kingdom would be disposed of at the will of the queen and her sister . . . who would be, as it were, a second queen," he wrote.

By the time of this Christmas party, Beatrice of Savoy understood the dynamics of the English political system as well as did most of its barons. She knew who wielded power and where potential trouble lay. Consequently, she focused her attention on her new son-in-law. Richard was made to feel that, because of his attractive young bride, he was now a part of one of the most desirable and cultured families in the world. Richard warmed to this vision.

The other focus of Beatrice's attention was Simon de Montfort and his wife, Eleanor. A supportive Simon was critical to maintaining Henry and Eleanor's political position, which was tenuous in the wake of the Poitou loss. It was Beatrice who approached Henry and asked him to be generous for his sister's sake. Henry, who loved this new family, was as happy that Christmas as he had ever been. He gave Simon and Eleanor a new living of five hundred marks and pardoned one thousand pounds of their debt. He promised his sister that he would reimburse her for the monies still owed to her from her first marriage, which the Marshal family had not yet paid. A month later he rewarded the earl of Leicester further with the gift of the fortified castle of Kenilworth. This represented a complete capitulation on Henry's part, a way of apologizing for what had gone before; the result was a grateful and loyal Simon de Montfort, and it was accomplished entirely by the gentle prompting of the king of England's mother-in-law.

Upon her departure from Dover the following week, hastened by the disquieting news that her husband, Raymond Berenger V, had fallen seriously ill in her absence, Beatrice of Savoy left behind her a much stronger and more united English royal family than could have been hoped for so soon after such disastrous international losses. Her daughter Eleanor, in particular, had benefited from her mother's experience and discretion. The earls of Cornwall and Leicester, formerly loose ends, had both been tied firmly into royal knots.

The service performed by the countess of Provence was exemplary, and it did not go unnoticed. Just before she left, at Eleanor's insistence, Henry lent his mother-in-law four thousand marks, secured by five Provençal castles, one of which was Tarascon.

Beatrice

Pope Innocent IV flees from the persecutions of Emperor Frederick II.

CHAPTER IX

AN UNLIKELY INHERITANCE

The countess of Provence came home from England in early 1244 to find her husband seriously ill; he did not improve over time. After languishing for more than a year, it became clear to everyone, including the count himself, that he was dying. It became necessary for Raymond Berenger V to put his affairs in order, and to consider the issue of succession.

This was not as straightforward a process as might be expected, and the count gave the matter much thought. Provence was not a wealthy county—the perpetual war against Toulouse, and Raymond Berenger's own lavish lifestyle, ensured that his expenses always exceeded his income, often by substantial amounts—but it was strategically placed, now more than ever. Louis IX's recent unequivocal military triumph over Henry III, Hugh of La Marche, and, most especially, Raymond VII of Toulouse, had pushed French boundaries up against Provençal borders. It would take very little, Raymond Berenger was aware, for France to swallow up the count's domain as well. Of course, Provence was a fief of the empire. Frederick II could be counted upon to resist any French encroachment into imperial territory, resorting to military intervention if necessary, but Raymond Berenger did not find this an attractive option. The count of Provence was a pious man (particularly while approaching death) and the emperor was still under the ban of excommunication. Moreover, imperial troops might be very difficult to dislodge once allowed a foothold in the area. It would be trading one unsatisfactory sovereign for another.

English interests, too, had to be weighed in the decision. Raymond Berenger now had two powerful sons-in-law from England who no doubt would be interested in maintaining Provençal independence against the French. Richard of Cornwall, in particular, was of sufficient international stature to succeed Raymond Berenger as count and he had no kingdom of his own to administer. There were also Raymond Berenger's relatives in Aragon to consider. By long tradition, the title of count of Provence had gone to a prince of Aragon.

Such an important decision could not be taken without consulting the countess; his chief adviser, Romeo de Villeneuve; and, most important, the countess's brothers from Savoy. Savoy was next door to Provence, and would naturally want a say in determining who would take over after Raymond Berenger was gone. Otherwise, Beatrice's brothers might reject the count's wishes after his death and support a different candidate for inheritance. Men like Thomas and Peter of Savoy could make a prospective heir extremely uncomfortable if they so chose.

At last the time came when the count could wait no longer to make known his decision. According to Matthew Paris, Raymond Berenger announced his last will and testament to the world by calling his youngest daughter, Beatrice, to his bedside with these words: "Dearest daughter, more beloved by me than all your sisters, I am aware that by the Lord's disposal all my daughters, except you alone, are exalted by marriage in a high degree, and to the admiration of all Christians. To you, therefore, at your marriage, I give and bequeath, by my will, the whole of my land, together with my money, castles, and all my other possessions; for your sisters do not need that the inheritance should be divided, in order for a portion of it to be given to either one of them." Then the count, satisfied with his legacy, breathed his last. After serious deliberation, he had left the whole of Provence—from the mountains in the northeast to the port of Marseille in the south, including land, property, allegiance of noblemen, and government administration—not to a strong adult male, but to a thirteen-year-old girl.

Matthew Paris's deathbed description might be picturesque, but Raymond Berenger's legacy was actually much more sophisticated than the chronicler realized. Although his daughter Beatrice did inherit everything, the administration of Provence fell largely to her mother, who was granted the use of the county for her lifetime. Moreover, by prearrangement, Romeo de Villeneuve was named as chief adviser to the young heiress, which meant an experienced, steady hand at the helm. So the count's last will and testament was really a clever bid for the continuation of the old regime, and reflected Raymond Berenger V's conviction, fully supported by his Savoyard brothers-in-law, that the person most qualified to protect Provençal interests against international incursion was his wife.

Beatrice of Savoy evidently felt herself and her youngest daughter equal to the delicate diplomatic challenge of maintaining Provençal cultural and political independence. Although only thirteen, the younger Beatrice was already exhibiting many of her older sisters' stronger qualities. In addition to beauty, she was self-assured and well-educated. Her parents had known for some time that she would inherit, and had trained her to rule. Provence was a hub for trade: from the Mediterranean came silks, spices, fish, wine, and vegetables; from the north, wood, metals, and animal skins. Tolls on these commodities were collected in Aix and at Tarascon, and would support the countess's household and help pay for any measures necessary to defend the regime. Fees could also be extracted from Provençal shippers, who benefited from the thriving crusader-and-pilgrim traffic to the Holy Land. Most important, Raymond Berenger had left his widow and daughter Provence's lucrative salt monopoly—it was from salt and not wine that the county derived its greatest source of income.

Together, Raymond Berenger V and Romeo de Villeneuve had fashioned one of the most efficient administrations in Europe to handle the increasing flow of commerce. The Provençal system was a model for other governments in the region, and both mother and daughter were familiar with its workings. Except for the port city of Marseille, which was sufficiently prosperous to entertain thoughts of independence, there had been none of the sort of civil unrest that had plagued France for decades. The count of Provence had always cooperated with the Church, and his rule was supported by important local prelates like the archbishop of Arles, who governed politically as well as spiritually. Beatrice of Savoy knew how to manipulate these relationships. She and her daughter had traveled extensively through the county during her husband's reign, and were acquainted personally with the lords of the realm, upon whom they could rely for defense. Additionally, Romeo had agents loyal to the family scattered throughout Provence. The wife felt ready to shoulder the burden of her husband's rule.

As for the daughter, the younger Beatrice benefited by a thirteen-year-old's natural self-absorption. All her life, her older sisters, the queens of France and England, had been held up to her as models of success, and she was a little jealous of their positions. Now she, as the sole heir to her father's fortune, was coming into her own. Although she had no doubt been told of the dangers of her position, she did not credit them; instead, she felt the pleasure of her new importance. The truth was that, as her father's favorite, Beatrice had been rather spoiled. She was used to being petted and made much of, and liked to call attention to herself.

In that regard, her father's will was immensely satisfying. As word of the inheritance leaked out, Beatrice acquired the attention not just of Provence, but of the world.

There was much lamenting in England and France upon the news of Raymond Berenger V's death. According to Matthew Paris, Henry, who was with an army in Wales trying to subdue the resident population, made a great show of sorrow, ordering that the bells be rung and dispensing alms at a memorial service, "at the same time strictly forbidding everyone from announcing this event to the queen, his wife, lest she should be overcome with grief." Marguerite, Eleanor, and Sanchia all mourned for their father, but lamentations quickly gave way to displeasure and disbelief as the terms of Raymond Berenger's legacy were revealed.

Beatrice *couldn't* have everything—Marguerite argued that she was still owed her dowry of ten thousand marks secured by her castles, of which Tarascon was one, while Eleanor reminded Henry that he had just lent her mother four thousand marks against her castles, including Tarascon, of course—and somewhere along the line the realization gradually dawned that Romeo de Villeneuve's much-vaunted financial strategy had simply been to pledge the same castles to everybody.

There was very little time to bicker, however, as the reality of Beatrice's inheritance provoked the expected response among eligible suitors. For all of the troubadours' rhapsodizing, the number of beautiful young heiresses actually available for the taking during the Middle Ages was limited. Beatrice's somewhat dramatic entry into this category therefore caused quite a stir. She and her mother were mobbed by potential husbands. Age was not a factor; fathers as well as sons proposed.

At the head of the list was that perennial suitor, Raymond VII of Toulouse. True, he had already wedded the daughter of Hugh of La Marche, but, like his previous marriage to Sanchia, this had never been consummated. Also, being the son-in-law of the count of La Marche was not as attractive a proposition now that the baron was a broken and defeated man.

To acquire a wife like Beatrice, who brought with her not only extreme youth and the concurrent expectation of sons, but the whole of Provence as well, was the answer to the count of Toulouse's prayers. He had to obtain an annulment from his new marriage in order to obtain the Church's sanction of a marriage to Beatrice; in fact, technically, he needed annulments from his two previous wives to marry Beatrice, but at least there was now a new pope, Innocent IV, to petition. The matter was too pressing and delicate to leave to intermediaries; this time, Raymond of Toulouse applied in person to the pontiff.

He didn't have far to go. Innocent IV was in Lyon holding an ecumenical conference, one of the purposes of which was to depose Frederick II. The pope claimed to have made a daring escape from imperial troops bent on his capture in Rome, riding his horse furiously under cover of night (followed more leisurely by his cardinals, who knew that the story was fictitious, a bid for world sympathy, and saw no need to hurry). Lyon was far enough away from the emperor's reach for Innocent to feel comfortable deposing him; but Frederick was already challenging the pope's authority to intervene in secular politics. In an open letter to the other kings of Europe, Frederick wrote: "Pope Innocent the Fourth, who, having summoned a general council, as he called it, dared to pass sentence of deposition on us, who were neither summoned to the said council, nor proved to be guilty of any deceit or wickedness, but which sentence he could not establish without great prejudice to all kings. For what will there not remain for each of you kings of each kingdom to fear from the face of such a prince of priests, if he attempts to depose us, who have been honored, as it were, from heaven with the imperial diadem, by the solemn election of princes, and with the approbation of the whole Church?" The argument was a persuasive one, and Innocent knew that he did not have the full support of the other monarchs, including Louis IX, for this action. But the battle between the papacy and the empire was engaged, and Innocent, who sensed he could win, had no intention of backing down.

Under these circumstances, though, the chances that the pope would allow Raymond VII of Toulouse, who was a known imperial sympathizer and decades-long heretic supporter, to annul his current marriage, or any of his marriages, in order to marry Beatrice and take over Provence were slim indeed. Innocent allowed Raymond VII to bribe him—the new pope liked to live well—and gave him his annulment, but there was no official papal sanction for a new wedding forthcoming. Raymond continued to nourish hopes, however, and even wrote to Blanche of Castile, begging her to use her influence with Innocent in his favor.

Still, the question of whom Beatrice should marry (there was no chance of her remaining single, not with the allegiance of Provence hanging in the balance) had to be settled, and the sooner the better. Richard of Cornwall put forward his son Henry, age ten, as a possible candidate; apparently, Sanchia had been promised five thousand marks at her father's death, which the earl was seeking to recoup. But not everyone was content to allow romance to take its natural course. Already, some of the suitors were growing impatient, and resorting to unorthodox means of provoking the young lady's ardor. The king of Aragon, for example, had directed an army to Aix to secure Beatrice for his son. Similarly, Frederick had dispatched the imperial navy to Provence to ensure that she marry one of his progeny.

Beatrice of Savoy did what she could in the face of this onslaught. She called a meeting of all of the townspeople of Aix, where she and her daughter had taken refuge in the local family castle, updated them on the situation (which was, in effect, that two separate hostile forces were converging on the city) and got them to agree to defend the castle against any possible intruders. She also had them swear to do their best to uphold all of the conditions of the count's will, which included that young Beatrice not be married without her mother's consent. She then instructed Romeo to put the Provençal ports on the alert for Frederick's ships, and this trusted adviser arranged matters so well that when the imperial fleet appeared it could not effect a landing and was forced to return home empty-handed.

But the countess knew she could not hold out alone for long. Rumors flowed in of the imminent approach of the king of Aragon's army. The emperor, also, had not given up. Frederick, frustrated in his attempt to take Beatrice by sea, now made plans to visit Innocent IV personally in Lyon at the head of an army, by which he meant to resolve favorably to the empire both the deposition question and the issue of succession in Provence. He tried to bribe Thomas of Savoy to desert his sister and niece's cause so that the imperial troops could pass through the Alps without fear of attack and catch the pope unprepared and unprotected. But Thomas was a family man and warned his sister. Beatrice of Savoy did not want her daughter married to the son of an excommunicate. She sent an urgent message to the pope alerting him of the impending danger and requesting official papal protection.

Papal protection meant that Beatrice of Provence was now a ward of the

Church; Innocent IV, stepping in as surrogate father, would decide (with her mother's approval) whom she married. With this valuable bargaining chip in his pocket, the pope turned for help against Frederick II to the one kingdom that he knew was a match for the empire: France.

Of all the sisters, it had been Marguerite (who had demonstrated her devotion to her father by arranging for his burial "in a very noble and beautiful sepulcher, which his daughter, the queen of France had built, as I saw with my own eyes," as the chronicler Salimbene attested) who was most furious when informed of the specifics of Raymond Berenger's will. The fact that she had brought a dowry of ten thousand marks, including an important fortification like Tarascon, with her to her marriage was a source of pride; she knew her mother-in-law looked down on her as a provincial, and the property allowed her a measure of self-respect. Moreover, it was a long-standing obligation upon which she and her husband's family had counted. The claims of Eleanor and Sanchia, she felt, were suspect. Everyone knew that Henry had accepted Eleanor without a dowry and that Henry had himself paid for Sanchia's. Vague promises of later bequests did not hold the same legal validity as an actual debt, which was the category into which her claim fell. As to the security for Henry's loan to her mother, Marguerite had held the prior title, and Eleanor had known it. The queen of England had been trying to usurp property that she knew had already been consigned to the queen of France. Marguerite was the eldest, the most mature, the most competent, and her position—thanks to Eleanor's encouragement of Henry's hopeless military campaign—the most prestigious. She was worth those ten thousand marks and she intended to have them.

The self-confidence Marguerite exhibited in arguing her case—which she did vehemently to both her husband and mother-in-law—was a reflection of the increased stature she now held within the French royal family. For the previous year Marguerite had fulfilled the role to which she had been aspiring since first becoming queen. On February 25, 1244, after a full decade of marriage, she had finally given birth to a son, Louis. More than that, she had followed up this achievement on May 1, 1245, by producing a second son, Philip.

The appearance of these two boys, so necessary to the succession of her husband's lineage, had transformed Marguerite's role within the family. Gone was the hapless victim of the White Queen's torments. In her place was a strong adult capable of defending her interests and those of her children. The years of enforced intimacy with Blanche of Castile and her methods had yielded fruit: Marguerite was now as attuned to the ebbs and flows of power and as sophisticated in her approach to politics as was her mother-in-law.

For once, the interests of Louis's wife and his mother coincided. Blanche of Castile also wanted those castles in Provence. A meeting between the French court and the pope was quickly arranged. In December 1245, Louis, Marguerite, Blanche, and Louis's younger, unmarried brother Charles of Anjou held a secret conclave with Innocent at the monastery at Cluny, northwest of Lyon. Also at this meeting, representing Beatrice of Savoy, were her brothers Boniface and Philippe of Savoy. Boniface of Savoy was in a particularly ticklish position at these talks; as archbishop of Canterbury he was supposed to be safeguarding English interests. If Henry and Eleanor had known where he was and what he was doing, they could have applied pressure or bribed him to resist the French. It appears, however, that the king and queen of England were ignorant of these proceedings.

With no opposing voice present, it took less than a week to strike a deal. In exchange for Beatrice's marrying Louis's youngest brother Charles of Anjou, Louis promised to recognize Innocent's deposition of Frederick and agreed to provide the necessary forces to protect him from imperial retaliation, should the emperor carry through with his threat to attack Lyon. The Savoyards agreed to the match on the grounds that all of the other provisions of Raymond Berenger's will be enforced. Provence was never to go to France outright through Charles. If Beatrice and Charles had children, the county would go to one of them. If there were no children, the county went to Sanchia. If Sanchia died without issue, Provence went to the king of Aragon. Moreover, the inheritance would not be split, not even for outstanding debts. Tarascon and the other castles were to stay in Beatrice's hands. Marguerite's claims, as well as those of her other sisters, were denied.

This was a compromise of Marguerite's interests and she resented it, but this was the best deal that she was going to get for the time being. At least Provence would be allied to her husband's family through Charles, which meant she had effectively marginalized Eleanor's claim. It still nettled her that her youngest sister had not been forced to surrender Tarascon or the 10,000 marks, but if there was one thing Marguerite had learned in her years of apprenticeship to the White Queen, it was patience.

With this understanding in place, the French acted quickly. Charles of

Anjou and Philippe of Savoy were dispatched with a force of five hundred knights, and Louis promised to follow quickly with reserves if necessary. On their way to Aix from Lyon, Charles and Philippe ran into Raymond VII, who was also on his way to Provence with a contingent of troops to woo Beatrice. But Charles and Philippe were quicker, and they had more men. The count of Toulouse was destined to be left at the altar yet again.

The officially sanctioned prospective bridegroom and his new uncle-in-law and their men-at-arms arrived in Aix to find the king of Aragon's forces already ensconced and besieging the castle where Beatrice of Savoy and her daughter were in hiding. There was a brief struggle and the king of Aragon retreated with dignity.

To be rescued, in true chivalric fashion, by a nineteen-year-old scion of the French crown—Salimbene called him "an admirable young man"—who was also athletic and well made (even if he did have a rather large nose), was a highly satisfactory resolution to the problem from the bride's point of view. Beatrice admired Charles's careless attitude and imperious bearing. "In kingly majesty he exceeded any other lord," the chronicler Villani observed. Charles was clearly used to getting his way, but then again, so was Beatrice.

The rest of Provence, however, was not as enamored of the pope's choice. It was widely viewed as the first step toward French domination. There was so much unrest in the capital that there was no question of a grand wedding in Paris or Sens, as Charles had evidently expected. Instead, the ceremony took place at Aix on January 31, 1246.

An effort was made to dignify the proceedings by attendance. Louis, Marguerite, Blanche, Boniface, and Philippe all stayed to witness the nuptials, and Thomas of Savoy made the trip from Flanders especially to give the festivities an extra infusion of celebrity (the chroniclers mentioned that the bride was escorted to the altar by her "famous" uncle). Still, it was by necessity a rushed, provincial affair, with soldiers on guard during the reception, and Charles of Anjou complained to his mother about the lack of pomp. Louis's wedding had been much grander, he insisted (although he must have been relying on hearsay as he was only seven at the time and had been left home in Paris). Charles was in determined competition with his eldest brother and often thought himself treated unfairly. "I am the son of a king and queen, and he [Louis] was not," he never failed to point out, referring to the fact that their grandfather Philip Augustus had still been king when Louis was born, so technically Louis had been the son of a crown prince and not a king. Of course, since Charles had been born after his father's death, the truth was that he had been the son of a *dead* king, but Charles did not see fit to remind anyone of that.

Marguerite did not appreciate the comparison between Charles and Beatrice's wedding and her own, nor the comment about Louis's ancestry. She had never liked Charles; she thought he was indulged and ambitious at her husband's expense. She hardly knew her sister Beatrice, who had been a toddler when Marguerite had left home to marry Louis. When it became clear that neither newlywed was willing to make concessions for Marguerite's claim on Raymond Berenger's estate, her opposition to the match hardened. After the wedding, she began to draw closer to Eleanor and Sanchia, and once back in Paris let it be known at court that she much preferred her English relatives to those of her husband's family.

Henry and Eleanor, who were informed of Beatrice's marriage only after the fact, were flabbergasted. Had not Eleanor's mother, Beatrice of Savoy, given her word that she would safeguard those castles for England? Had the king of England not given her four thousand marks only last year at her request for the purpose of fortifying those very castles? Had Henry and Eleanor paid to renovate fortresses that were now to be occupied by the French? "The king, however, did not meet with compassion or condolence from any one on account of this loss and disgrace," observed Matthew Paris. His barons had never approved of the loan to the queen's mother, or the liberal hospitality that Henry had displayed during her visit. They did not trust Beatrice of Savoy, as they did not trust the queen's other relatives, and the chronicler spitefully reported that the countess had been heard to say, "I am sorry that I have given my daughters (whom, according to the vulgar phrase in Provence, she called *her boys*) in marriage to this king and his brother."

If Beatrice of Savoy did really say that—which seems unlikely as she was much too skilled a diplomat to be so straightforward—she soon changed her mind. Her trials with her new son-in-law began almost immediately. Although Charles made use of Romeo de Villeneuve as an adviser immediately after the wedding, and even promoted him, he excluded his mother-in-law from the business of running Provence. He imported a throng of French bureaucrats, mainly accountants and lawyers, to investigate and arbitrate disputes during the transition of authority, and then used their findings to transfer power, castles, and fees away from Beatrice of Savoy and the other Provençal lords and into his own hands. He demonstrated in every decision, every conversation, every mannerism that he considered the culture and society of Provence inferior to that of France, and his attitude reflected his conviction that his subjects should be grateful for the improvements he was making on their behalf.

This was not a formula destined to endear him to the local inhabitants. A Provençal troubadour, Bertran d'Alamanon, who had in former days been used to the gracious ambience of the court of Raymond Berenger V, eloquently outlined the difference in Charles's approach to government:

> To my great annoyance and under duress, I have turned my whole attention to what I heartily dislike. I have to think about lawsuits and lawyers in order to draw up notarial acts; then I look out along the road to see if any courier is coming, for they arrive from all directions, dusty and saddle-sore . . . And if they say something stupid I wouldn't dare reproach them. Then they tell me: "Get on your horse, you're required in court; you will be fined, and you won't be pardoned if the hearing can't go ahead because of you." You see what I've come to, my lords: now look and see whether or not I'm properly kept to heel [on a leash]: for I prefer ice to meadow flowers, and I don't know what is happening to me.

Beatrice of Savoy did more than complain—she removed herself to Forcalquier and actively began plotting against her son-in-law. Marseille threw his officials out of the city. Both Arles and Avignon expelled papal representatives and sided with Beatrice of Savoy. The pope was forced to intervene.

In this power struggle between her mother and her husband, the new young countess of Provence sided with her husband. It wasn't simply that she had been her father's favorite. In Charles, Beatrice recognized someone whose interests, ambitions, and background were remarkably similar to her own. They were both the youngest of large families, and as such had tended to be alternately ignored and indulged. Each had grown up in the shadow of much older, highly accomplished siblings who had been held up to them as yardsticks of achievement since they were old enough to reason. Both had felt the comparisons, either spoken or unspoken, between their own performances and that of the revered eldest child. Each felt themselves to be secretly superior and took every slight, real or imagined, as acutely as they would have a wound from a sharpened sword; similarly, each had developed a façade of fiercely arrogant poise to compensate for the resulting pressure and inevitable self-doubt. The one overwhelming ambition of each was to overtake their eldest sibling—Louis in Charles's case, Marguerite in Beatrice's—in the eyes of the world; to garner that unquestioning adoration and respect that seemed to come so easily to the king and queen of France.

With her marriage, Beatrice felt herself to be finally on the way to attaining her objective. She was fourteen years old, beautiful, rich, and married to a member of the French royal family. She and Charles got along well. He gave her robes and furs and jewels and took her with him when he traveled. Charles enjoyed the privileges of his position and they journeyed in style. In May the couple was in Melun, just outside Paris, where Louis knighted Charles and Charles officially did homage to him for the counties of Anjou and Maine. The ceremony and subsequent feast were sufficiently opulent to satisfy even a man of Charles's advanced taste. As an additional wedding present, Louis made him lord of Vendôme and viscount of Laval and Mayenne, and gave him an annual income of five thousand livres parisis, just to get him started in married life. It was the first time Beatrice had been out of Provence and not even Marguerite's obvious coolness could spoil the headiness of the experience or shake her faith in Charles.

And now there was promise of even greater adventure, and a chance for honor and fame. The king and queen of France were going on a crusade to the Holy Land. All of the king's brothers would be accompanying him, and Charles had assured her that she could come along as well.

Marguerite

King Louis IX, ill in bed, takes the cross.

CHAPTER X

A VOW

ike the rest of his army, Louis IX had contracted dysentery while campaigning against Henry III and Hugh of La Marche in 1242, and returned to Paris much weakened. Two years later he fell ill again, this time critically. He lay dehydrated with a high fever, passing in and out of consciousness. The best physicians in Paris were called to the royal bedchamber, but medieval medicine being limited at the time to scholastic parsing of the works of Aristotle, there was not much they could do for him. The diagnosis, however, was unanimous: the king was dying. Certainly, Louis himself believed this to be so. In one of his rare moments of lucidity, he soliloquized, "Thus it comes that I, who was most rich and most noble in this world, and exalted above all others by my treasure, my arms, and my alliances, cannot now force grim death or my illness to a truce, were it even for an hour. What then are all these worth?"

Marguerite, Blanche, and their ladies-in-waiting held vigil by Louis's side. The illness reached its crisis. The king stopped breathing. There was a small argument between two of the ladies-in-waiting as to whether to confirm his death by drawing the sheet over his head. Later, Louis recounted to Joinville that as he "lay listening to the dispute between the two ladies our Lord worked within him, and quickly brought him back to such a state of health that although up till then he had not been able to utter a word he now recovered his speech. As soon as he was able to speak he asked for the cross to be given him; and this was promptly done. When the queen mother heard that the power of speech had come back to him she was as full of joy as it is as possible to be. But on learning that he had taken the cross—which she heard from his own lips—she mourned as much as if she had seen him lying dead."

Taking the cross—vowing to go on crusade—was probably not an unusual reaction under the circumstances. Louis naturally attributed his miraculous recovery to God, and sought to demonstrate gratitude through reciprocation. In medieval Christianity, there was nothing a man could do to please God more than to fight for the Holy Land. Individuals who embraced the cross were absolved of all sin, even terrible sins like murder, rape, and pillage; and since murder, rape, and pillage were the inevitable byproducts of the ordinary knight's lifestyle, going on crusade was an attractive option. It provided convenient redress for one's soul as well as the opportunity to engage in more murdering, raping, and pillaging, this time in the name of the Lord.

For Louis, the impulse to go on crusade was more in the nature of an epiphany; he implied to Joinville that he had weathered some divine test of faith by recovering. It is also certain that Louis had been nursing this idea for some time—at the very least, since Thibaud of Champagne's embarrassingly abortive effort of 1239. It cannot have been pleasant for a man as profoundly (and proudly) religious as Louis to have had to stand by and watch his brother-in-law, Richard of Cornwall, an Englishman, cover himself with glory by rescuing captured French knights abandoned by their own countrymen. Similarly, to have had these same knights so overwhelmed with appreciation that they defied their own sovereign and protected Richard and his brother on the battlefield was disconcerting. There was, in this episode, a tacit rebuke of French honor that stung.

The king's immovable conviction that his mission was divinely inspired led him into direct conflict with the queen mother. To Blanche, the idea of Louis leading a crusade was anathema. He was frail and sickly. Pray, by all means, she told her son, live a moral life, build churches, dispense alms, wash the feet of paupers if you feel you must, but do not leave the realm on a false caprice. The Holy Land needed protection, certainly—but so did France.

She did what she could to stop him. She reasoned, she commanded, she withheld affection. Nothing worked. At last, she enlisted the aid of William of Auvergne, the bishop of Paris. William consulted the scriptures and discovered that an oath taken under duress could be broken with impunity. "My lord, recollect, when you assumed the cross, you made the vow suddenly and unadvisedly," the bishop observed during an interview with the king arranged by Blanche. "You were ill, and, to speak the truth, were deprived of your senses; your blood was carried to your brain, and you were not of sound mind, wherefore the words you then uttered were devoid of the weight of truth and influence. His holiness the pope will benignly grant us a dispensation, when he knows the necessitous condition of the kingdom and the weak state of your bodily health." Blanche interjected her own logic: "My dearest son," she said, "remember what a virtue it is, and how pleasing it is to God, to obey and to comply with the wishes of your mother."

For the first time, Blanche did not prevail. Louis was fierce in his determination to go. To ensure that there was no doubt about his pledge, he first laid aside the cross, and then resumed it, saying, "My friends, now I am not devoid of reason or sense; I am not powerless or infirm; therefore I now require my cross to be restored to me." The decision to go on crusade was tantamount to a declaration of independence, and it marked a turning point in the king's life. At thirty-one years of age, Louis had finally found the strength within himself to confront his mother.

This small act of defiance had immense repercussions. Sheltered by his faith and the firm conviction that he was acting under instructions from God, the king of France was transformed from a diffident, insipid figurehead into a strong, active ruler. He threw himself into the planning and direction of his crusade. It was to be the best organized, best prepared, most efficient military strike in history. No detail escaped his attention. Blanche was forced to acquiesce in the face of her son's overwhelming energy and grim determination.

Marguerite watched her husband's performance with quiet satisfaction. Louis's taking of the cross would not have been her first choice—she, too, worried about his health and generally delicate constitution—but if that was to be the vehicle of her husband's assertion of adulthood, so be it. She would support him in his efforts and encourage him in his drive to succeed. To more fully demonstrate her faith in him (and to ensure that he was properly looked after while abroad), she, too, took the cross and announced her decision to leave the children with Blanche and accompany her husband to the Holy Land. Three months—the ordinary term of medieval military service—was not such a long time to be away.

Assembling a crusading army on the scale Louis envisioned was going to require significant manpower and resources, and the king felt that some foreign support would be very helpful. A united international venture (led by Louis, of course) would serve the dual purpose of lending legitimacy to the mission and defraying French expenditure by spreading the cost, which promised to be significant. Since all participants had to accept the cross of their own free will, Louis turned to diplomacy to try to put together an international coalition of volunteers.

He did not have much success. Henry and Eleanor, still fuming over Beatrice's clandestine marriage to Charles of Anjou and the usurpation of English rights in Provence by the French, declined to participate, and when Simon de Montfort heeded Louis's call, they hurried to dissuade him by naming him seneschal of Gascony. If anything, the crown of England sought to use the French crusade to angle for advantage, just as Blanche had feared. Henry sent Richard and Sanchia to Paris in the fall of 1247, just before Louis left, to revisit the issue of the return of English fiefs in Normandy in exchange for an extension of the truce during the period of the king's absence in the Holy Land. Louis successfully put off the question and renewed the truce until after he returned from crusade, but the only military aid he received from the English was one conscience-stricken knight and a small band of retainers, hardly the lethal fighting force for which he'd hoped.

Nor did he have much luck with other kingdoms. The king of Aragon was in no mood to help the French—besides, he was already busy fighting to take over Valencia. Hungary had just spent several months under a devastating Mongol occupation and was unable to help itself, let alone send a force to the Holy Land. There was some initial interest on the part of the king of Norway, but it turned out that he just wanted to use the promise of a crusade to raise money to fund an army to contend against the rest of Scandinavia.

Even the pope was reluctant to help. He had already called for a crusade against Frederick II, which many German barons had answered, and he wanted Louis to join that effort instead. This Louis refused to do. The king of France then asked the emperor for support. Frederick facilitated French procurement of ships and supplies from Genoa and Sicily, but he did not himself join, being too occupied with repulsing the pope's German forces. Also, Frederick was a very good friend of the sultan of Cairo—such a good friend that he made sure to warn the sultan of Louis's impending campaign and surreptitiously kept him apprised of French troop movements.

Of more concern to the king of France was the distinct lack of enthusiasm for the undertaking among much of the French aristocracy. Although the king's brothers as well as several important noblemen including Peter

Mauclerc, Hugh of La Marche, and Raymond VII of Toulouse (all of whom had reason to curry favor with Louis) had signed up right away, Thibaud of Champagne had declined to enlist, and many of Louis's other vassals were equivocating. Louis, however, remained true to his purpose. According to Matthew Paris, during the Christmas season of 1245, the king played a trick on the French aristocracy to encourage participation. He had special robes prepared "made of the most costly cloth, with divers skins let into them, and crosses made of fine gold-work, to be sewed on the shoulder part of the cloaks," to be given away to his nobles. Acceptance of the robe was akin to taking the cross. "And as it would seem unbecoming and disgraceful, as well as unworthy, for them to lay aside these crosses, they [the recipients], with a smile . . . and with floods of pleasant tears, called the French king, on account of this . . . a hunter of pilgrims and a new fisher of men."

Marguerite's decision to accompany her husband on crusade was of considerable benefit to Louis's recruitment. When it became known that the queen of France was committed to accompanying the king to the Holy Land, many other wives also agreed to go. Not having to separate from their families made it easier for their husbands to volunteer.

The manpower deficiency thus alleviated, Louis turned his attention to the accumulation of supplies. With approximately 2,500 knights and their attendants, 10,000 men-at-arms and 5,000 crossbowmen planning on making the journey, Louis had to arrange for the purchase of ships, horses, and crossbow bolts, not to mention food and wine. Unwilling to rely on the good will of Sicilian shippers, Louis went to considerable trouble to build his own port, Aigues-Mortes (today called Port-Saint-Louis-du-Rhône), just next door to Marseille.

Ports and ships (Louis contracted for thirty-six ships in all, to be built in Genoa and Marseille) all cost a great deal of money. The initial price tag for Louis's crusade, not counting expenses incurred after he sailed, came to a whooping 1,500,000 livres. The royal income, which could be counted upon for some 250,000 livres annually, was clearly insufficient. Louis turned to the pope, who graciously allowed him to take a tenth of the revenues of every church in France for three years, provided that His Eminence himself could take a twentieth as well, to be used in the crusade against Frederick. "The French kingdom was now wonderfully and pitiably impoverished . . . For the French king . . . oppressed that kingdom in manifold ways, by extorting large sums of money on the plea of fulfilling his pilgrimage in a manner suited to his rank," said the chronicler. Louis raised one million livres in this way; the rest came from expanded fees and fines, and from the plundering of the Jewish population.

It took more than three years, but at last all was in readiness. On June 12, 1248, Louis received the pilgrim's staff from the papal legate at St. Denis, heard mass at Notre Dame, and then, accompanied by Marguerite and his three brothers and their wives, rode off to the royal castle at Corbeil to say good-bye to his mother.

He left her not only the care of his children, but the regency of France. Once more, the queen mother was the official head of state. Although, in truth, Blanche had been running the country for the past twenty years anyway, she did not want the position. She was sixty years old, and tired. She understood the magnitude of the forces that would work against France in her son's absence, and the strength she would have to muster to hold the kingdom together. She knew it would speed her death. Upon his leave-taking she said simply: "Alas, my fine son, I will never see you again in this mortal life." She was right.

The crusaders took many detours on their way south to Louis's new port. The king made a point of stopping at all the major religious houses along the way to ask the various monks and friars to pray for his success. Salimbene observed the king and his brothers, dressed as pilgrims, on this journey when they stopped at Sens to pray. "Truly, he [Louis] was closer to the monk in the devotion of his heart than to the warrior in the pursuit of war," the chronicler declared. To reciprocate for the monks' spiritual support, Louis feasted his hosts, and Salimbene was lucky enough to have been invited:

We had, first of all, cherries and, later, the finest white bread; wine also in abundance and of the best was presented, as was worthy of a king's magnificence. And in the Gallic manner many were invited and "compelled to drink," although they "were not willing." Afterward, we had fresh beans cooked in milk, fish, crabs, eel-cakes, rice in almond milk and grated cinnamon, roasted eel in splendid sauce, cakes, cheese, and fruit in abundance. And all things were done with the utmost decorum and courtesy.

Marguerite and Beatrice accompanied their husbands on this extended procession through France. They seem to have put their differences aside for the moment, in order to help create an aura of competence and command.

Beatrice was pregnant with her first child, and would perhaps have leaned heavily on her sister. More than that, Marguerite understood that a populace made anxious by any sign of disunity would be more difficult for Blanche to control in the king's absence. Naturally, the people in the towns and cities along the way came out to get a glimpse of the king and his entourage as they passed, and Louis and Marguerite hoped by decorum to instill confidence in the citizenry. Salimbene, who came from Italy, was rather disappointed in the humble nature of the crowds; the women, he said, "look like servants. If the king of France had taken his way through Pisa or Bologna, the finest ladies of those famous cities would have turned out to meet him. But then I remembered the French custom, for in France only the bourgeoisie live in the cities while the knights and their noble ladies live in villas on their estates."

To ensure that Provence also remained quiet while the king and his brothers were away on crusade, the royal party stopped in Beaucaire, near the castle at Tarascon, on their way to port. There, Charles and Beatrice met with Beatrice of Savoy to try to reconcile their differences. Relations had by this time deteriorated to the point that the pope felt it necessary to send representatives as well in order to give the negotiations the best chance of success. A treaty of sorts was struck whereby Beatrice of Savoy surrendered her right to the castle at Aix in exchange for a percentage of the county's revenue. A special committee was established to look into the question of the disputed castles and other areas of contention. (Charles favored committees.) The agreement was more in the nature of a truce than a practical document—all of the really divisive issues were put off until Charles and Beatrice's return—but at least the family was again on speaking terms.

The citizenry of Provence, however, remained unmoved by the new family détente. In a scant two years, Charles of Anjou had succeeded in making himself very unpopular. This became evident as soon as the royal entourage reached Avignon. There, the crowds did not come out to cheer the king but to assault him. Matthew Paris claimed that the citizens of Marseille actually launched an attack against the king and his knights, and that it was only with great difficulty that the king of France restrained his forces from retaliating. This incident embarrassed Charles and Beatrice greatly, and would not be forgotten upon their return.

On August 25, Louis and Marguerite finally set sail from Aigues-Mortes. With them on the ship were Charles and Beatrice, and Louis's brother Robert of Artois and his wife. The king's other brother, Alphonse of Poitiers, stayed behind to help Blanche govern, but promised to join the royal army as soon as the queen mother had established a reliable administration. Other French nobles, such as Joinville, also sailed from the port, but in separate ships. The rendezvous point was Cyprus.

The crusade of Louis IX had begun.

> We should not be ashamed to acknowledge truth from whatever source it comes to us, even if it is brought to us by former generations and foreign peoples. For him who seeks the truth there is nothing of higher value than truth itself.
>
> —al Kindi, Islamic philosopher, ninth century

The Islamic empire of the ninth through the twelfth centuries was the most influential and advanced civilization of its age. Its borders stretched from Spain to Persia, encompassing all of present-day Morocco, Algeria, Tunisia, Libya, Egypt, Jordan, Israel, Lebanon, Syria, Turkey, Saudi Arabia, Iraq, and Iran. Tolerant of the Christians and Jews who lived under its rule (although non-Muslims were required to pay higher taxes, which did wonders for the conversion rate to Islam), the empire benefited from a rich and varied intellectual heritage, and as a result, its store of accumulated knowledge dwarfed that of the Europeans. Arab scholars were familiar with the Indian numbering system (now called Arabic) while the north still grappled tortuously with unwieldy Roman numerals; Arab physicians, schooled by translations of recovered Greek manuscripts, were acknowledged the best in the world; Arab philosophers were so learned that their commentaries on Aristotle were required reading at all of the European universities, including the one at Paris. Undisturbed access to African gold mines ensured the caliphs and sultans of Arabia a fairy-tale affluence envied at the courts of their Christian counterparts. Joinville described huge ingots formed by pouring molten gold into king-size earthenware wine casks that one sultan used for decorative purposes, while a tenth-century historian recorded the magnificence of the reigning Caliph's headquarters, whose crowning triumph was a rare tree growing out of a basin of water: "The tree has eighteen branches . . . on which sit all sorts of gold and silver birds, both large and small. Most of the branches of this tree are leaves of different colors. The leaves of the tree move as the wind blows, while the birds pipe and sing."

By the time of Louis's crusade, however, the caliphate was under attack from both external and internal forces. Its boundaries had been pushed back in the north by the militant kings of Aragon and Castile, and in the east by the ferocious descendants of Genghis Kahn. Within its reduced borders, differences over religious doctrine further fragmented the political structure. Gone were the days of a single, all-powerful caliph at the head of an organized realm. In his place were squabbling war lords called sultans, who claimed sovereignty over specific regions and cities. They spent their time feuding with each other, often employing mercenaries in an attempt to usurp neighboring territory, and weren't above cutting side deals with foreigners if expedient.

Nowhere was this confused state of affairs more apparent than in the immediate vicinity of Jerusalem. There were no fewer than five sultans—Cairo, Kerak, Damascus, Homs, and Aleppo—vying for power among themselves, with a small swatch of Christian territory, encompassing Jerusalem, Acre, Tripoli, Antioch, and Edessa, carved out between them. Although ostensibly protected by the Knights Templar and the Knights Hospitallers, the Crusader States, as this area was known, owed their continued existence to the goodwill of the Sultan of Cairo, with whom Frederick and later Richard of Cornwall had negotiated a treaty. Unfortunately, however, in 1244 the sultan of Cairo, whose name was Ayyūb, had felt it necessary to employ mercenaries against his archrival, the sultan of Aleppo. The mercenaries were difficult to control, and they had taken it upon themselves to sack Jerusalem on their way to Cairo to meet their new employer. Nearly all of the Knights Templar and the Knights Hospitallers were killed, and losses to the Christian population were estimated at sixteen thousand.

Ayyūb hadn't intended to provoke French intervention; that was just the way his luck was going. Son of al-Kāmil, a great warrior and highly educated man who had allied himself with Frederick II, Ayyūb had hoped that his father's old friend would intervene on his behalf and discourage the French king from attacking. "In 1249 when the King of France, one of the great Frankish kings, attacked Egypt, the Emperor sent him a message in which he tried to dissuade him from the expedition and warned him of the consequences of his action, but the French king did not take his advice," wrote Ibn Wasil, an historian and diplomat of the time.

Frederick's failure to convince Louis was unfortunate as the sultan was already preoccupied with a much more serious threat. The Mongols, led by the grandsons of Genghis Kahn, were once again on the march and heading toward Baghdad, with the intention of taking over all of the Islamic empire. The last time this pestilence had turned its attention to Islam had been twenty years before, when the great Kahn's sons had led an army into Persia; the slaughter had been terrible. Whole towns, including important libraries and mosques, were burned to ashes and the inhabiting populations systematically plundered, ravaged, and then destroyed. The victors celebrated each conquest by erecting monuments consisting of huge, grisly pyramids of the heads of their victims. The French threat seemed civilized by comparison.

Ayyūb was a sick man. He was suffering from an advanced stage of tuberculosis, which resulted in prolonged, violent coughing fits during which he had trouble catching his breath. These attacks did nothing to enhance his image as a strong leader and it was whispered among his people that the sultan was dying.

Louis, Marguerite, Charles, Beatrice, and Robert of Artois reached Cyprus in mid-September 1248. Theirs was among the first of the French ships to arrive. Louis was so anxious to begin his quest to save the Holy Land that it was only with difficulty that his advisers convinced him to stay on in Cyprus and wait for the rest of his army.

Evidence of the king's painstaking preparations greeted the royal party. In the middle of a field the wine barrels purchased for the expedition were stacked one upon the other; there were so many that "any one approaching them from the front might have taken them for barns," said Joinville, whose party of knights arrived soon after the king's. Similarly, "the wheat and the barley had been heaped in great mounds . . . the rain had been beating down so long on these heaps that it had caused them to sprout, and consequently appear to be covered with grass, so that, at a first glance, you might have imagined they were hillocks. However, when the time came to transport the grain to Egypt, it was found, on removing the first layer of green, that the wheat and barley underneath were in as good a condition as if they had only just been threshed," he wrote. The spectacle of the mass of supplies was comforting; it bespoke good management and leadership and augured well for the success of the king's venture.

The royal party made its way to Nicosia, the capital, and immediately took over the palace and all the best houses in the city while it waited for the rest of the French ships. Evidently, Louis's intentions were well-known throughout the Middle East, for soon after he had ensconced his household in Cyprus he received an embassy from the court of the Mongols (or Tartars, as they were known in Europe). The envoys suggested that, as the Mongols were also interested in attacking the Muslims, they and the French might combine forces in a coordinated military action. The Tartars were prepared to help Louis take Jerusalem as his share of the deal. The ambassadors were extremely friendly and solicitous. They even hinted that their countrymen might be amenable to conversion to Christianity.

Although Louis knew that these were the very same marauding, merciless barbarians who had just occupied and devastated Hungary, the temptation to convert the Tartars to Christianity was irresistible. He treated the Mongol representatives as honored guests, and sent his own emissaries back to the "king of the Tartars" to discuss the proposal. As a further demonstration of his goodwill, he sent along an extremely expensive tent that doubled as a portable chapel. It was made of crimson cloth and was ornamented with carved figurines of the Virgin Mary, the baby Jesus, and the Apostles.

Although the crusade would not go as planned, and a joint Christian-Mongol attack would surely have beaten the sultan of Cairo's forces, the French were actually lucky that nothing came of the Tartar proposal. Louis was no match for the descendants of Genghis Kahn, for whom piety was merely a ploy to obtain assistance in the short term. Given the history of Mongol behavior, of which there was substantial precedent, the alliance would have been broken as soon as the Muslim forces were subdued. Louis, Charles, and Robert would have been beheaded with ruthless efficiency, Marguerite and Beatrice would have been sold into slavery, and the course of European history would have changed forever. As it was, the French envoys had so far to travel, and were detained so long upon their arrival at the Mongol court, that it took more than two years for Louis's negotiators to return to Cyprus. By that time, Louis and his army had long since left for Egypt.

What with waiting for everyone to assemble and the advent of winter, the French army did not leave Cyprus until the spring of 1249. The weather was balmy, there was plenty to eat and drink, and the reigning monarch was friendly and rich. Beatrice gave birth to a son, whom she and Charles christened Louis. Robert of Artois wrote home to Blanche about it: "Know: that the Countess of Anjou [Beatrice] did bear at Cyprus a most fair and well-knit son, which she hath put to nurse and left there," he said.

Louis had one last duty to discharge before embarking: the composition of an official declaration of war, meant as a sportsmanlike warning to one's opponent that you intended to come over and annihilate him. So, as was customary, before sailing, the king of France sent the sultan of Cairo the following message:

You will be aware that I am the head of the Christian community, as I acknowledge that you are the head of the Moslem community . . . I have given you sufficient demonstration of our strength and the best advice I can offer . . . If this country falls into my hands, it will be mine as a gift. If you keep it by victory over me, you may do as you will with me. I have told you about the armies obedient to me, filling the mountains and the plains, numerous as the stones of the earth and poised against you like the sword of destiny. I put you on your guard against them.

To which Ayyūb replied:

Fool! If your eyes had seen the points of our swords and the enormity of our devastations, the forts and shores that we have taken [from you] and the lands that we have sacked in the past and the present, you would gnaw your fingers in repentance! The outcome of the events you are precipitating is inevitable: the day will dawn to our advantage and end in your destruction. Then you will curse yourself.

The final condition of chivalry and modern warfare being thus satisfied, Louis IX and his crusaders prepared to embark.

CHAPTER XI

THE CRUSADE OF LOUIS IX

The French fleet left Cyprus on May 13, 1249. It must have made an impressive picture. Louis had arranged to bring everything along—men, horses, siege equipment, weaponry, armor, wine, wheat, even ploughs to be used by future Christian communities. Joinville, who was there, put the number of French ships at 1,800: "It was indeed a lovely sight to look at, for it seemed as if all the sea, as far as the eye could reach, was covered with the canvas of the ships' sails." Marguerite sailed with Louis and his brothers; similarly, the other French wives sailed with their husbands, as Matthew Paris mentions that the queen of France was accompanied to Damietta by a party of noblewomen.

There was a storm along the way, which separated half the fleet, so that only about seven hundred ships arrived at the intended target, the Egyptian port of Damietta. The rest were blown nearly two hundred miles off course, all the way to Acre. The royal barge was one of those that made it to the correct port. On June 4, the king and queen of France saw the outline of Damietta on the shore.

Ayyūb had had ample warning of Louis's approach. Frederick had sent a spy to the sultan who reported "that his journey to Egypt had been made in the guise of a merchant, and that no one heard a whisper of his visit to the Sultan and the Franks never realized that the Emperor was intriguing with the Muslims against them." Too sick to confront his nemesis in person, the sultan of Cairo had delegated the task of defending Egypt to his best general, Fakhr ad-Din. Fakhr, unsure of Louis's intended landfall, and with almost two hundred miles of coastline to defend, assembled the majority of the army inland so as to be able to move quickly to intercept the French. He put the bulk of the Egyptian forces at Mansourah, between Louis and Cairo, so the invaders could not reach the capital city. Strongly suspecting, however, that the French would come ashore at Damietta, the general personally led a small advance guard to the beach outside the city, to try to repel the crusaders before they could effect a landing.

Thus the French beheld what they thought was the sultan's main army lined up on the beach when Damietta came into view: "We found the full array of the sultan's forces drawn up along the shore. It was a sight to enchant the eye, for the sultan's arms were all of gold, and where the sun caught them they shone resplendent. The din this army made with its kettledrums and Saracen horns was terrifying to hear," Joinville recalled. There was a brief discussion about waiting for the rest of the army, which had been blown off course, to arrive but this time Louis was adamant: the king's forces would attack first thing in the morning.

At daylight the crusaders put on their armor and got into galleys for transport to shore. Some of these vessels were magnificent; the Count of Jaffa's, for example, was painted all over with his coat of arms. "He had at least three hundred rowers in his galley; beside each rower was a small shield with the count's arms upon it, and to each shield was attached a pennon with the same arms worked in gold." Louis was so anxious to lead his troops personally into battle, that when he heard that another nobleman had landed before the royal galley had reached the shore, he leapt out of his vessel into neck-deep water, holding his standard high above his head. "When he had reached land and scanned the enemy, he asked who they were, and was told they were Saracens [Muslims]. He put his lance under his armpit, and holding his shield before him, would have charged right in among them if certain sagacious men who were standing round him had allowed it," said Joinville.

The Muslim advance guard was outnumbered, and the French crossbowmen, with an unrestricted, flat terrain in front of them, inflicted heavy losses. As Marguerite and Beatrice watched from the safety of the harbor, General Fakhr sounded a retreat. He tried to burn the bridge to Damietta behind him, but the French knights were pursuing too closely, and he did not have time. Instead of falling back on the city and taking a stand, Fakhr chose to go around Damietta and regroup with the main army. Damietta had its own defensive force, but when the city's soldiers saw the sultan's army retreat, they deserted their posts. Ibn Wasil wrote: "The people of Damietta

feared for their own lives if they were besieged. There was of course a garrison of brave Kinanites in the city, but God struck terror into their hearts and
they left Damietta, together with the population, and marched all night . . .
On the morning of Sunday 23 safar [June] the Franks appeared before Damietta and found it deserted, with the gates wide open. They occupied it without striking a blow and seized all the munitions, arms, provisions, food, and
equipment that they found there. It was a disaster without precedent."

After that, it was only a matter of singing a *Te Deum*. Marguerite and
Beatrice were probably on shore by nightfall. Louis had captured Damietta
for France and the Church in a single morning.

The offensive was not without casualties, however. When the crusaders
began the process of gathering and identifying their dead, they counted
Hugh of Lusignan, the count of La Marche, among the fallen. He who, with
his wife, Isabella, had started and survived two rebellions, and come so close
to dominance and autonomy, had been felled at last on a remote, alien shore
by a Saracen scimitar, in the service of the king of France.

The arrival of King Louis IX's ships.

★ ★ ★

General Fakhr fell back on Mansourah, where the rest of the Muslim army
was stationed, and duly informed the sultan of the size of the invading army
and the loss of Damietta. Ayyūb was so furious that the local defenders had
abandoned their posts that he had them all hanged.

While these executions no doubt satisfied the sultan's ire and need for a
scapegoat, they did nothing to address the immediate problem of expelling
the French army from Egypt. According to Matthew Paris, who seems to

have been reliably informed by letters sent back to Europe from the crusaders themselves, Ayyūb tried mediation first—Jersusalem for Damietta, a straight trade. But Louis rejected the offer, based in large part on his brother Robert of Artois's advice.

Diplomacy failing, Ayyūb had no choice but to fight. He sent an emissary to Louis, officially challenging him to a battle at Mansourah on June 25. The magnitude of the threat was such that, sick as he was, the sultan felt it necessary to make the journey personally to Mansourah to rally his troops. Accordingly, he gathered his entire household around him and arranged to be carried, writhing and coughing, by litter across the desert. Just before he left, as an extra precaution, the sultan of Cairo sent once more for the mercenaries.

Louis chose not to respond to the sultan's June 25 challenge. Instead he waited at Damietta for the rest of his ships, which had been blown off course during that first storm. This took several months. He and his army simply sat in Damietta until November, when the last of the crusaders, including his brother Alphonse of Poitiers, finally arrived.

Even those unversed in military tactics understand that enforced idleness does not improve an army's morale. There were disagreements among the knights about the manner in which the rather meager spoils captured with Damietta were to be divided. "The total value of the goods . . . amounted to no more than six thousand livres," Joinville sniffed. "As for the main mass of troops, they took to consorting with prostitutes, and because of this it happened that . . . the king discharged a great number of his people."

Worse, the sultan's forces, perceiving that the enemy had inexplicably decided to remain quiescent, began a series of daring midnight raids aimed at diminishing troop strength by attrition. Crusaders dozed off at their own peril. Their compatriots would find their headless bodies sitting at the table in the morning.

Finally, however, with Alphonse of Poitiers's arrival, Louis called a council to decide on the army's next move. The debate centered on whether to take Alexandria, Egypt's other important port, or to head directly for Cairo. Most of the barons favored Alexandria "because the city had a good harbor, where the ships bringing food for the army could land their supplies." But Robert of Artois strongly disagreed, arguing instead that the French should march straight to Cairo. "If you wished to kill the serpent you must first of all crush its head," he urged. "The king," Joinville reported, "rejected the barons' advice in favor of his brother's."

The army rode out of Damietta on November 20, 1249. Louis left Marguerite, Beatrice, and the other aristocratic wives behind with a token force of five hundred soldiers under the command of the duke of Burgundy to guard the city. Many of these soldiers were sailors from Pisa and Genoa who had manned the ships that had brought the crusaders to Egypt. They had been recruited in the euphoric aftermath of the victory at Damietta to stay to fight with the French. Both the queen of France and her sister the countess of Provence were pregnant again when their husbands rode off to do battle with the Egyptians.

The trip across the desert had drained Ayyūb of his remaining strength, but he managed to reach Mansourah alive, and had the presence of mind to order the construction of additional fortifications to try to thwart Louis's progress. Walls were built, weaponry distributed, and troops were brought by barge up the Nile. But the sultan fell into a coma on November 20, the very day the crusaders moved out of Damietta. Four days later, he was dead.

Panic seized the sultan's advisers. Ayyūb's death would certainly demoralize the army, causing defections, just at a time when troop strength was most demanded. The sultanate needed to be passed immediately to Ayyūb's eldest son, Tūrān-Shāh, but Tūrān-Shāh had been sent north on a political errand, and it would be several weeks before he could get back. The counselors vacillated over what would be the most effective policy.

Into this political void stepped Shajar al-Durr (Tree of Pearls), Ayyūb's favorite wife. Shajar, an Armenian slave who had captured the sultan's eye as the worthy spoil of a previous battle, demonstrated the statecraft of a seasoned campaigner. Gathering the immediate family and servants in the corpse's tent, she convinced them to conceal the death from the public. The masquerade was extensive: Shajar continued to have food prepared and delivered to Ayyūb's tent as before, and those in the administration who were not in on the scheme and who requested an audience with the sultan were told to come back another time when the sultan was feeling better. Shajar then had General Fakhr ad-Din compose a letter to the people of Cairo, categorizing the effort as a jihād, and exhorting the citizenry to rise up and resist the French. "Come out, heavily or lightly armed and fight for God's cause with your money and your life." To add to the illusion, she had the general forge Ayyūb's seal on the document, so it looked as though it had come from the sultan himself. It all worked; reinforcements poured in and the secret was kept from the army, although the French seemed to have learned the news quickly from spies.

The French army's slow progress from Damietta along the right bank of the Nile also worked to Shajar's advantage. Hampered by five hundred horsemen sent as snipers by General Fakhr, the crusaders took a month to reach Mansourah. When Louis and his army finally arrived, they found the enemy encamped in great numbers on the other side of the river "to prevent our passage—a thing which they could easily do, for no one could get across to approach the enemy, except by swimming over," said Joinville.

The crusaders tried for a month to ford the river by building a fortified bridge, complete with towers. However, no sooner was a tower built than the Arabs burned it down with flaming projectiles launched from catapults built for just this purpose; as for the bridge, the enemy waited until it was nearly finished and then destroyed it by digging channels in the Nile so that the weight of the rushing water caused the bridge to collapse. "Thus it happened that in one day they undid all that we had done with three weeks' labor; for as fast as we dammed up the stream on our side, they broadened its course by the holes they made on theirs," Joinville reported glumly. Bridge work was debilitating as well as fruitless, and disease preyed on the knights and their men. Frustration and discouragement ran high.

Then the French were the beneficiaries of a piece of luck. In exchange for five hundred bezants, a Bedouin traitor offered to show the crusaders a spot farther upstream where it was possible to ford the river on horseback. This was quite a bit of money, but it seemed worth it. Louis decided to send a select force, led by his brother Robert of Artois, to cross the Nile first and test the information before risking the entire army on the excursion. If all went well, the army would follow.

Robert of Artois's initial foray across the river was a great success. The Bedouin's information proved reliable; there was a sandbank in the middle of the Nile at just that point, and the horses and riders were able to scramble to the opposite shore. They surprised a force of three hundred Arab soldiers, who fled before them. The count of Artois and his forces pursued closely, burst into a forward army camp that the Arabs called Jadila, caught General Fakhr ad-Din in the bath, and killed him and everyone in sight.

At this point, the plan called for Robert to sit tight and wait for Louis and the rest of the army before proceeding. Unfortunately, Robert, having tasted victory, yearned for more, and, rejecting the sober advice of his more experienced knights, led his force directly to Mansourah. The city gates had been left open for those Muslims trying to escape the French, and the crusading force entered Mansourah and thundered down its streets, killing all in their way, until it reached the very palace that housed the sultan.

But an army is only as good as its discipline, and the French knights, perhaps assuming that the lack of resistance signaled surrender, were distracted by the possibility of spoils. They dispersed through the streets of the town, hunting for plunder. Their Arab opponents, who had not in fact retreated, but were stationed on balconies and roofs all over the city, began raining projectiles down on them. "When our men tried to return," Joinville wrote, "the Turks in Mansourah threw great beams and blocks of wood down on them as they passed through the streets, which were very narrow." What had been a small but formidable unit disintegrated into scattered pockets of crusaders unable to regroup.

And then the mercenaries struck.

They were the Mamlūks, Turkish horsemen from the north. Once slaves, they had been trained in warfare and found both freedom and wealth as hired killers. Consequently, they fought with a ferocity unmatched in medieval times: it would be the Mamlūks who later repulsed the Mongols and saved Egypt from the grandsons of Kahn. Seeing the enemy trapped and isolated, they flew at them through the streets: "At the moment of supreme danger, the Turkish battalion of the Mamlūks . . . lions in war and mighty in battle, rode like one man upon the enemy in a charge that broke them and drove them back. The Franks were massacred one and all with sword and club," wrote Ibn Wasil.

Meanwhile, Louis had brought the rest of the army across at Jadila, only

The crusading army attacked by the Saracens.

to discover that, against orders, his brother's unit had gone on ahead to Mansourah, leaving the bulk of the soldiery, who were having trouble crossing the Nile, unprotected. Moreover, the Muslims, now aware of the location of the French crossing, had stationed additional troops at Jadila who attacked Louis's battalions as soon as they had crossed. Joinville was with the king:

> While we were coming back down the bank of the river, between a brooklet and the main stream, we saw that the king had come up close to the river. The Turks were driving back his other battalions, slashing and striking at them with swords and maces, and gradually forcing them, together with the king's own battalion, back upon the river. The rout there was so complete that many of our people attempted to swim across to join the Duc de Bourgogne; but they were unable to do so, for their horses were weary, and the day had become very hot. So, as we were coming downstream towards them, we saw the river strewn with lances and shields, and full of men and horses drowning in the water.

Louis's troops held their position across the river, but were unable to march on Mansourah. Robert of Artois and his entire command, constituting approximately a third of the French forces, died in the streets of the city at the hands of the Mamlūks. Louis lost hundreds more crossing the river, and although he held the enemy camp of Jadila, he came under constant attack from the Muslims, now under the command of a Mamlūk general.

And then the stupendous folly of not having secured Alexandria before attempting to take Cairo was made clear to the French. The Muslims had brought barges filled with warriors down the Nile from this second port and stationed them between Louis and Damietta, cutting off the crusaders' supply lines and avenue of retreat. The king of France was trapped.

Robert of Artois had launched his disastrous offensive on February 8; the French army sat in Jadila through April, repelling enemy attacks and slowly starving. They ate anything they could find, including diseased fish. Consequently, a deadly illness spread through the camp. "On account of this evil circumstance, and because of the unhealthy climate—for not a drop of rain ever falls in Egypt—a disease spread through the army . . . with those who had this disease the flesh on the gums became gangrened; and none who fell a victim to it could hope to recover, but was sure to die," wrote

Joinville. To try to halt the progress of the disease, French surgeons operated on the soldiers, shaving off the black gum tissue. "It was pitiful to hear around the camp the cries of those whose dead flesh was being cut away," said Joinville. "It was just like the cry of a woman in labor." The king himself was stricken.

Increasingly desperate, with no hope of taking Cairo, Louis tried to revive the sultan's original offer of Damietta for Jerusalem. But Tūrān-Shāh, the sultan's son, had by now returned from his journey north and, with the Egyptian forces clearly holding the superior position, he refused to negotiate. There was nothing left for Louis to do but retreat. The French recrossed the Nile and resumed their original camp, and on April 7, under cover of darkness, what remained of the army tried to make it back to Damietta.

It was a harrowing trek. The king ordered the remaining barges to carry the sick and wounded, but to signal the retreat they had to build bonfires, which also alerted the enemy to their intentions. "The crews who manned our galleys had made great fires to attract the attention of the sick who had managed to drag themselves to the bank of the river," Joinville remembered. "As I was urging my sailors to let us get away, the Saracens entered the camp, and I saw by the light of the fires that they were slaughtering the poor fellows on the bank." Much to the frustration of Charles of Anjou, who understood that his brother's slow progress was endangering the retreat, the king refused to travel by boat. Louis was so ill with dysentery that he could barely stay upright upon his horse; he had to stop so often to relieve himself that "they had to cut away the lower part of his drawers," said Joinville. Charles urged him repeatedly to hurry. "Count of Anjou, count of Anjou, if you think I am a burden to you, get rid of me; but I will never leave my people," Louis cried.

Charles was right to press him: Louis only made it to the small village of Sharimshah, about halfway between Mansourah and Damietta, before collapsing. He was carried, barely conscious, to the private home of some sympathetic citizens of French ancestry. "It was thought, at the time, that he would not last the night," said Joinville. With Louis's permission, one of the knights with him tried to arrange a truce with the Egyptians, but before the terms were accepted, a frightened French sergeant began shouting for the crusaders to surrender; in the confusion, "everyone had thought that the king had really issued such orders, and had given up their swords to the Saracens." The truce was consequently denied, the house where the king and his brothers were hiding was surrounded, and all were taken prisoner.

Those foot soldiers and knights who had managed to escape from Sharim-shah during the night were caught farther upstream the next morning. "As Wednesday dawned the Muslims had surrounded the Franks and were slaughtering them, dealing out death and captivity. Not one escaped. It is said that the dead numbered thirty thousand," wrote Ibn Wasil. Louis, Charles, and Alphonse of Poitiers were taken back to Mansourah and placed in chains under armed guard. The sultan of Cairo confiscated Louis's scarlet, ermine-trimmed cloak and sent it to an emir in Damascus as a souvenir.

The Mamlūks had once again been at the forefront of the fighting. As befits mercenaries, the profit motive spurred them to new heights of valor. It seems that they worked on commission. By public pronouncement before he died, Ayyūb had promised ten gold coins for every Christian head, five for every right hand, and two for every foot. As a result, the surviving spectral vision from Louis's crusade, so meticulously planned, so fervently executed, was of a flat plain littered to the horizon with headless French corpses minus hands and feet, among them the peers of France, each mutilated knight still encased in his cross-emblazoned armor, left to rot in the desert sun or be eaten by vultures.

CHAPTER XII

THE QUEEN'S GAMBLE

Now you have already heard of the great suffering of the king and all the rest of us endured. The queen (who was then in Damietta) did not, as I am about to tell you, escape from tribulations herself.

—Joinville

Damietta, cut off from communication with the main part of the army by the enemy blockade of the Nile, was ignorant of the extent of the disaster. But as the months passed with no word from Louis, Marguerite and the remaining French forces became increasingly anxious. By Easter it was clear that something had gone wrong, but in the absence of reliable information, the queen and her advisers could not devise an effective course of action. Then there was the added complication of Marguerite's pregnancy. (Beatrice had already given birth to a daughter, Blanche.) The French queen was due to deliver at the end of April.

Then, three days before the baby was due, the soldiers on watch from the lookout towers shouted that an army was moving toward Damietta. From a distance it looked like it might be the French troops returning in triumph, and there was some preliminary rejoicing, but the guard was soon disillusioned. It was the Egyptian army, brandishing the shields and standards of the captured Christians, "in order that, having the appearance of Frenchmen, they might obtain admission into the city, and, as soon as they were admitted, might kill all therein," wrote Matthew Paris. The watchers at Damietta were not fooled, for "the nearer they approached, the more unlike Frenchmen they appeared."

Panic ensued, particularly upon the news of the capture of the king and the complete destruction of the French army. Still, the duke of Burgundy's forces, while not in a position to attack so massive an enemy force, were sufficient to put up enough of a fight in defense of the city that the Egyptians did not attempt to storm the gates. Instead, the enemy made camp just outside the walls, on the bank of the Nile. Towers and pavilions were erected in anticipation of the sultan's approach, and weapons and catapults poured in. Damietta would soon be under siege.

Marguerite, fearful for Louis's sake as well as her own, had nightmares, but, determined that she should not be taken prisoner, kept an older knight by her bedside, even during childbirth. "If the Saracens take this city," she ordered him, "you will cut off my head before they can take me."

"Rest assured that I will do so without hesitation," replied the knight.

Just as she went into labor Marguerite was informed that a large number of the sailors and foot soldiers from Pisa and Genoa, who had originally agreed to remain in Damietta with the French troops to provide additional support, were now planning to evacuate. Their desertion would put the entire city in jeopardy, for without the Pisan and Genoese ships Damietta could not be supplied with provisions against the siege. Those remaining in the city would be forced either to surrender Damietta to the sultan or face a prolonged blockade with limited supplies, which would inevitably result in starvation. In this moment of panic and confusion, Marguerite's instinctive appreciation of the military and political realities told her that these soldiers must be induced to stay, that she must hold Damietta if at all possible. It was the one asset that the French possessed that was valuable enough to trade for Louis's life.

Marguerite had her baby, whom she called Jean Tristan as a reminder of the sorrow attached to his birth (after the legendary Sir Tristan, a hapless knight at King Arthur's court who, distraught over a miscommunication with his lover, Isolde, committed suicide). Immediately after giving birth, not being able to get up herself, she called all of those who planned to abandon the city to her bedside; apparently, the room was quite crowded. "Gentlemen," she said, "for God's sake, do not leave this city; for it must be plain to you that if we lose it the king and all those who have been taken captive with him would be lost as well. If this plea does not move you, at least take pity on the poor weak creature lying here, and wait till I am recovered."

The gentlemen were moved, but not enough to change their minds. "My lady, what can we do? We're dying of hunger in the city," they replied.

Marguerite saw her opening. "I will order all the food in this city to be bought in my name, and from now on will keep you all at the king's expense," she countered.

They knew she had the money—indeed, they had brought it themselves. According to Matthew Paris, the French at Damietta had received "as much money in talents, sterling coin, and money . . . as eleven wagons, to each of which were four strong horses, could be loaded with."

Her bribe was accepted. It cost her 360,000 livres, but the French held Damietta.

By taking this decision on herself when the reigning knight, the duke of Burgundy, was floundering, Marguerite prevented the slaughter or starvation of hundreds of Frenchmen, the residue of the huge force whom Louis had brought to the desert. With this one act, the queen saved what was left of her husband's crusade.

Marguerite had solved the immediate problem, but she still did not know where her husband was, or what the Egyptians planned to do with him. There was nothing to do but wait.

It was perhaps lucky that the queen of France was ignorant of her husband's true situation. Immediately after Louis's capture, Tūrān-Shāh apparently toyed with the idea of further humiliating the king by exhibiting him, chained, all over Egypt—either that, or beheading him. Nonetheless, he sent his own doctors to cure Louis, as Tūrān-Shāh needed to keep his asset alive in order to keep his options open.

At first the sultan tried to extract excessive concessions from the French. He sent envoys and translators to the main body of captured French noblemen, of whom Joinville was one. "My lord," said the Saracens, "the sultan has sent us to you to inquire if you wish to be set free?" The count of Brittany, who was acting as spokesman, answered that yes, they did wish to be set free. The Egyptian agents then asked if the French were willing to barter their own castles and lands, or the castles and lands of the Knights Templar in the Holy Land for their freedom. The count of Brittany declined to do so. "At this [the sultan's envoys] remarked that it seemed to them we had no desire to be set free, and told us they would go and send us men who would make sport of us with their swords, as they had done with the others of our army. Then they went away," wrote Joinville.

The negotiators then approached Louis with the same requests. When he, too, replied in the negative, they threatened to torture him. But the king was in despair, refusing all food and drink. The shame of his present circumstances, coupled with the horror he felt at having led so many of his subjects to their deaths, made him apathetic to his own fate. "In reply to these threats the king had answered that he was their prisoner and they could do with him as they pleased," reported Joinville.

His initial overtures having failed, the sultan fell back on the traditional demand for ransom. "When the Saracens had seen that they could not prevail over our good king with threats, they . . . asked him how much money he was prepared to pay the sultan, and whether he would also surrender Damietta," wrote Joinville. "The king had replied that if the sultan was willing to accept a reasonable sum he would send and advise the queen to pay that amount for their ransom. 'How is it,' they had asked, 'that you won't tell us definitely whether you'll do this?' The king had answered that he did not know whether or not the queen would consent, since, as his consort, she was mistress of her actions."

There was no duplicity in Louis's response; the king was not a man to dissemble, not even to gain advantage against the enemy. In the absence of the king, it was Marguerite who was entrusted with sovereign responsibility.

The sultan asked for a million gold bezants, a sum equal to five hundred thousand livres, and the return of Damietta. Overwhelmed by guilt and remorse, Louis agreed passively to the Egyptian demands. When messengers informed Tūrān-Shāh of the French king's reaction, the sultan exclaimed: "By Allah! This Frank is a very generous-minded man not to have haggled over paying so great a sum! So go and tell him I'll let him off a hundred thousand livres of the ransom money," reported Joinville. The deal was struck, and the sultan ordered that Louis and the more important prisoners, including Joinville, be brought to the camp outside Damietta so that they could open communications with Marguerite.

But Tūrān-Shāh, who was young and inexperienced, was not as popular with his troops as his father had been. Worse, he seems to have reneged on Ayyūb's original offer of gold for Christian body parts. This upset the Mamlūks. It occurred to their leaders that, as they had done the brunt of the fighting, they were entitled to the preponderance of the spoils. But when they made this point strongly to the sultan they were rebuffed. On May 2, just as the French prisoners arrived by barge, the Mamlūks took matters into their own hands. Tūrān-Shāh had had a large tower erected next to his tent, and he often climbed to the top to have a look at Damietta. The Mamlūks waited until Tūrān-Shāh was in his tower and then set fire to it. When the sultan ran out, they chased him to the bank of the Nile and assassinated him. None of his own people came to his aid, although he cried out for help. One of the mercenaries cut out Tūrān-Shāh's heart and left his body to rot by the river. "He was still young, not yet thirty, I think," wrote Ibn Wasil. "He ruled over Egypt for two months."

The French king and his party were now in the singular position of eavesdropping while the Mamlūks argued among themselves over what to do with their prisoners. The majority seemed to have favored killing them outright: "My friends, if you'll listen to me and to those who think as I do, you'll kill the king and all the people of any importance who are with him," said one. "Then, for the next forty years we'll be in no danger, since their children are young, and we hold Damietta." Still, a vocal minority opposed the plan: "If we kill the king [said another], after killing our sultan, everyone will say that the Egyptians are the wickedest and most treacherous people in the world."

Although it seems an odd time to have suddenly become concerned with appearances, the Mamlūks were rightly worried that their military coup would not translate into stable political gains. They would have to acquire legality in order to rule Egypt, or they would not be able to command the respect of the inhabitants and eventually they would be overthrown. A creative solution was therefore employed. Shajar al-Durr, the former slave who had been Ayyūb's wife, and who had demonstrated such initiative after the death of her husband, was declared sultan, "an event without precedent throughout the Muslim world," said Ibn Wasil. The head of the Mamlūks then married Shajar.

Political legitimacy thus established to everyone's satisfaction, Shajar and the Mamlūks were free to turn their attention to the French. It was fortunate for the king of France that the Mamlūks appreciated large ransoms. The new sultan decided to uphold Tūrān-Shāh's original arrangement. There was a big conference between the leading Egyptian advisers and the French prisoners to hammer out the details. It was agreed that Louis and the French men of rank would be released immediately upon the surrender of Damietta, and that all of the French would be allowed to go unmolested to the city of Acre, still held by Christian forces. Marguerite would have to agree to pay two hundred thousand livres before the king left the Egyptian military camp; the balance would be paid from Acre. The Egyptians promised to protect those French too ill or wounded to be moved from Damietta.

The emirs were so impressed with Louis's sincerity that they seem actually to have weighed the idea of making him sultan of Egypt. "The king asked me if I thought he would have taken this kingdom if it had been offered to him. I told him that if he had done so he would have acted very foolishly, seeing that these emirs had killed their former lord," said Joinville. "He told me, however, that in fact he would not have refused it." In the end, though, the emirs, noting that the king of France never left his tent without first lying down on the ground and crossing himself all over, and reflecting that this habit argued against an easy conversion to Islam, withdrew the offer.

Early the next morning, Geoffroy de Sargines, a trusted French nobleman, was dispatched to Damietta to inform the queen of the details of the surrender. Marguerite was relieved to hear that Louis was alive, and that an arrangement had been negotiated for his release. But the magnitude of the ransom shocked the count of Burgundy and his advisers; moreover, they did not trust the enemy's integrity. There was a heated discussion as to whether to honor the treaty and evacuate the city; in the end Marguerite managed to convince the soldiers to pay the ransom and abide by the conditions of the agreement.

Gathering up her infant son in her arms, the queen of France then led her people, including her sister Beatrice and her baby, to the ships of those Genoans and Pisans whom she had so presciently paid to stay, and soon afterward rendezvoused with her husband's four galleys, which were anchored by the shore of the Nile nearby. She brought the money with her.

It took two whole days to count out the silver. Marguerite watched the transfer made and the outline of the city fade away in the distance as the French fleet sailed for Acre.

She was more fortunate than she knew. As soon as the French had evacuated Damietta, the Mamlūks rushed in and immediately violated the terms of the treaty by slaughtering the sick and wounded and burning the stockpiled weaponry and remaining provisions.

It took six days for the French ships to reach Acre. Marguerite, still weak herself from childbirth, and nursing Jean Tristan, had sailed ahead in a separate galley; she did not actually see Louis until he disembarked at Acre. She was shocked by her husband's appearance. He was very ill and could barely stand. He had nothing left of his own, and consequently appeared in clothing provided by the sultan, which included a black satin robe trimmed in squirrel's fur and decorated with gold buttons. But it was in manner that he was most changed: gone was the strong, determined young king. In his place was a grieving, guilt-ridden depressive.

This change caused a rift in the royal family. Louis's two brothers, Alphonse of Poitiers and Charles of Anjou, neither of whom felt personally responsible for the fiasco, had taken the same ship as their elder brother, but they avoided the king's company. Alphonse seems to have blamed his brother for poor judgment; Charles, who was much younger and used to having fun, simply did not want to be around someone so miserable. He much preferred to spend his time playing dice. When Louis found out, he was furious. "One day, having asked what the Comte d'Anjou was doing, the king was told that he was playing a game of chance with Gautier de Nemours," wrote Joinville. "Weak as he was through his illness, His Majesty tottered toward the players. He snatched up dice and boards, flung the whole lot into the sea, and scolded his brother very soundly for taking to gambling so soon. My lord Gautier, however, came off best, for he tipped all the money on the table—and there was plenty of it—into his lap and took it away with him."

Louis's brothers' behavior affected Marguerite's relationship with them and with her own sister Beatrice. Beatrice may not have been of much practical help during the long months at Damietta, but she was company, and would have commiserated with her sister. Beatrice, too, had feared for her own husband's life as Marguerite had feared for Louis's; she, too, had borne a child at Damietta. The two had faced a common threat in the prospective siege, and shared danger tends to bring people closer.

But reunited with Charles at Acre, Beatrice sided with her husband against Louis. As far as she was concerned they were free of the Muslims; as soon as the money was paid at Acre they would return home and get on with their lives. It had all been rather terrible, but why dwell on the past? Charles was not sick the way Louis was. Why should he not enjoy himself? As for Beatrice herself, she was anxious to get back to Cyprus to reclaim her son.

Her brother-in-law's callous behavior on board ship antagonized Marguerite. In her opinion, neither Charles nor Beatrice demonstrated proper concern for the king's health, or respect for his predicament, and this Marguerite could not abide. She began, once again, to hold herself aloof and to treat Charles and Beatrice with scorn.

The queen of France understood that the danger was not yet over. There still remained the problem of raising the remaining two hundred thousand livres in ransom. Marguerite knew that her mother-in-law would do everything in her power to save Louis, so messengers had been sent on ahead to Paris to apprise Blanche of the situation and to formally request the remittance of the necessary funds.

Blanche's regency had faced a number of challenges in the two years since Louis's departure. Raymond VII of Toulouse had promised to follow the king of France on his crusade to the Holy Land, but he died in September 1249, just prior to embarkation. The great terror of his life—that he would perish without a male heir—had come to pass, but as Alphonse, the new count of Toulouse, was by this time on his way to Egypt to help his brother, it was left to Blanche to arrange for an orderly transition of power. As always, she acted quickly, sending official representatives to Toulouse in her name and organizing a special ceremony whereby the county's leading citizens all swore fidelity and homage to Alphonse of Poitiers; thus did once-mighty Toulouse, which had dared to defy orthodoxy, slip meekly into French hands.

The king of England, too, had caused her problems. Henry was asserting his authority in Gascony through his regent, Simon de Montfort, and Blanche worried that French influence in Poitou would be affected. The queen mother appealed to the pope to put pressure on Henry to adhere to the truce negotiated by Louis and Richard of Cornwall two years before, and was again successful: on March 8, 1250, Henry wrote her a letter agreeing to a short extension. But the continued presence of a strong English regent and English soldiers in Gascony was provocative, and the situation could deteriorate at any time.

Of course Blanche worried about the progress of her eldest son's crusade, but the news had initially been very encouraging. Robert of Artois had written to his mother immediately after the taking of Damietta, reassuring her that everyone was in good health, and bragging that the city had been taken "without a blow . . . the which was done by the pure gift of God and the generosity of the Almighty Lord." The queen mother knew, too, that Alphonse had arrived safely, and she was aware of Louis's plan to take Cairo. Her son's cause was righteous and he had done all in his power to assure success; moreover, the queen mother had seen her people fight and had faith in the valiancy of the French knights. She was thus completely unprepared to learn the truth.

News of the French defeat leaked out slowly. Richard of Cornwall had an early letter from his chancellor warning that initial reports of the French offensive against the Egyptians were not good. "Whereas, sometimes, the minds of the great are wearied and tortured by the statements of various rumors, until the truth is known, I have thought proper to intimate to you some lamentable and mournful rumors concerning the French army, in a definite and true form, which reports are not yet made public, but the particulars of which I learnt by word of mouth, as he did not bring letters, but only credulous reports, from a former clerk of mine, who was sent to the queen of the French," he wrote. Blanche, too, heard the rumors, but they were so terrible that it was difficult to credit the information. Louis, so thoroughly armed, so intensively prepared, a prisoner of the sultan? The legions of French soldiers annihilated? Her son Robert of Artois slaughtered by Saracen mercenaries? It seemed preposterous—so preposterous that whoever dared even to whisper such ill tidings must be an enemy of France. "When the news of these mournful events was brought to the knowledge of the Lady Blanche and the nobles of France, by some people returning from the eastern provinces, they could not or would not believe them, and ordered the bearers of it to be hung; and these men we believe to have been manifest martyrs," wrote Matthew Paris. "At length, as they heard the same facts from repeated reporters of it, whom they did not dare to call storytellers, and when they saw letters containing accounts of the same, and other unmistakable credentials, the whole of France was covered with grief and confusion."

Fearful that even after she had raised the money for his release her son would prolong his stay in Egypt, Blanche wrote to Louis, urging him to return quickly. She used as her excuse her inability to extend the truce with England. It wasn't true, of course—Henry had agreed to an extension in March—but Louis wouldn't know that.

Louis, Marguerite, and the other French nobles arrived safely in Acre, where there was a substantial Christian population. The royal party were given accommodations; there was food, including meat, and even a chance to bathe. The process of recovery began and with the return of health and the promise of an imminent departure, spirits rose; Alphonse and Charles played dice openly, Alphonse distributing his winnings in careless handfuls to whichever knight or lady was in attendance. Marguerite, too, felt hopeful. Jean Tristan was doing well and her husband was taking regular meals under her watchful eye. It would be a long and dangerous sea journey back to Provence, but at least they would depart refreshed.

Only Louis remained bleak; only Louis wondered. Then, one Sunday, Blanche's letter arrived. Louis called for a meeting of the barons. "'My lords,' he said to them, 'Her Royal Highness the Queen Mother has sent me a message begging me most urgently to return to France, because my kingdom is in great peril, since neither peace nor truce has been established between myself and the King of England. However, the people of these parts whom I have consulted tell me that if I go away this land will be lost, where the people are so few. I therefore beg you to give serious thought to the matter."

Only Joinville and the count of Jaffa spoke in favor of remaining, and the count of Jaffa held castles in the area, which he naturally wanted to protect. All of the other nobles, including both of his brothers, urged Louis to leave immediately. They argued that, with hardly a hundred knights remaining, there was no point in staying; the thing to do was to go back to France (which is what everybody wanted to do anyway) and raise a new force and come back and try again. It meant leaving those who had followed the king but who were not noble in Egyptian jails, but the barons appeared sanguine about an extended incarceration on the part of their servants and other retainers. Marguerite added her voice to those of his vassals: they had their children to think of, as well as the kingdom; Blanche had said she needed him; their duty was clearly to France.

But Louis was not to be swayed. "My lords," he said at a second meeting the following week, "I have come to the opinion that if I stay there will be no danger of losing my realm, since the Queen Mother has people enough to defend it . . . I have therefore decided that I will not on any account abandon the kingdom of Jerusalem, which I came here to reconquer and defend. So I have finally determined to remain here for the present." Louis then asked for volunteers to remain with him, and offered to pay all of their expenses.

There was remarkably little enthusiasm for the king's decision. Almost no one elected to stay, including Alphonse and Charles and their wives. Louis sought to save face by commanding his brothers to leave and charging them with the task of entreating Frederick II for additional troops and aid, "but whether this was at their own request or by his wish I cannot really say," Joinville reported laconically. Nearly every ship that had arrived from Damietta left the following month for France. Joinville, who did volunteer to remain with Louis, added that, just as Charles of Anjou boarded his ship to leave, "he showed such grief that everyone was amazed. All the same, he went back to France."

Beatrice, too, no doubt, displayed sorrow, and wept over Marguerite and Jean Tristan. But the queen of France was not deceived. Louis's brothers had betrayed him. They were saving themselves; they would not return. Marguerite knew that if she wanted to, she, too, could have taken the baby and sailed back to France. But if she did, France would lose its king. Dislike deepened to animosity and, finally, to hatred. She would never forget, and she would never forgive.

And so Marguerite watched as her sister Beatrice and her brothers- and sisters-in-law and all the other nobles and their wives sailed away, leaving her and Louis alone and without resources in the desolate atmosphere of Acre.

Eleanor

The royal coat of arms of King Henry III.

CHAPTER XIII

QUEENSCRAFT

arguerite's struggle in the Holy Land coincided with a period of increasingly provocative challenges for Eleanor. Although the difficulties confronting the queen of England were largely political, and perhaps not as dramatic as those with which her elder sister was coping, they were nonetheless demanding, and no less significant for being subtle.

The early to mid-1240s had produced a series of grievous setbacks to English interests abroad. The disastrous, ill-fated strike against French encroachment in Poitou, which had been meant as a stepping-off point to the larger, all-important goal of reclaiming Normandy, had failed utterly, scotching whatever small pretense to influence England could claim in the region. Eleanor and Henry had barely time to recover their bearings when Raymond Berenger V died and the couple's reliance on her mother to safeguard their interests in the succession had proved embarrassingly shortsighted. Beatrice of Savoy had been outmaneuvered by the combined efforts of the French crown and the pope; she had not been able to help herself, let alone England. Now, French troops guarded Provençal castles whose upkeep was paid for with Henry's money, and French lawyers administered justice and dispersed largesse at the whim of the new count, Charles of Anjou and his wife, Beatrice (or, at least, they would once the couple returned from crusade). Worst, all of these diplomatic failures had proved disconcertingly expensive, particularly as Henry and Eleanor were forced to follow up each new disappointment with a grand show of pomp as a way of distracting the populace and reestablishing the dignity of the monarchy. As a result, the royal family was heavily in debt.

There was no question that they had lost respect in the eyes of the world. Already, the kings of Castile and Navarre, seeking to exploit English weakness, were making inroads in Gascony, a province historically recognized as falling within England's sphere of influence. Suddenly, there was the very real danger of losing the last of their continental possessions, an insupportable loss. It was unthinkable to Eleanor that her eldest son, Edward, should inherit a realm so dramatically reduced during his father's reign.

Eleanor was an extremely devoted mother. She spent most of her time with her four children at the royal castle at Windsor. As early as 1241 she had convinced Henry that she and Peter of Savoy, and not Richard of Cornwall, were best suited to guard Edward's interests, and Henry had issued documents commanding that, in the event of his death, various fortresses and lands be delivered to the queen or her uncle for safekeeping until Edward came of age. In 1246, when Edward came down with a high fever while visiting the Cistercian Abbey at Beaulieu with his parents, Eleanor insisted upon staying with him and nursing him personally. It was completely against Church policy for a woman to live with the Cistercian monks; the prior protested vehemently, but Eleanor stayed three weeks until Edward was fully recovered.

She was just as solicitous with her other children. Edmund was a sickly child and to cajole him she bought him barley sugar and sent for her own doctors to cure him. When her daughter Margaret, who married Alexander III of Scotland when she was eleven, complained by messenger that she was being held under house arrest by her husband's regent, Eleanor, Henry, and an army of knights sallied forth to rescue her. When her youngest daughter, Katharine, died in childhood, Eleanor grieved so intensely that she made herself ill.

Eleanor had recognized early that Edward's interests in Gascony must be protected and that the region was in danger of slipping away. Henry must be made to act. But after a decade of marriage, the queen was under no illusions about her husband's capabilities—nor, for that matter, was anyone else in the kingdom. Henry had no aptitude for leadership. His military skills were nonexistent. Domestically he could not control his own barons. Time and again, when he asked for money, he was refused and humiliated, and so was forced to take measures that only further alienated his subjects. In January 1248, when Henry called a general parliament to discuss the state of the realm, "which was now greatly disturbed, impoverished, and injured," as Matthew Paris observed, the English aristocracy used the occasion to officially upbraid their sovereign.

Even worse, in Eleanor's view, were the king's wild mood swings. He was subject to self-destructive fits of pique and equally self-destructive bouts of credulity. He took up new people impulsively, establishing immediate intimacies that threatened his older relationships. Originally, this quirk had worked to Eleanor's advantage and that of her family. But in 1247 the children of Henry's mother, Isabella (now deceased), and her husband, Hugh of Lusignan (on crusade, soon to be deceased), had come to England, and the king's magnanimity toward and confidence in these new half-siblings threatened to displace Provençal and Savoyard interests.

Faced with these realities, Eleanor began building her own power base. This was a significant departure for Eleanor; before their defeat at the hands of the French she had worked with Henry, had trusted in his ability to shepherd the family's interest, to translate ambitious intent into solid gain. Afterward, she worked around him. Not that they didn't still have the same goals—international respect, an expanding empire, increased wealth—but the queen had evidently decided that the king might not be the best person for the job, so she attempted to take matters into her own hands. Events thrust Marguerite into a leadership position; Eleanor seized it.

The simplest way of expanding royal influence, of course, is to recruit intimates who are entirely dependent upon the goodwill of their sovereign, and so it was that Eleanor, aided by her ever-present Savoyard uncles, began encouraging trusted friends and subordinates from Provence and Savoy to immigrate to England. This was not difficult to do, as the king and queen of England had a reputation for easy generosity; accordingly, over the next decade or so, approximately three hundred of Eleanor's and her uncles' countrymen and -women elected to relocate. Some of these people secured administrative positions at court; some served the august archbishop of Canterbury (Uncle Boniface) or the equally powerful earl of Richmond (Uncle Peter). Eleanor took a number of these transplants into her own household, and employed them as diplomats or as royal protectors of the interests of her children. The more prominent of the queen's relatives were the beneficiaries of extremely advantageous marriages, designed to dilute the power of the native English aristocracy. The daughter of Eleanor's first cousin was married to the future earl of Lincoln; the lord of Vescy took her sister. The queen also arranged for another of her first cousins, Thomas of Savoy's daughter, to be married to the son of the earl of Devon. It worked in reverse as well: Eleanor managed to convince the earl of Gloucester that the best man to marry his wealthy young daughter was her cousin the marquis of Montferrat.

Three hundred new friends and associates made a very satisfactory addition to Eleanor's social and political circles, of which Sanchia, Uncle Boniface, and Uncle Peter formed the nucleus. Peter of Savoy spent his time shuttling back and forth between Switzerland, where he engaged in lengthy and highly successful assaults on his neighbors' property, and England, where the numerous gifts lavished on him indicated that he was still very much in Henry's favor. (In 1246 the king presented the earl of Richmond with a house in the Strand for the extremely reasonable sum "of three barbed arrows per annum." Peter made substantive improvements to the original structure; as a result, its magnificence rivaled the palaces of Europe, and it became known simply as "The Savoy"—thus originated the name of one of the most famous hotels in London.)

Boniface of Savoy had finally found the time to tend his English flock, although it took the new archbishop of Canterbury and the local clergy a little while to get used to each other. As one of his first official acts as head of the Church in England, he tried to "visit" the canons of St. Bartholomew in London—*visit* being the medieval euphemism for a critical review of the manner in which the clergy carried out its duties—and, when the prior resisted, he beat up the sub-prior, an elderly man, and had to be restrained from killing him with his sword. These differences were soon smoothed over, however, and Uncle Boniface retained a position of authority in England, adding leverage to the growing circle around the queen.

This influx of influential new foreigners represented a shortcut to power, and like all shortcuts they provoked resistance. The native English gentry were especially unhappy about the arranged marriages. In 1247 Matthew Paris reported that "Peter of Savoy, the earl of Richmond, came to the king's court at London, bringing with him from his distant province some unknown ladies, for the purpose of giving them in marriage to the nobles of England . . . which circumstance was evidently annoying and unpleasant to many of the native nobles of England, who considered that they were despised."

It was not a perfect strategy by any means, and resentment would build over time until it finally boiled over, but the queen was working with limited options and under time pressure. Gascony hung in the balance.

Gascony operated loosely as a colony. Henry appointed an Englishman as royal seneschal—a sort of governor—to live in Bordeaux and represent the crown. The seneschal was aided by an advisory group of local barons, and a large check drawn on the royal treasury. Although the native population, a hardened, fractious, combative group, generally did as they pleased without regard to the seneschal's orders, this system at least had the utility of maintaining the appearance of English rule.

All of this changed in 1248, when Louis went off on crusade and a vacuum was created in his absence. Some of the Gascon barons to the south, aided by fat Thibaud of Champagne (now the king of Navarre), began marauding around the country killing people and taking other barons' castles. The most ferocious and influential man in the duchy, Gaston de Béarn, retaliated with the support of the king of Castile. Gaston just happened to be Raymond Berenger V's half-brother, and therefore Eleanor's uncle on her father's side. Fighting also broke out among the barons of the north, particularly in the area around Dordogne.

The current seneschal, a minor functionary, was completely unequipped to handle the situation, and Henry was forced to recall him, as he had been forced to recall the man's two predecessors. It was clear that Gascony required a much stronger, more prestigious seneschal, one capable of intimidating both Gaston de Béarn and the meddling kings, if the colony was to be pacified. Henry and Eleanor cast around for the right man for the position.

The obvious choice was Richard of Cornwall. He had every qualification. He was a skilled and seasoned negotiator, as his time spent in the Holy Land attested. He was the king's brother and a man of great international standing in his own right; it would flatter the Gascons to have such an important person take up the role of seneschal, and they would be more likely to listen to him. After all, Louis had given Poitou to his brother Alphonse, so the appointment of Richard would put Gascony on the same footing. Richard was also very rich, which was an absolute prerequisite for the job. The Gascon government could not function without bribes. Lastly, the earl of Cornwall was familiar with the area and knew the players well. He had first visited in 1225, when he was only sixteen years old, in the company of a band of seventy knights, and had managed, even at that early age, to secure the region for England.

And that was exactly the problem. Henry had more or less given Richard Gascony way back in 1225 (or at least, he granted him a charter of enfeoffment, which had given Richard the expectation of ownership when he came of age) and then had promised him the duchy outright in 1243 when Richard saved Henry from ignominious capture by the French at Taillebourg. It was only after Eleanor convinced Henry that Gascony should be reserved for Edward that the king rescinded his promise to his brother. Richard was still fuming over Gascony; even his marriage to Sanchia had not quelled his anger over the broken pledge. If they sent Richard, he would no doubt demand to be given the lordship of the country in perpetuity, and this Eleanor would not countenance. Better to lose Gascony altogether than to have it go to Richard and not Edward.

They sent Simon de Montfort instead. He was Eleanor's choice. Simon would not have been Henry's candidate—the king had never really gotten over Simon's comparing him to Charles the Simple after the loss of Poitou. But he let his wife and her uncles convince him.

Eleanor had been drawing closer and closer to Simon. It is not difficult to see why. Simon was everything Henry wasn't. He was strong where Henry was weak, courageous where Henry was cowardly, steadfast where Henry was fickle. He was also a warrior, a scholar, and a natural leader. The two men could not be in a room together without the earl outshining the king just by his mere presence, and the two were in a room together often.

It wasn't love, but respect and admiration. Eleanor was very close to Simon's wife, Henry's sister Eleanor, and to Adam Marsh, a brilliant Franciscan friar and Oxford theologian, who was a member of Simon's circle of intimate friends. Adam Marsh would go on to become one of Eleanor's most trusted spiritual and political advisers.

Simon de Montfort was under no illusions as to the difficulty of the task ahead and the character of the man who would send him. He did everything he could to protect himself in advance. Knowing Henry's tendency to inconstancy, he fixed the term of his appointment unconditionally at seven years, the time he deemed necessary to both quell the resistance and institute an accepted rule of law. Clearly, he did not want to be recalled on some new whim of the king's. Also, as the earl of Leicester was most definitely not rich, he refused to accept the commission unless he was given an army at the outset and assigned all of the revenues of Gascony, which ordinarily would have gone to the crown. If he had to go to war against either the king of Navarre or the king of Castile, Henry was obligated to send him even more money and more troops "as though he were defending his own land." Mostly, he asked that he not go as an appointed seneschal, but as Henry's vice-regent, with the power to govern Gascony as he liked.

But the very qualities that made him such an appealing candidate in England—his unwavering determination, strength of character, and blunt manner—worked against him in Gascony. Where Richard saw nuance, Simon saw black-and-white. Where the earl of Cornwall would have used money and practical negotiation, overlooking minor offenses and taking into account local customs, the earl of Leicester acted on instinct, locking up all of those he considered troublemakers without regard for ducal law, taking sides in various disputes, putting down rebellion grimly. As he was also simultaneously engaged in recovering certain portions of his wife's dowry that were in dispute, instead of spreading money around, he took it. This gave some of his actions, at least to his new constituents, the flavor of extortion. His very name excited resentment—Gascony was in the south of France, bordering Languedoc, and no resident of the duchy would ever forget the elder Simon de Montfort's merciless slaughter of the Cathars, nor his usurpation of Toulouse and its environs. Sending the younger Simon to Gascony was like trying to stitch up a wound by using a sword instead of a needle. Within a year, the Gascon barons, who were practiced at going behind the seneschal's back anyway, began complaining directly to the king about Simon's contemptuous, rough treatment.

Even when Simon did score a triumph, it was reversed in England. He captured and subdued Gaston de Béarn, the leader of the opposition to English rule, brought him to terms, confiscated his lands, and sent him back to England, only to have Henry and Eleanor treat him like a beloved relation visiting on holiday. Henry pardoned Gaston of all wrongdoing and Eleanor, who was used to doing business with family, naively insisted that his lands be restored to him. Uncle Gaston was then allowed to return to Gascony on the promise that he wouldn't make any more trouble; upon his arrival he immediately began conspiring again with the king of Castile against the English.

Yet Simon, despite his methods, was in large part succeeding in his task. In 1250 Matthew Paris wrote that "the said earl, studying to take after his noble father in all respects, and to follow in his footsteps or to go beyond them, so checked the insolence of the king's rebellious subjects at Bordeaux, and throughout the whole of Gascony, that he put to flight, disinherited, and condemned to banishment William de Solaires, Rustein, and other proud men who were raising the heel against the king; and many too he consigned to the gallows."

But all Henry heard were the complaints; messenger after messenger appeared from the Gascons, followed by personal appearances from those victims who could steal away. Within two years Henry was grumbling that he was spending a great deal of money on Simon and getting very little in return; in four years Simon was obliged to return to England a year before his commission officially expired to stand trial for charges of inhumane treatment and extortion brought against him by the Gascon barons, who now had the full support of the king. The earl of Leicester was understandably incensed; he stated in court "how, when he was on the point of starting to Gascony for the first time, the king had advised him to crush the traitors; how he had given him his charter for holding the guardianship of the country for six years; and how he had promised to afford him effectual aid and counsel, which had not been fulfilled."

Some of the most important noblemen in England, including Richard of Cornwall (who, according to Matthew Paris, "was well pleased at the trouble of the Gascons"), came to London specifically to support the earl of Leicester against the king, "for it was much feared that the king, in his impetuous haste, as he was known to be so favorable to foreigners, would order the earl, a man of noble birth, and his natural subject to be seized and detained as a prisoner, as if he were a convicted traitor, which could by no means be allowed." Henry dared not defy his own peerage and find Simon guilty, but he indulged in a fit of passion against his former friend, which did not compare well to the earl's frigid composure.

This episode concluded in 1252 with Simon's resigning his commission, for the sum of seven thousand marks, in favor of Henry and Eleanor's eldest son, Edward, and decamping for Paris. As Edward was still only thirteen years old, somebody else was going to have to pacify Gascony for him. There was no casting around this time; Henry determined to go himself.

Although Eleanor did not attempt to influence or control her enraged husband during the trial, her sympathies were with the earl of Leicester. She was in communication with Adam Marsh during the entire affair, and used him as an intermediary to reconcile Richard to the investiture of Edward with Gascony. Richard had hoped to use the proceedings against Simon to regain Gascony for himself. After Henry calmed down, Eleanor undertook to salvage matters as best she could. Henry balked at paying Simon what was owed, but Eleanor convinced him to repay the loans.

It is easy in retrospect to condemn Eleanor since it was she who had insisted that Gascony be kept for Edward against Richard's legitimate claims and she who chose Simon de Montfort to govern in Richard's stead. In fact, however, every decision Eleanor made during this period was well thought-out, reasonable, and politically astute. If she put the wrong man in the job, at least she kept the more dangerous man out. Richard gave every sign of being a much greater threat to Henry than did Simon. Richard had sided with the other English barons against Henry in the past. Richard knew himself to be a much more qualified leader than his brother, and he was also of royal blood. The barons would surely have followed him. If Richard had been allowed to keep Gascony, his powers might have overtaken those of the king. No one in England in and around 1250 could have possibly anticipated that Simon de Montfort, who had no claim at all to the English throne, and was not even royal, would later try to unseat Henry. Richard's political leanings, on the other hand, were well-known. There was a much greater chance of the earl of Cornwall, and not the earl of Leicester, being the man to try to depose Henry. That he did not cannot be directly attributed to Eleanor's denying him Gascony, but she certainly helped to redirect his political ambitions, at least in regard to the English throne.

More than that, Eleanor's desire to save Gascony for Edward was founded in something more than vanity. Even at thirteen, Edward was showing signs of becoming a much greater statesman and warrior than his father. He was very tall—he would be known as Longshanks—and a superior athlete, who was called "the best lance in all the world" by the troubadours. Nicholas Trevet, an English knight who knew Edward, wrote of him as an *"animus magnificus."* His mother saw in her eldest son what Dante saw: "the simple king who sat apart, Henry of England . . . He has a better issue in his branches." Edward was England's best hope for a glorious future, not Henry, not Richard; and his mother was determined that he should have his chance. Events would prove her right.

Eleanor walked a very narrow line during these years while she struggled to manage the escalating crises without alienating her husband. There is every reason to believe that Henry suspected that the queen was gaining power at his expense. In a wholly unrelated incident, just as Simon's troubles with Henry were coming to fruition, Eleanor made a present of a certain church living to her personal chaplain, William of London. Henry gave the same church living to a man of his choice, and then, when he found out that Eleanor's chaplain had already taken possession, exploded. "How high does the arrogance of woman rise if it is not restrained!" he is reputed to have roared before firing the unfortunate chaplain. It didn't improve matters when Robert Grosseteste, the venerable bishop of Lincoln, who was a good friend of Adam Marsh's, took Eleanor's part and Henry was forced to take the whole matter to court. It grew even worse when Eleanor's candidate won.

The queen was too clever not to know that her husband's reaction was more severe than was warranted and she enlisted the aid of Henry's sister Eleanor to try to soothe him. She might have succeeded had not the queen become involved in yet another entanglement, this time with one of Henry's half-brothers, Aymer de Lusignan. Henry had made Aymer the bishop of Winchester, which put him into direct conflict with Uncle Boniface, the archbishop of Canterbury. There was a disagreement between the two over the presentation of another church living, and Eleanor naturally took Boniface's part. Henry took his half-brother's side. There was another scene and this time Henry did more than complain. He confiscated Eleanor's lands and banished her from London.

This must have been quite frightening for Eleanor. Although this was before the time of Henry VIII, who preferred to cut off his wives' heads rather than argue with them, there was still precedent for long-term punishment. Henry II had kept Eleanor of Aquitaine under house arrest for years.

Henry III, however, was much more of a family man than his grandfather. He also genuinely loved his wife. There was the added difficulty that he could not seem to reconcile the disagreement between Aymer and Boniface without her, so Eleanor was back at court, with her lands restored to her, in less than a month. Still, it was a significant quarrel and the king and queen didn't really make it up until just after the New Year when everybody in the family, the Lusignans included, got very expensive Christmas presents and a semblance of family unity was reestablished.

Eleanor was much more careful over the next few months to be seen working in tandem with her husband. She must have done a very good job of redeeming his trust and affection, for when Henry left for Normandy in August 1253, he appointed her regent of England in his place.

Sanchia

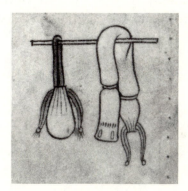

Purses, symbols of money.

CHAPTER XIV

A ROYAL WINDFALL

B eauty can be as effective a social or political tool as wealth or breeding, but it must be coupled with another, stronger trait such as determination or ruthlessness. Sanchia had neither Marguerite's resourcefulness nor Eleanor's ambition. The queen of England's campaign to wrest Gascony away from the earl of Cornwall put Sanchia's position with her new husband on delicate footing. Richard naturally expected his wife to use her relationship with her sister to help further his interests, while Eleanor depended upon her sister to reconcile the earl of Cornwall's political aspirations with those of the English Crown. It was the sort of balancing act that would have taxed the talents of even the most experienced diplomat, and Sanchia, who had been in England less than five years, was unequal to the task. While doubtless aware of the conflicting expectations of her husband and sister, she had not the skills to resolve the situation to either's satisfaction. Her inadequacies were a continuing source of frustration and disappointment to Richard, and would later affect their marriage.

Of all the sisters, Sanchia was the only one to have married a man who had been previously married. Richard's first wife, Isabella Marshal, had been a woman from an extremely important, influential English family whom he had known since childhood. Isabella had grown up with English politics, and had become attuned to the nuances of shifting alliances, the ebb and flow of power. As such, she had been a partner to her husband in the fullest sense of the term, both as a source of emotional strength and as an astute adviser. Her family connections were of enormous strategic value to the earl of Cornwall. Her brothers, leading members of the aristocracy, could be rallied at a moment's notice to take the earl of Cornwall's side in any argument, even against his brother the king. Richard had been tied to Isabella by a myriad of shared experiences and a sense of inherited leadership, a vision of the kingdom as it was meant to be. Theirs had been a union so marked by affinity that Richard had taken it for granted.

Now he had married a foreign woman half his age. Sanchia could not be expected to provide the same insights as had Isabella Marshal, and in the beginning Richard did not require this of her. She was an asset to his estate as a particularly impressive castle or a valuable horse would have been. She was stylish and looked well at court functions; she was sweet and impressionable in private. If she was not excessively clever, well, what of it?

Sanchia was pleased when she conceived within a year of her marriage; she hoped that having children of her own would bring her closer to her husband. Already she understood that the difference in their ages and backgrounds was creating a distance between them that Eleanor did not seem to experience with her husband. A family provided a logical way to bridge this gap. When she gave birth to a son in the fall of 1246, it seemed her expectations were rewarded; Richard took it as a good omen, and gave a great feast to celebrate.

But Sanchia's newborn son died a scant month later, "that worldly joy might not be free from sudden and frequent griefs." The loss was wrenching. Eleanor was sympathetic, but Eleanor was queen; she could not devote herself to comforting her sister. Sanchia reached out to her husband, but this death was too reminiscent of the deaths of his other children by Isabella. Richard drew away from his wife and instead threw himself into his work, a formula against affliction which would eventually become routine.

The pathos of Sanchia's position lies in her awareness of her husband's diminishing affections, and her efforts to carve out a life for herself in the face of his negligence. She went through all the motions of being a great lady. She was present at all the major court functions. When Richard was sent to Paris in 1247 to renegotiate the peace with Louis before the French king went on crusade, she and Richard's son Henry went, too. She was an accepted member of the English nobility, particularly among the women; she even belonged to a book group. There is a handwritten note attributed to Matthew Paris extant in a copy of the *Life of Alban* addressed to the countess of Arundel, asking her to return "the book about St Thomas the Martyr and St Edward, which I translated and illustrated, and which the Lady Count-ess of Cornwall [Sanchia] may keep until Whitsuntide."

But she was never a political force in England. Eleanor never quarreled with Sanchia, never objected to any of her activities. She was always wel-comed into the queen's circle, even when Sanchia, through Richard, be-came even richer than her older sister. Eleanor was not the sort of person to share power, so clearly she did not view her sister as a threat. Matthew Paris had been wrong when he prophesized that Richard's marriage to Sanchia would result in the kingdom's acquiring two queens.

Possibly because Sanchia's influence was proving to be so ineffective, Henry and Eleanor, who were in debt to the earl of Cornwall themselves, were forced to appease Richard by the customary means of bribery. This was how, in 1247, Richard came to take over the national mint.

By the mid-1240s it had become clear that English money was badly in need of recoinage. The value of the silver penny (the only coin in existence at the time) had been seriously compromised by the practice of "clipping," a process by which, every time a coin changed hands, its outer rim was shaved off, "so much so that the inner circle was barely left remaining, and the let-tered border wholly cut off." Collect enough shavings from enough coins and an enterprising clipper could accumulate the silver necessary to produce his own pennies; consequently, the procedure had acquired a devoted and enthusias-tic following, particularly among "the merchants of the countries adjacent to England, especially the Flemings." By 1247 the problem was serious enough for Henry to consider a kingdomwide recall of the debased specie, followed by the replacement of the entire English mintage with new coins.

Such an ambitious endeavor was beyond the resources of the crown itself, so Henry turned to Richard, already the wealthiest man in England. In ex-change for agreeing to undertake the supervision of the recoinage personally, and supplying an initial loan of ten thousand marks to get the business started, the earl of Cornwall was allowed to write the terms of his own contract with the king. These were: (1) that his loan of ten thousand marks be repaid in new coinage before anyone else received any profit from the deal; (2) that he would exercise complete control over the mint, and that the king himself would have to adhere to his brother's financial decisions; and (3) that he and Henry would split the profits of this exercise fifty-fifty for the next twelve years.

So, from 1247 to 1259, the inhabitants of England were obliged to bring their old coins for replacement to one of the seventeen mints that Richard had established for this purpose. For every pound of old coins brought in, each citizen lost sixteen-pence value—ten pence to pay the expenses of the recoinage and six pence as a fee to Richard.

Even given that he split this six-pence-per-pound profit with Henry, it was an astounding amount of money for a private citizen to earn. It represented nothing less than a fundamental redistribution of the kingdom's wealth toward Richard and away from every other inhabitant, on a scale "only matched, in later centuries, by the reforms of Henry VIII, Elizabeth, and William III. Like Elizabeth and William (or rather Sir Isaac Newton, the then Master of the Mint), Richard made a profit. But if the available figures are even approximately reliable, his profit vastly exceeded theirs," wrote N. Denholm-Young, Richard's biographer. Twelve years of taking three pence from every pound owned by every man, woman, and child in England (and in 1251 Henry contracted with him to do it in Ireland for twelve years as well) vaulted the earl of Cornwall's net worth into the realm of the fantastic. Before his appointment as Master of the Mint he had merely been the richest man in England. Afterward, it was just possible that he was the richest private individual in the world.

These activities occupied a great deal of Richard's time and energy. Sanchia, by default, claimed less and less of his attention. On December 26, 1249, the countess of Cornwall finally presented her husband with a son, Edmund, who lived. But this time the earl did not arrange for a party.

Reverse of the new penny of 1248.

★   ★   ★

A year later, an event occurred that would have enormous influence on the lives of all four sisters. On December 13, 1250, the Holy Roman Emperor, Frederick II, called "the greatest of earthly princes" and "the wonder of the world" by the chroniclers, died unexpectedly of dysentery. "His death was kept secret for some days," Matthew Paris wrote, "that his enemies might not so soon exult in the circumstance; but on St. Stephen's Day it was publicly made known and announced to the people."

His enemies did exult, and none more so than the pope, Innocent IV. There was no one Innocent had hated more than Frederick II. The antipathy between the two men had caused the pope to go to prodigious lengths to eradicate his opponent. Innocent had not only excommunicated the emperor, he had called for and funded a crusade against the empire that had taken badly needed resources away from Louis's crusade against the Saracens. Not content with raising an army of German mercenaries to assail imperial forces, the pontiff had also intrigued with the emperor's personal physician to have Frederick poisoned, although the assassination attempt had been unsuccessful. The poison had been discovered in time and given to a condemned prisoner instead, and the doctor responsible had had his eyes gouged out and undergone other, similarly excruciating tortures before finally being killed. Frederick unearthed the source of the plot and vowed vengeance on the Curia, and Innocent, still hiding out in Lyon and noting the severity of the punishment meted out to the doctor, had worried over imperial retaliation. Now, suddenly, providence had intervened and removed the man the pope had labeled "the AntiChrist" as a threat.

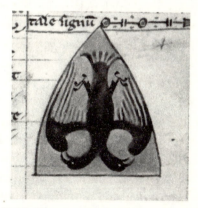

Inverted shield of Emperor Frederick II, indicating his death.

Innocent IV knew that his papacy was still in jeopardy. Frederick had two adult sons, Conrad and Manfred, both of whom were strong enough to carry on their father's work. Conrad, who was the eldest and the legitimate heir, lived in Germany. Upon hearing of the emperor's death he immediately made plans to travel to Sicily to claim his inheritance. It was his eighteen-year-old half-brother, Manfred, Frederick's illegitimate son by a beloved mistress, who was the real warrior, however. Manfred had been raised at the emperor's court and had been his father's favorite. There was likely to be some friction between these two over the imperial succession.

And therein lay Innocent's opportunity. If, during this transitional period, Innocent could somehow split the empire into two separate kingdoms—Germany and Sicily—by offering the crown of Sicily to a friendly third party, the danger from the emperor's sons would be eliminated. Someone else just might be willing to go to the trouble and expense of fighting Conrad and Manfred if it meant papal support for a kingship; accordingly, the pope looked around for a suitable candidate.

He turned to Charles of Anjou. Charles and Beatrice, along with Alphonse of Poitiers and his wife, had arrived in Lyon during the summer of 1250, five months before the emperor's death, with the grievous news of Louis IX's defeat at the hands of the Egyptians. They had first gone from Acre to Frederick II's court, where they had begged the emperor to send an army to rescue the king of France, an appeal Frederick had been forced to refuse on the grounds that he needed every last imperial soldier to fight against the pope. Charles and Alphonse had then come to Innocent to try to compel him to make peace with Frederick so that the emperor could use his army in Louis's defense rather than his own. They threatened to throw the pope out of Lyon if he refused, and only Frederick's untimely death had saved Innocent from having to relocate to Bordeaux and avail himself of the questionable protection of Henry III.

As a way of mollifying his French hosts, Innocent offered the kingdom of Sicily to Charles of Anjou. All Charles need do was to repay Innocent for expenses already incurred (Innocent had already spent quite a lot of money trying to unseat Frederick and wanted to recoup as much as possible), raise an army of his own, and sail to Rome, where, as an extra inducement, Innocent promised personally to crown him king. From there it would be a simple matter of marching south and engaging imperial troops in battle; a man as fiercely talented as the new count of Provence, the pope felt, should have no difficulty imposing his will on either Conrad or Manfred, depending upon which of the two was in power at the time.

Charles of Anjou was not, in principle, against this offer—in fact, he was rather inclined to accept, but he was prevented by his elder brother's obstinacy in remaining in the Holy Land. Louis had charged Charles and Alphonse with the task of mustering new troops for a renewed attack on the Egyptians and, as this had been Charles's excuse for leaving his brother

North Sea

Baltic Sea

Brabant
Hainaut

Cologne

Aachen

Westphalia

Mainz

BOHEMIA

Swabia

Bavaria

GERMANY

N

Lyon

Mont Cenis

Savoy

Asti

Genoa

Provence

PAPAL
STATES

Aigues-Morte

Aix-en-Provence

Pisa

Spoleto

Marseille

Orvieto

Adriatic Sea

Viterbo

Mediterranean Sea

Rome

Benevento

Naples

SICILY

The Holy Roman Empire
in 1250

in the first place, he couldn't simply abandon his obligation to the king of France in favor of a more personally advantageous proposition (however tempting). As long as Louis remained in Egypt, Charles was obligated to at least go through the motions of reviving his eldest brother's failed crusade, so he regretfully declined Innocent's offer. Besides, he did not have the money.

Beatrice was likely relieved not to have to support Charles in yet another foreign entanglement so quickly. She had only just returned from a two-year sojourn in the desert, the last few months of which had been harrowing. There was still unrest in Provence, and her mother's claims to settle. Beatrice knew everyone of importance in the county, and they knew her. She could do much to smooth and legitimize the transition of power away from her mother and toward her husband. And it might be best to address these problems while Louis and Marguerite were still away—Beatrice was aware that her older sister would throw her support with the king behind their mother's position and against that of Beatrice and Charles.

Both Beatrice and Charles resented Marguerite's interference in the affairs of the county. Beatrice was aware that Marguerite still hoped to inherit Provence, even though it was supposed to go to a child of Beatrice's on her death. But children can get sick and die, as Beatrice had discovered when she had returned to Cyprus after leaving Louis and Marguerite at Acre. The son she had left behind with a nurse had not survived. It is possible she blamed Louis and Marguerite for his death—if the crusade had not dragged on in the disastrous fashion it did she might have returned in time to save her son. She still had her daughter, Blanche, of course, but a daughter was not enough to ensure that her older sister did not succeed in reclaiming the county. Perhaps spending time with her husband in the unhurried atmosphere of her native land, where they would not be troubled by Saracen assassins, or Mamlūk mercenaries, or all of the other inconveniences associated with a prolonged stay in the Holy Land, might help her to get pregnant again, this time with another son.

Not that it wouldn't have been nice to be crowned a queen.

Undaunted by the count of Provence's refusal, the pope resumed his search for an acceptable king of Sicily. It did not take him long to settle on a new candidate: Richard of Cornwall.

Richard had probably been Innocent's first choice all along. In fact, it is possible that the pope, who had been nursing the idea of separating Sicily from the rest of the Holy Roman Empire ever since he had first excommunicated and deposed Frederick II at the Council of Lyon in 1246, had offered the kingdom to Richard even before the emperor died. Richard had made a personal visit to Innocent in April 1250, where, according to Matthew Paris, the earl and the pontiff "held many secret and lengthened conferences between them; and all who witnessed these proceedings wondered at them, and especially at the great and unusual hospitality of the pope."

There was nothing to wonder at—the pope was a man who appreciated wealth, and Richard made no secret of his immense resources. The earl may not have been a king but he traveled like one. When Richard came to visit Innocent, he was accompanied by Sanchia, her baby Edmund, his son Henry, five earls, three bishops (including the bishop of London and Robert Grosseteste, the bishop of Lincoln), and forty armed knights. "The number of his pompously-equipped retinue and his sumpter-horses was so great, that the citizens, as well as all who had come to the court to transact business, were astonished at the arrival of such a great prince." Innocent sent all his cardinals but one out into the street to meet their honored guests, and afterward got up from the papal throne to embrace the earl of Cornwall and invite him to dinner.

Innocent offered the kingship of Sicily to Richard with the same provisos he had outlined for Charles. In exchange for the pope's personally crowning the earl of Cornwall the legitimate king of Sicily, Richard would agree to underwrite all the expenses of the military campaign, including the reimbursement to the papacy of any monies already expended in the cause. After Richard had won the battle and taken over the kingdom he would not try to unite Sicily and Germany as Frederick II had tried to do, but would be content with wealthy Sicily and the pope's goodwill. Thus "was unraveled the mystery to why the pope had formerly done so much honor to Earl Richard at Lyons, as to treat him as a relative, and took so much pleasure in his company as to excite the astonishment of all."

But Richard surprised the pontiff and refused. Although he wanted a kingdom, it turned out he did not want that particular one. He wrote a letter politely declining the honor, but privately he laughed at the proposal. Richard, who was neither "brave nor skillful in war," as Matthew Paris so candidly expressed it, had no intention of raising an army to try to take over a kingdom so far away, whose terrain and customs were unknown to him, and which was guarded by an entrenched, ferocious warrior like Manfred.

It was "the same as if any one said to him, 'I give or sell you the moon, climb up and take it,'" he snorted to his friends.

Sanchia doubtless approved of her husband's decision. There is nothing in her life to indicate that Sanchia desired to rule as her sisters did; certainly she would not have wanted to endure a battle and live in Sicily. Reports were just filtering back about Marguerite's ordeal in Egypt. Better the loneliness of neglect than to face the hardships of war.

Marguerite

King Louis IX and Queen Marguerite embarking from Acre.

CHAPTER XV

THE RETURN OF THE QUEEN

After the exodus of the French baronage from the Holy Land in the summer of 1250, Louis, Marguerite, their newborn baby, Jean Tristan, and a handful of knights including Joinville remained at Acre to continue working toward the goals of the crusade. Louis had dispatched letters with Alphonse and Charles outlining the status of the current operation—that is, he admitted having suffered a crippling defeat—and requesting that additional monies be forwarded and a new army recruited for a rendezvous with the king at Acre. He specifically asked that these reinforcements be transported by no later than August of the following year. Louis still had hopes of redeeming himself by launching a fresh assault against the Muslims. Marguerite resigned herself to another year in the desert.

While awaiting the arrival of his new forces, Louis worked to free those in the French army captured by the Egyptians during the terrible retreat from Mansourah. There were apparently thousands of these unfortunates, the vast majority of them foot soldiers, many of whom had already been sold into slavery by their captors. This was one of the principal reasons Louis had not sailed back to France with his brothers; mindful of Thibaud of Champagne's shameful behavior in deserting his prisoners during the previous crusade, the king of France was determined to set a more honorable example. The lives of the men *he* had led to this hellish place would not be dependent for their freedom on another Richard of Cornwall's coming along.

Although the Mamlūks had agreed to give up these prisoners as part of the original settlement at Damietta, they evidently did not feel any urgency about doing so, particularly as two hundred thousand marks of Louis's ransom had yet to be paid. The king of France was obliged to send one of his knights to Cairo to remind them of their obligation under the terms of the treaty. While he was in the process of negotiation, emissaries arrived from another power in the region, the sultan of Aleppo.

The sultan of Aleppo, whose name was an-Nasir, was a cousin of the late sultan of Cairo. Although an-Nasir had never liked Ayyūb, and in fact had spent most of his career at war with him, either fending off Ayyūb's attacks on his territory or trying to take over territory belonging to Ayyūb, he had been greatly disturbed by the news of the murder of Ayyūb's son Tūrān-Shāh by the Mamlūks. There was more at stake here than simple family feeling. Tūrān-Shāh had been the legitimate heir to the sultanate of Cairo. It wouldn't do for the sultan of Aleppo to stand by and let a common mercenary disrupt the hereditary bloodline. It violated the justification for rule by one man over another; in the Arab world, only a descendant from a member of Muhammad's family could claim to lead. Besides, an-Nasir had been known to employ mercenaries himself on occasion.

Louis's force was small, but an-Nasir was going to need all the men he could get, so he asked the king of France to join him in fighting the Mamlūks, and offered him the old city of Jerusalem, currently under the sultan of Aleppo's control, as incentive. This proposition was very tempting, particularly when the knight Louis had sent to Cairo to bring back the French prisoners returned with only two hundred noblemen, and not the promised thousands. Instead of either accepting or declining an-Nasir's offer outright, however, the French king decided to engage in some diplomacy. Louis implied in his reply that he was strongly considering allying himself and his army with an-Nasir, and then used the sultan of Aleppo's offer to try to force the Mamlūks to abide by their original agreement: "The king now gave his answer [to the Mamlūks]. He told them he would make no treaty [with them] unless, in the first place, they sent him all the heads of Christians they had hung round the walls of Cairo since the time when the Comte de Bar and the Comte de Montfort were taken prisoner [that was Thibaud's crusade]; secondly, unless they handed over all the children who had been taken young and renounced their faith; and lastly, unless they let him off payment of the two hundred thousand livres he still owed them."

Unless the Mamlūks agreed to these conditions, the king continued, he would most certainly join forces with the sultan of Aleppo against them.

Unhappy about the prospect of fighting both the sultan of Aleppo and the remaining French, the sultan of Cairo hurried to placate his former hostage. He waived the two hundred thousand marks remaining on the ransom and allowed Louis to repurchase the last of the French prisoners from their new owners. He also agreed to remit the heads and whatever remained of the corpses of Christian soldiers that could be found. By 1252 Louis had so far forgiven the sultan of Cairo that he reversed himself completely and agreed to fight on the side of the Mamlūks against the sultan of Aleppo. To this end, he gathered up his small army and relocated to Jaffa in May 1252, to wait for an Egyptian force to arrive for a coordinated attack against an-Nasir's army.

Marguerite, who by this time had had another child, Peter, watched these negotiations with mounting frustration. She knew her husband's character very well. He would stay until he had no choice, no matter how adverse the circumstances, in order to do penance for his military loss. The time had long since passed when Alphonse and Charles were supposed to have returned with a new army; clearly, they weren't coming. "The most Christian king of the French . . . remained at Acre waiting assistance . . . he also, as has been before stated, sent his brothers, in whose bosom was reposed his greatest hope and confidence. They, however, forgetful of their Joseph, performed the duty enjoined on them in a very lukewarm way, and so delayed matters that they seemed to be unwilling to assist him." Still, the king showed no signs of surrendering his hopes of salvaging the crusade, even though, as Joinville remarked, "During all this time, I may say, the greatest number of men-at-arms we had available never amounted to more than fourteen hundred." The loss at Mansourah was a blot that Louis was desperate to remove. The Church offered indulgences to those who helped fortify Christian settlements in the Holy Land, so the king of France used his spare time to embark on an ambitious construction program, building walls and towers. He carried the rocks and dirt with his own hands to maximize the benefit to his soul.

But walls and towers cost money, and Louis was spending all he had and more in fortifying Acre and Jaffa. Joinville wrote: "I will not attempt to give you an accurate account of the huge sums the king spent in fortifying Jaffa, for they are too great to be reckoned . . . To give you some idea of what the king spent on all this I will tell you that I asked the legate how much the gate and part of the wall had cost him . . . He told me—as God was his witness—that wall and gate together had cost him full thirty thousand livres." The money Blanche had sent wouldn't last long at this rate, even given the

Mamlūks' forgiving what had remained of the ransom, and they would need to reserve money for the voyage home.

Going home was the focus of Marguerite's attention. They had been away too long. She had left her other children, including her son Louis, heir to the throne, in Blanche's hands; he would be eight by now, and she hadn't seen him since he was four—what of him? For that matter, what of the two sons she had with her now? Did Louis want his children raised in such a place? What of their responsibilities to France? Marguerite did not trust the king's brothers, especially Charles. Charles was too ambitious for the French queen's taste and Blanche, who was getting older, might not be able to control him. Younger brothers had been known to use absence as an excuse to usurp an older brother's authority. If Marguerite did not get Louis back to Paris soon, she feared he might not have a kingdom to return to.

The queen's unhappiness over the king's policies caused a serious rift between them. Even without her continued pleas to renew their old lives, she and the children were a living, breathing reminder of his temporal responsibilities, and these, in his desperation for salvation, he dismissed as irksome. When, as was inevitable, the Mamlūks did not meet Louis in Jaffa as promised, but instead made a separate peace with the sultan of Aleppo behind his back, and an-Nasir demonstrated his displeasure at the French king's having reneged on his original agreement by sacking the Christian town of Sidon, Louis took his army to Sidon and left Marguerite in Jaffa to have a third child alone. In order to rejoin her husband, the queen was forced to confront the dangers of a medieval sea voyage on her own with three children under the age of three. Louis, who loved doing penance, and who embraced the most gruesome tasks as a way of flaunting his piety, did not leave his chapel to greet her ship when it finally arrived. (In Sidon, where the French army arrived too late to prevent a massacre, and was reduced to burying the dead, he "had carried some of the rotting, evil-smelling corpses to the trenches to be buried, and that without ever holding his nose, as others had done.") Joinville, who did hurry to meet Marguerite on this occasion, commented upon the king's behavior toward his family:

> The queen, who had but lately recovered from her confinement on giving birth to the Lady Blanche at Jaffe, now arrived at [Sidon] having come there by sea. As soon as I heard that she was there, I got up from where I was sitting beside the king and went to meet her, and escorted her back to the castle. When I returned to the king, whom

I found in his chapel, he asked me whether his wife and children were well. On my telling him they were he remarked: "When you got up and left me I knew very well that you were going to meet the queen, so I have asked them to postpone the sermon until your return." I am telling you this because during all the five years I have been with the king he had never once spoken to me of his wife and children, nor, so far as I know, to anyone else. In my opinion it does not seem right and proper for a man to be so detached from his own family.

There is more in this statement of Joinville's than simply pity for the queen. His affection for Marguerite is palpable. He mentioned her often in his journal and sent her gifts. He sought out her company and she his; he comforted her in her grief and escorted her through dangerous terrain.

This raises the question of whether there was more to their relationship than platonic friendship. Joinville apparently did enjoy a reputation as something of a ladies' man. While at Acre, he set up his bedroom "in such a position that no one could enter without seeing me as I lay there. I did this to prevent anyone harboring evil suspicions of me with regard to women," he wrote. At the least, Joinville's account of his adventures while on crusade suggest that the knight and the queen shared a sense of mutual regard and a growing sympathy of purpose. And, although the chronicler always spoke deferentially of the king, noting his holiness and piety, there was often an edge to his compliments.

Marguerite could have gone home alone, of course. Louis would have provided her with a ship and a retinue and would not perhaps have been sorry to see her go. But if she went, he might never return. So she endured his indifference, and remained in Egypt with the children.

And then, in Sidon, came unexpected news: the regent, Blanche of Castile, was dead.

Blanche had done what she could to help her son. As soon as she heard of his capture (after pleading with him in a letter to come home), she went about the business of raising the money for his ransom. It was such a large sum that she tried to disguise the actual amount, for fear of rebellion. Matthew Paris guessed at it: "The number of those slain of the French king's army, owing to the pride of the count of Artois, was more than sixty thousand, and twenty thousand men at arms, besides those drowned, others who were dispersed in fight, and those who voluntarily gave themselves up to the enemy . . . The amount of the ransom-money for the king, who was made a prisoner through God's anger, did not differ much from the number of those slain, being sixty thousand pounds of the best and purest gold, sterling money, besides some other common money of Tours and Paris, amounting to an immense sum."

The queen mother got permission from the pope to take a tenth of the Church's income in France for two more years and raised the taxes on the towns, accepting whatever she could get, no matter how small. By 1251 she had most of the ransom collected and shipped to Acre, but fate intervened once more. "The mother and brothers of the French king transmitted a large sum of money for his ransom; but whilst the ship in which it was embarked was at sea, a storm arose, and the vessel, with everything on board, was sunk. When the most Christian king of the French heard of this event, he said, 'Neither this nor any other misfortune shall estrange me from my affection for Christ'; and thus this noble-minded king comforted and strengthened those whom he saw were faint-hearted; so that he seemed to be a second Job; and even the infidels pitied him and admired his constancy and firmness of mind." It was of little comfort to his mother, however, who had to start all over again.

She was even less successful at organizing a new crusading army. None of the barons who had been with Louis originally, including his brothers, had any intention of returning, and their obvious reluctance affected new recruitment. Worse, thousands of peasants, called the *pastoureaux,* led by a rogue monk who styled himself the "Master of Hungary," marched on Paris in an unruly fashion, announcing their intention of embarking for the Holy Land to save the king. At first Blanche, who had hopes of actually sending Louis this untrained, rambunctious force, fed the mob out of her own funds and rewarded its Master with gifts. But it soon became clear that these were not crusaders but thugs. The *pastoureaux* robbed and looted wherever they went; they harassed the mendicant friars and attacked and murdered Jews for their money. Blanche finally had the Master of Hungary and several of his accomplices hanged, and others arrested. The mob disintegrated into small groups; the last of these made it as far as Bordeaux, where Simon de Montfort made quick work of them.

All of this was in addition to the ordinary administration of the affairs of the kingdom. By 1252, Blanche had begun to wonder, like her daughter-in-law, if the king would ever come home. In November Blanche became seriously ill while visiting Melun. The Bishop of Paris was called to hear her confession and administer the last rites. True to her own vision of the Church, Blanche took the veil at the end, which she wore over her crown and ermine, and requested that she be buried in this costume. Then, on either November 26 or 27, the woman who had steered France safely through a quarter century of turmoil, and who, despite the six-year absence of its king, had left the kingdom a thousandfold stronger and more united than when she first acquired it, died.

"Thus, therefore, languished in desolation and prematurely died that most noble lady Blanche . . . a woman in sex, but a man in counsels . . . leaving the French kingdom comfortless and devoid of all consolation," wrote Matthew Paris.

Her body was carried by Alphonse and Charles on a funeral bier back to Paris, where an all-night vigil was held and the citizenry mourned in the streets. She was buried the next morning in the abbey of Maubuisson.

According to Joinville, Louis, who had been on the move with his small army of knights throughout the first six months of 1253, did not find out about his mother's death until June of that year. "It was while he was in Saida [Sidon] that the king received news of his mother's death," the knight wrote. "He was so prostrated with grief that for two whole days no one could speak to him." Marguerite's reaction, however, surprised the chronicler. She was "plunged in grief" and "in tears." (Again, it was Joinville who was summoned to the queen's apartments to soothe her.) As the knight knew of Blanche's long-standing animosity toward her daughter-in-law, he could not resist registering his astonishment at Marguerite's display of emotion. "'For,' said I, 'the woman who hated you most is dead, and yet you are showing such sorrow.' She [Marguerite] told me it was not for Queen Blanche that she was weeping, but because of the grief the king was showing in his mourning over the dead, and also because of her own daughter—later Queen of Navarre—who was now left in the sole guardianship of men."

Louis still did not hurry home to reclaim his kingdom. Instead, he contented himself with writing letters commanding the French clergy to pray for his mother's soul. He evidently intended to stay where he was and continue fortifying the Christian settlements, hoping by these means to keep his crusade alive. Marguerite must have pressed him hard to return home, because he sent her and the children away from him once again, even though the army was in hostile territory. "Some time later the king sent for me and ordered me to arm myself," wrote Joinville. "On my asking him why he told me that it was to escort the queen and her children to Es Sur, some seven leagues away. I did not say a word in reply, though he was sending me on a very dangerous errand, for at the time there was neither peace nor truce between us and the Saracens of Egypt, or of Damascus. God be thanked, we got to Es Sur by nightfall, quite peacefully and without hindrance, though we had to dismount twice to make a fire for cooking our food, and to give the children something to eat, or let them be suckled."

In the end, though, Blanche's death did free her daughter-in-law. Only his mother had cared enough to send Louis the money he needed to maintain his present pace of construction and support his small band of loyal knights. After she died, Alphonse and Charles evidently considered that the kingdom's donations to this particular cause had been quite sufficient already. Alphonse had suffered a stroke and was not fit to assume a leadership role, and Charles, as Marguerite had feared, was only too happy to accumulate power.

Even the citizens of the Christian settlements encouraged Louis to leave, particularly after it became clear that he had no more money to spend. "Your Majesty," the barons of Sidon told him before he left, "you have fortified the city of Saida [Sidon] and . . . greatly strengthened the defenses of Acre by the walls and towers you have built around it. We have talked things over among ourselves and we do not see how it will profit the kingdom of Jerusalem for you to remain here any longer. We therefore strongly advise you to go to Acre in the coming Lent and prepare for your journey home, so that you may be able to return to France after Easter." The inhabitants of Sidon may have felt less safe for the French king's presence, despite the gift of the new walls, than they had previously. Louis's inept handling of diplomatic relations between Cairo and Aleppo had caused the rival Arab tribes to turn on innocent Christians. Between the ransom, the provisioning of the army, and the fortification of a few settlements, the French king had nearly bankrupted his kingdom, spending upward of three-quarters of a million livres of his countrymen's money, and with it bought nothing but death and uncertainty.

And so, with reluctance, Louis marched from Sidon to the port at Acre, stopping briefly in Es Sur to pick up Marguerite and the children. The army that disembarked on April 25, 1254, was so small that it needed only thirteen ships.

A little more than a decade after Louis's departure, the reigning Mamlūk sultan attacked Caesarea and Jaffa, killing and enslaving their populations. In 1291, despite its walls and towers, Acre was besieged and fell to the Syrians, followed by Sidon. Sixty thousand Christians were sold as slaves or murdered.

★ ★ ★

The journey home was terrifying. The ship that contained Louis, Marguerite, the children, and Joinville ran aground at Cyprus due to fog, barely
avoiding crashing into some submerged rocks, "where our ship would have
been dashed to pieces, and all of us have been wrecked and drowned." The
king did what he always did in these situations, which was to lie prone on
the deck in front of the portable altar, making the sign of the cross with his
body. Afterward, he refused to save himself and his family at the expense of
the other people aboard. "If I leave this ship," said Louis, "there are five
hundred people or more on board who will land on this island of Cyprus for
fear of danger to themselves—for there's not one of them who doesn't love
his life as much as I love mine—and these, perhaps, will never return to their
own country." The ship was repaired with all of its passengers aboard.

No sooner had the vessel been dislodged than a fierce wind forced the
ship against the rocks again, and only the sailors' throwing out five anchors
in the opposite direction saved the passengers. Marguerite, being informed
that if the wind continued to blow, the company would all be drowned,
went to consult Joinville. She asked what to do; the knight suggested that
she promise to have made a miniature ship of silver worth five marks if she
and Louis and the children all survived (Joinville himself had already pledged
to take a pilgrimage to visit the shrine of Saint Nicholas as a way of warding
off the previous night's danger). "When the queen—may God show her
mercy!—had come back to France, she had the silver ship made for her in
Paris," said Joinville. "In it were figures of herself, the king, and their three
children, all in silver. The same metal was used for the sailors, the mast, the
rudder, and the rigging of the ship, while all the sails were sewn with silver
thread. The queen told me it had cost a hundred livres to make." Marguerite
gave the model to Joinville so he could present it to the shrine of Saint
Nicholas when he made his pilgrimage.

Marguerite tried to make the voyage as easy for the children as possible;
when the crew feared drowning during yet another storm, she refused to
awaken them, saying that she preferred that they die in their sleep. When
the small fleet passed an island, Marguerite asked Louis to please send some
men to collect fresh fruit for the children. The men were put into some galleys and told to catch up with the ship when it passed the harbor. But the
men stayed in the orchard eating the fruit and so failed to arrive at the appointed time. Louis, attributing their absence to an Arab attack, ordered his
ships to turn around. "When the queen heard of this, she began to show

great distress, and said: 'Alas! This is all my doing!'" The king eventually discovered that it was greed and not Saracens that had detained his servants; furious, he had the men chained like criminals to a longboat aside the ship. "The queen and all of us did what we could to make the king change his mind; but he would not listen to any of us," said Joinville. Turning the ships around cost the company an extra week at sea.

Here again Joinville's sympathies were with the queen. In a later incident, he certainly credits her with courage and quick thinking. A maidservant left her mistress's kerchief too close to a burning candle one evening, and the queen woke to find the clothes in her cabin on fire. Instead of calling for help, Marguerite "jumped out of bed quite naked, picked up the kerchief, and threw it all burning into the sea, and then extinguished the fire on the cloths," Joinville wrote admiringly. The chronicler claimed to have been sleeping in his own room when he was awakened by the commotion. He could see the burning clothes floating in the sea, so he went on deck to investigate. "While I was there my squire, who had been sleeping at the foot of my bed, came and told me that the king was awake, and had asked where I was. 'I told him,' said he [the squire], 'that you were in your cabin'; and the king said to me; 'You're lying,'" Joinville wrote. Perhaps Marguerite had had some help putting out the fire after all.

It took ten weeks, but at last they came in sight of Provence. Marguerite recognized the coastline; there was a familiar castle nearby. "The queen and all the council agreed that the king ought to disembark there, because the land belonged to his brother," said Joinville. But Louis wanted to sail on until they reached Aigues-Mortes, the port he had built at such expense, some six weeks away. It must have been terrible for Marguerite to have Provence so near after such a fearful journey and yet be unable to put to land. It took the queen and the barons two whole days to get Louis to change his mind. Joinville told the king that it was foolish to persist in sailing to Aigues-Mortes when a friendly port was at hand. "The king accepted the advice we gave him, and this decision greatly delighted the queen."

On Friday, July 3, 1254, the royal ships docked at the port of Hyères, about thirty miles east of Marseille. The king and queen and their three children were met by the abbott of Cluny, and escorted to the closest castle to rest and await fresh horses for the journey on to Paris.

In twenty years, this event marked Marguerite and Blanche's one and only collaboration. It had taken both of them, but the king of France was finally home.

Eleanor

Symbolic embrace of the kings of England and France.

CHAPTER XVI

A ROYAL RECEPTION

Although Henry III had resolved to travel to Gascony in order to manage the crisis there as early as the spring of 1252, he did not actually embark on this expedition until August 1253. The reason for the delay was once again the reluctance of the English ruling barons to invest in yet another foreign military campaign. The king simply could not raise the money.

Finally, Eleanor's uncle the archbishop of Canterbury, and Henry's half-brother, the bishop-elect of Winchester, agreed to allow the crown to collect a tenth of all Church proceeds in England for three years. Although ostensibly this money was to be used by Henry and Eleanor to fund an expedition to the Holy Land—the king and queen had taken the cross in 1250, prior to the news of Louis's defeat—everyone understood that the king was really going to Gascony. To demonstrate how little they trusted their sovereign, however, at a parliament held in May 1253, the nobles made Henry promise once again, on pain of excommunication, to uphold the Charter of Liberties. They brought the actual document signed by his father, King John, into the room, to be sworn over rather like a Bible. "So help me God, all these terms will I faithfully observe, as I am a man, a Christian, a knight, and a crowned and anointed king," Henry swore.

The barons' insistence on excommunication for the breaking of any of the covenants of the Great Charter reflects their knowledge both of Henry's character and of his pecuniary difficulties. The degree to which the king and queen of England were in debt was signaled by the extremely unpopular measures they took to raise funds. "As the king was about to partake of a repast at . . . Christmas, the citizens of Winchester sent him a most handsome present of eatables and drinkables, which excited the admiration of all beholders; and the king, by way of thanks, obliged them to pay him two hundred marks in a brief space of time . . . and thus the festivities of Christmas were turned into sorrow and lamentation for them." When a fight broke out in London between some young gaming men and the royal attendants, and the royal attendants (who had started the affair by insulting the Londoners) got the worst of it, Henry, "resorting to his usual kind of vengeance," imposed a harsh fine on the Londoners. He allowed sheriffs and other officials to engage in dubious practices, such as extortion, and then took a royal percentage of the proceeds.

Of course Henry and Eleanor knew that their fund-raising activities were widely condemned, but they felt they had no choice. The king of France, who could count on taxes and fees from the affluent former English possessions of Normandy and Poitou, and whose mother had conquered mighty Toulouse and stripped its citizenry of its wealth, had access to revenues that dwarfed those available to the English monarchy. While Louis could squander three-quarters of a million livres on his crusade, Henry and Eleanor had trouble pulling together a quarter of that sum. The average annual income to the English crown for the years 1238 to 1259 was a paltry £36,000 (approximately 162,000 livres). Running a kingdom and holding Gascony on a budget was a challenging prospect. Yet hold Gascony they must. In the king and queen's opinion, the barons' discontent was a reliable sentiment; they were always discontented. Experience had taught that the crown usually got its way in the end.

By August 1253, when Henry finally sailed, he and Eleanor were once again firmly united and working together toward a common goal. The strategy they pursued was intelligent and efficient, and, because Eleanor and her uncles were involved, included a diplomatic initiative to supplement the military campaign. Specifically, a plan was underfoot to marry Prince Edward, heir to the English throne, to the king of Castile's half-sister Eleanor.

Alfonso X, the king of Castile, was the greatest threat to English interests in Gascony. In 1252, when Simon de Montfort had been abruptly recalled to London to stand trial, Alfonso had resurrected an old claim to sovereignty as his excuse for military intervention and established a formal alliance with the rebel leader, Gaston de Béarn. With their ferocious English overlord absent and disgraced, several Gascon towns had judged it best to shift their allegiance from England to Castile, with the castle at La Réole serving as the stronghold and base of the operation.

Even though the rebels seemed to have the upper hand, the king of Castile was evidently unsure of his ability to consolidate his authority in Gascony because he was willing to entertain the suggestion of a prestigious marriage between his sister and the heir to the English throne. So, even before he set sail for Gascony, Henry sent one of his most influential counselors, John Mansel, to Castile to begin negotiations. Mansel was an intimate of both the queen and Peter of Savoy; he was often employed to carry discreet messages back and forth between the two. He would not have been charged with so delicate a mission without the full knowledge and approbation of the queen, who concerned herself with every detail of Edward's existence.

The prospect of a royal wedding was the carrot, but Henry and Eleanor knew that they must use a stick as well. If Alfonso's interference in Gascony was not met by a definite show of English force, the king of Castile would take over the province easily and then he would have no need to treat with England. To force Alfonso to take the diplomatic alternative seriously, Henry embarked from Portsmouth on August 6 in the company of some three hundred warships. Edward, who was fourteen, came to see him off. "The boy, Edward, after his father had kissed and wept over him at parting, stood crying and sobbing on the shore, and would not depart as long as he could see the swelling sails of the ships." This was not mere filial affection. Gascony had been promised to Edward, and he was desperate to go; to stay home was humiliating, and so he cried. Already, Henry and Eleanor's first-born was demonstrating the passion for warfare that would mark his reign.

Eleanor, too, watched the ships set sail and no doubt pondered the future. She had observed Henry's behavior as commander-in-chief a decade before in Poitou, and it had not been a reassuring performance. Could he now succeed when he had failed so abjectly in the past?

Eleanor was five months pregnant when Henry sailed; this was one of the reasons she stayed behind. Her third child, Beatrice, had been born in Gascony in 1243 and the queen still had vivid memories of her hosts threatening to give her up to the French. It was not an experience she cared to repeat, nor would her presence in Gascony have materially aided her husband's efforts. He must be free to move about and strike without regard to the requirements of a pregnant wife. Henry needed someone he trusted in England, someone who could anticipate his needs and act in his stead, someone who could keep the kingdom focused on winning the war.

Henry left her regent, with Richard to advise her. This was outside English custom; certainly neither Henry's despised father John nor his revered grandfather Henry II had ever allowed their wives to rule in their place, and the idea apparently took some getting used to. Matthew Paris reported that the king appointed both "Earl Richard and the queen [as] guardians of the kingdom," but the chronicler was wrong. It was Eleanor who was trusted with Henry's great seal for safekeeping, Eleanor who was named "keeper and governor" of England in the king's absence. Her task was to keep order and supply Henry's needs abroad. Neither party was under any illusion as to what this meant. Eleanor was in charge of raising money.

And Henry needed all the money she could get him. The army was expensive to maintain. Famine had seized war-torn Gascony "to such a degree, that a hen was sold for sixpence sterling; a measure of corn for twenty shillings; a quart of wine for two shillings and more . . . so that a hungry knight could scarcely support himself, his esquire, his page, and his horses for two shillings of silver [a day]." Moreover, the king much preferred to bribe his subjects than to fight them, and since this policy was also acceptable to many Gascons, his expenditures rose accordingly.

Henry's faith in his wife's abilities was well-placed. Eleanor fought for his interests tenaciously and squeezed every mark she could out of the populace. When Henry asked her to pay Alphonse of Poitiers £3,226 sterling to keep France out of the war, she took the money from her own allowance. She borrowed from bankers in Florence, and had Richard pressure the Jews of England for funds. (Church policy forbade Christians from loaning money at interest, so the practice had devolved upon the Jews. A despised minority, the Jews were an easy target for plunder.) According to Matthew Paris, "Earl Richard having convoked them [the Jews] to a meeting, demanded of them for the use of the king—who, he said, was highly indignant with them—a large sum of money, under penalty of imprisonment and ignominious death." So attuned was the queen to the king's need for funds that even the royal Christmas gift, usually an expensive robe or engraved cup, was eschewed; instead, Eleanor sent Henry five hundred marks in cash.

The arrival of her daughter Katharine in November did nothing to slow Eleanor's efforts on Henry's behalf. By January 1254, she and Richard were lobbying the barons and the clergy for more assistance, both financial and military, at the annual parliament. The queen and the earl of Cornwall were only partly successful. The native aristocracy distrusted Henry's reports from abroad, particularly his worry that the king of Castile was preparing to invade imminently, and the clergy felt that the tenth of their income appropriated ostensibly to the crusade was quite enough of a sacrifice already.

In spite of these obstacles, Eleanor kept the money flowing, and the result was that Henry began to make progress. He bought back several castles, and began a siege of the rebel stronghold at La Réole. Almost as soon as he began he recognized the difficulty of this task, swallowed his pride, and appealed to Simon de Montfort, who had taken up residence in Paris after his trial, to return to Gascony and help him. Despite the amicability of his French hosts, which stood in direct contrast to his recent treatment in England—the French baronage admired the earl of Leicester so much that they had tried to make him regent after the death of Blanche of Castile—Simon obeyed Henry's summons. Eleanor, alerted to Henry's appeal, also helped to get Simon back to Gascony by quickly paying the earl of Leicester the money still remaining on his initial contract.

The arrival in Bordeaux of their former tormentor caused many of the rebels, who feared Simon de Montfort more than they feared Gaston de Béarn, to revert their allegiance to Henry. The king of England showed great foresight by conferring clemency on these returned subjects; his generosity extended even to the bestowal of expensive Christmas presents. The Gascons began to remember the advantages that had formerly accrued to the duchy under the administration of this benign and usually absentee English king, and the movement for independence faltered. The number of rebels dwindled to a hard core of seasoned warriors, but the king's Lusignan half-brothers, who had accompanied him from the beginning, were also fierce fighters. Henry, gratified by their valiancy, began to reward them by assigning them the property of those whom they had conquered, which spurred them on to greater efforts.

The success of Henry's policies can be measured by the sudden capitulation of Alfonso to the idea of an alliance through marriage in March 1254. The announcement of Edward's engagement was accompanied by the initiation of serious peace negotiations between England and Castile.

Cautiously optimistic—the marriage was not yet consummated and Alfonso had proved treacherous in the past—Eleanor went about the process of transferring property to Edward, so that he would be sufficiently moneyed in his own right to take his place in the world as a married man who would one day rule England. Edward got, in addition to Gascony, of course, all of Ireland, the Channel Islands, several important castles in Wales, the town of Bristol, the county of Chester, and other assorted English properties. It was an endowment sufficiently munificent as to provoke comment; the strengthening of the son's estate weakened that of the father.

This accomplished, Eleanor arranged for herself, Edward, her younger son Edmund, and her uncle Boniface to embark for Gascony. Preparations for this expedition were marked by frustrating delays due to regional squabbling. The ship builders of Yarmouth, who had been assigned the task of providing Prince Edward with a suitable vessel, delivered a much-admired state-of-the-art warship that excited jealousy among the ship builders of Winchelsea, who were under contract to furnish the queen's ships, and whose efforts had yielded a distinctly inferior product. "The people of Winchelsea . . . finding that the [ship] sent for the prince was much larger and more handsome than theirs . . . treacherously and suddenly made an attack on it, destroying the ship, and wounding and slaying some of the crew; and in order to palliate their crime, they took the mast of the destroyed vessel, and fitted it to the queen's ship, as though they had acted as they did for her benefit and advantage." Then, just as Eleanor had reorganized her party to accommodate the loss of Edward's ship, an urgent message arrived from Henry, informing her that Alfonso was mustering troops for an invasion of Gascony after all, and ordering her not to leave the country.

It was a critical moment. If she sailed, she risked taking her two sons into danger, where there was a possibility they might be killed or captured. But if she did not sail, she risked losing Gascony and a diplomatic achievement much to her own advantage. The plan for Edward's marriage was in the final stages; was she now, through fear of personal safety, to abandon that goal and scuttle all that had been accomplished so far? "Thus tormented . . . she said in her vexation, 'Troubles arise on all sides; everything is ready for setting sail; I have bade farewell to all; the wind blows most favorable; and shall I go back? No.'" And she sailed.

This act of courage and decisiveness was rewarded. Alfonso did not attack Gascony (Henry had misinterpreted his spies' information; Alfonso's troops had been mustered for an assault not on Gascony, but against Navarre, with whom Alfonso was also feuding). Edward was sent on to Spain "in great pomp and splendor" to be knighted and married at the end of October 1254. Neither Henry nor Eleanor attended the wedding, believing their presence in Gascony to be a stabilizing force during the precarious period preceding their son's marriage, but Edward was back in Bordeaux three weeks later with his thirteen-year-old bride in tow, "and was received with the greatest rejoicings, as though he had been an angel of God." John Mansel, the ambassador who had so deftly negotiated the terms of the alliance, also returned, bearing a peace contract dated November 1, marked by Alfonso's gold seal, "by which he [Alfonso], for himself and his heirs, quitted claim to the whole of Gascony to the king of England and his heirs."

There was now no longer any doubt as to the efficacy of the king and queen's efforts: Henry and Eleanor, working together, had succeeded for the first time in eighteen years of marriage in bending events to their will. They had pacified Gascony and secured Edward's birthright; arranged a brilliant marriage for their eldest son; and turned the king of Castile, a potentially dangerous enemy, into a reliable family ally.

So satisfied were Henry and Eleanor with their accomplishment that they decided to take a holiday before returning to England. Henry had always wanted to visit Fontevrault, where his mother and grandparents were buried. "He had, also, a wish to see the French kingdom and the cities of it, of which he then only knew the names," said Matthew Paris. Henry and Eleanor knew that Louis and Marguerite were back in Paris, so Henry sent ambassadors to the capital city to ask for permission to travel through France. He wasn't sure what Louis's reaction would be; he had heard that Louis was greatly altered by his experiences on crusade. Both he and Eleanor were consequently pleased when the king of France not only granted the safe-conduct, but invited his brother and sister-in-law to spend Christmas in Paris with the royal family.

Louis was indeed much changed. The guilt he felt for his role in leading thousands of Frenchmen to their deaths in the Holy Land shrouded his every gesture. "The king of the French, cast down in heart and look, refused all consolation: musical instruments afforded him no pleasure; no cheerful or consolatory speeches drew a smile from him; he felt no joy at revisiting his native country and his own kingdom, nor at the respectful salutations he received, nor at the acknowledgments and gifts made by his subjects to him as their lord; but with downcast looks, and with deep grief and frequent sighs, he thought of his capture [by the Saracens], and through it of the disgrace brought on Christianity in general." He eschewed the trappings of royalty. "After the king's return from oversea he lived with such a disregard for worldly vanities that he never wore ermine or squirrel fur, not scarlet cloth, nor were his stirrups or his spurs gilded," said Joinville. More than this, he took to wearing a hair shirt under his robe; when his skin became so inflamed that he could no longer bear it, he still insisted upon wearing a hair belt at Lent. He paid no attention to his food, eating whatever was put before him in moderation, and had himself regularly scourged with a rod and chains. (Upon his death, he would leave both the hair belt and the chains to his daughter Isabelle as fond mementos.)

Much of his grief was associated, not simply with his past performance in the desert, but with the interruption of his work in the Holy Land. He insisted that "he had not yet concluded his pilgrimage, but had only suspended it for a time." He had evidently mulled over the disaster and concluded that the reason for his initial failure was that both he and his kingdom were sinful. Within six months of his return he had issued a series of laws with the stated intent of imposing morality on his subjects. The general ordinance of 1254, issued by the king in December, prohibited all officers of the crown, including "bailiffs, sheriffs, provosts, mayors, and all others" from accepting gifts valued in excess of ten sous for either themselves or their families; from neglecting their duties or robbing or extorting money from the citizens under their jurisdiction; from impeding justice, levying fines except in open court, engaging in nepotism, or bribing a higher official. The purpose of these measures was obviously to relieve the general populace of corrupt officials and to encourage fairness in the average citizen's dealings with government representatives. "By such ordinances the king did much to improve conditions in his kingdom," Joinville observed approvingly.

The decree also contained a series of laws monitoring personal behavior. Swearing, gaming, or frequenting taverns was forbidden. To make his point, upon his return, Louis had the lips of a Parisian shopkeeper convicted of blasphemy burned off. When the court reacted with horror, Louis replied: "I would willingly allow myself to be branded with a hot iron on condition that all wicked oaths were banished from my realm." Prostitution and the production of dice were also forbidden. The Jews had already been expelled, and their property appropriated, by virtue of an edict issued while Louis was still in the Holy Land; apparently, however, some had remained because the king renewed his attack on them upon his return.

Marguerite did her best to moderate his behavior, but was only partially successful. She tried to persuade him to dress in a manner more fitting to his station, but he replied that he would only improve the quality of his robes if she cheapened the material of hers (a condition she found less than appealing). She begged for mercy in several cases where Louis's moral code imposed a particularly harsh punishment, including the case of a noblewoman who was to be hanged in her hometown for having arranged her husband's death. The woman had sincerely repented, and Marguerite asked that she be put to death in a different venue so that the rest of her family would be spared the pain and humiliation of watching her die in so public a manner; Louis refused. But when Louis came to her with the suggestion that they both give up their secular responsibilities and retire to separate religious houses in order to pursue a more spiritual existence, Marguerite was adamant in her opposition. She hadn't brought him out of the desert so he could become a Dominican friar. She retorted shortly that they could do more to promote God's will as king and queen of France than they could ever accomplish by seclusion.

In fact, her experience in Egypt had changed Marguerite as well. She had the strength, self-assurance, and faith in her own abilities that comes from having faced and survived extreme adversity. The French queen's sojourn in the Holy Land had affected her standing at home and abroad; she had gained international prestige for her fortitude. Marguerite was recognized as intelligent, practical, and fair, and, after her return, was often asked to mediate disputes. Her husband, bereft of his mother's counsel, frequently turned to her for advice. It was Marguerite who had prevailed upon Louis to extend the Christmas invitation to Henry and Eleanor. The sisters' mother, Beatrice of Savoy, would be there as well; the older woman had joined Marguerite, Louis, and the children soon after they had landed in Provence, and at her daughter's urging had agreed to accompany the royal family back to Paris and to stay for the holiday. Marguerite wanted her husband to move closer to her family in order to isolate Charles of Anjou. This meant establishing peace with England.

Louis also wanted peace. His principal objective was to return to the Holy Land. This could not be accomplished if his kingdom was at war with another European power. Henry and Eleanor, too, had their own reasons for seeking a more permanent understanding with the French crown. They accepted Louis's invitation and made plans to travel from Gascony to Paris.

The Christmas gathering of 1254 represented the apex of English prestige during Henry and Eleanor's reign. They were enormously popular in Paris. "Crowds . . . assembled, rushing in masses, and vying with one another in their endeavors to see the king of England in Paris, and his fame was carried to the skies by the French, on account of his munificent presents, his hospitality during that day, his munificent almsgiving, as also on account of his select retinue; and again, because the king of France had married one sister, and he, the king of England, another," wrote Matthew Paris.

Face-to-face for the first time in their long history of animosity, each under the influence of his wife and her charming family, Henry and Louis discovered that they had much in common. They were both extremely religious, with a taste for architecture. Henry, buoyed by his recent victory, was at his best. There were no fits of pique or irrational temper on display; instead, he felt confident enough to be magnanimous toward Louis, offering him the place of honor at the banquet and complimenting him on the exquisite design of the newly completed Sainte-Chapelle. Louis, in turn, was very impressed with Henry's piety. "The king [Louis] asked me once if I washed the feet of the poor on Maundy Thursday," wrote Joinville. "I replied that I did no such thing, for I thought it unbecoming. He told me I should not disdain to perform such an act, seeing that our Lord had done so. 'I suppose,' said he, 'you would be very unwilling to follow the example of the King of England, who washes the feet of lepers, and kisses them.'"

This Christmas party was a glittering social success and stunning diplomatic triumph. The issues of Gascony, Poitou, and Normandy were discussed and settled in principle. Henry would renounce all claim to Normandy and Poitou in exchange for a substantial monetary settlement; Louis would recognize and respect England's dominance in Gascony, asking only for the symbolic gesture that Henry do him homage for the duchy. This arrangement was much to England's advantage, as Henry, who had no hope of reacquiring Normandy, was to be paid a sum that would eventually be set at 134,000 livres in the final treaty of 1259. The French baronage protested to Louis that the settlement with England was too generous, but the king did not listen.

The family of sisters from Provence had completely recast relations between two of the greatest powers in Europe. For the next fifty years there would be differences, but they would be negotiated within the context of an implicit understanding that the interests of England and France were ultimately allied.

Henry and Eleanor returned to England in January 1255, secure in the friendship of the king and queen of France. Henry was impressed by this, his first truly international experience, and Eleanor had confirmed a heightened social status. She and Henry were finally on a par with Louis and her sister

Marguerite. This newfound standing did not disintegrate once they had returned home; to further cement the alliance Louis sent them an elephant, "the only elephant ever seen in England, or even in the countries on this side of the Alps," and Marguerite gave them a washing bowl in the shape of a peacock, encrusted all over with precious stones, including pearls. "So richly was this jewel ornamented, and so new and wonderful was the workmanship, that it created admiration in the eyes of all beholders," Matthew Paris marveled.

Thus armed, Eleanor and Henry felt sufficiently emboldened to reveal to the native English aristocracy the terms of a new scheme, which they had accepted some months before, and which had the strong support of the queen's Savoyard uncles. Edward's coming into his inheritance had highlighted the inequity of the meager legacy set aside for their second son, Edmund. This imbalance was now to be righted. Henry, at Eleanor's urging, had accepted in Edmund's name the pope's offer of the crown of Sicily, so recently rejected by Richard of Cornwall as an impossible prospect, comparable to asking for the moon.

It was a gamble of immense proportions, a throw of the dice motivated in equal parts by the interests of a cherished second son and vainglorious ambition. In the end, it would cost them 135,541 marks, the respect of their peers, and the kingdom.

Sanchia

Thirteenth-century shields. Richard of Cornwall, King of the Romans' shield is in the first row, second from the left. It depicts a crowned lion surrounded by gold coins. His is the only coat of arms to reference money.

CHAPTER XVII

QUEEN OF THE ROMANS

When Sanchia learned that her mother and sisters and her sisters' husbands were all to gather in Paris to celebrate Christmas, she wanted to go as well. She was very close to her mother, whom she hadn't seen since 1248 when Beatrice of Savoy had made a special trip to London to reassure Henry and Eleanor that she had not, in fact, surrendered the castles that Henry had paid for to Charles of Anjou, but was fighting to keep them for England. Henry had been appeased by this visit, and was once again on good terms with his mother-in-law. It was unlikely that the countess of Cornwall would ever have the chance to visit her mother in Provence, so she pressed to attend the Christmas reunion. If everyone else in the family was going to be in Paris in December 1254, Sanchia observed to her husband, they should go, too.

Richard did not disagree. He understood that a Provençal family gathering was as much a diplomatic and political event as it was a social affair, and that agreements in principle would be settled on important policy issues under the guise of holiday gift-giving and banqueting. But when Eleanor had joined Henry in Gascony she had left the regency of the kingdom in her brother-in-law's hands, and he could not now shirk that responsibility. So it was decided that Sanchia should attend without her husband. To ensure that she was taken seriously as his representative, and "that her condition might not appear inferior to her sister's, the queen," the earl of Cornwall outfitted his wife with a retinue of such splendor and magnificence that she might have been mistaken for a visiting empress.

Sanchia did very well by Richard on this occasion. Her clothes, jewels, and entourage added greatly to the general spectacle, which served to enhance English prestige at a time when Henry and Eleanor were grateful for the boost. She was firmly in her mother's camp, which meant that she was with Marguerite and Eleanor and against her younger sister, Beatrice. Her retiring personality and general piety recommended her to Louis, who also held Richard in high esteem, and allowed her mother and sisters, who were very involved in their different political schemes, to speak freely in front of her.

One of these schemes was Henry and Eleanor's plan to procure Sicily for Edmund. Eleanor would have used the Christmas gathering to acquaint her mother and Marguerite with her desire to provide her second son with a kingdom of his own. It was impossible for Henry to accept the pope's offer without the tacit approval of Louis, Marguerite, and Beatrice of Savoy. Edmund's English troops would have to have royal permission to cross France and sail from Provence in order to invade Sicily. It was also highly unlikely that the gambit in Edmund's name (he was only ten years old) would have any real chance at success without a recognized peace between the two kingdoms. Eleanor was aware that after Richard had formally refused the kingship of Sicily in 1252, the pope had offered the crown to Charles of Anjou, and only Louis's insistence that French military focus be kept on the Holy Land had prevented his brother's accepting the honor. Now that Louis was back, Eleanor wanted to make sure that the king of France did not change his mind and that Sicily went to her son and not to Charles.

She found willing allies in Marguerite and Beatrice of Savoy, both of whom had their own reasons for hating Charles. There was evidently an unspoken agreement among the two eldest sisters and their mother that they would work together to promote peace between England and France and to support each other's interests in Provence, which included wresting what each considered to be her fair share of the inheritance away from their youngest sister. There are letters extant between Marguerite and Eleanor, which indicate a coordinated effort to secure a treaty.

Sanchia was once again in a difficult position. Richard of Cornwall's support was essential to the Sicilian undertaking. He was still the leading figure among the baronage, and Henry would expect his brother to argue in favor of Edmund's kingship in parliament. But Richard was still upset that Henry and Eleanor had taken Gascony away from him and given it to Edward. Richard might find it galling to have Edmund now invested with Sicily.

★ ★ ★

Richard did indeed find it galling. His indignation was conspicuous and took the tangible form, at least in the short term, of refusing to lend his brother any more money. That this refusal was a consequence of his anger over "the Sicilian business," as it was then being called in England, is reinforced by his decision at around this time to deny a request for credit by the pope as well. At a parliament in 1255, "The earl would not listen to the entreaties either of the king or the pope, and the more especially because the king was bewitched by the underhand instigations of his transalpine advisors [Eleanor's Savoyard uncles], and had undertaken the expedition to Apulia [Sicily] without asking the advice or consent of him (the earl) or that of his barons."

Richard certainly had reason to oppose his brother's arrangement with the pope. The situation in Sicily in 1255 was, if anything, even more unmanageable than it had been when the earl of Cornwall had flatly refused to undertake the task of conquering the kingdom the year before. Frederick II's son Conrad, the legitimate heir, had ruled for only two years before dying of fever at the age of twenty-six. His one accomplishment had been to poison his fifteen-year-old half-brother, the son of Frederick II and Isabella of England (Henry III's sister), who had been the next in line. This had left Manfred, the emperor's illegitimate son, in undisputed control. The pope had already tested Manfred's resolve by sending an army of sixty thousand men (which Henry, as part of the deal, had promised to pay for) to wrest Sicily from this unworthy usurper. But Manfred had retained the loyalty of the imperial forces, a substantial percentage of which were of Saracen origin. These troops, inspired by the recognition that there would be no place for them in a Sicily administered by the pope, fought with such grim determination that "they approached the papal troops with the rapidity of a whirlwind," overwhelming their opponents. The Christian forces were "slain, or made prisoners, or dispersed . . . and the whole Roman church were overwhelmed with grief at the news," Matthew Paris observed solemnly.

It is customary among medieval historians to view Henry and Eleanor's Sicilian project as unmitigated folly, and Richard's vociferous opposition to it as the product of the earl of Cornwall's disinterested good sense. But Richard's condemnation of his nephew's advancement was so vehement, and so public, that it betrays a quite different rationale: fear that the plan would succeed. Taken in the context of its time, Henry and Eleanor's pursuit of the Sicilian crown for their second son was not the hopeless quest history later judged it. The king and queen of England had very good reason to believe that this goal was attainable, and that reason, as Richard well knew, had to do with his wife's family.

By the 1250s, Sanchia and Eleanor's Savoyard uncles, particularly Thomas and Peter of Savoy, who were the motivating forces behind this project, controlled almost all of Switzerland and northern Italy—everything east of the Rhône, almost to Milan. They were the gatekeepers to the passes through the Alps, and seasoned fighters. They were adept at the delicate task of navigating between the Church and the empire. The pope, who often employed one or the other as diplomats, and who recognized and promoted their authority in Switzerland, could not do without them. Manfred, too, had close ties to the family, having married one of Thomas of Savoy's nieces. If Sanchia's uncles and their vassals chose to accompany Edmund's forces to Sicily—and they had every incentive to do so—what to the barons of England seemed an outlandish scheme had actually a very good chance at success.

If the earl of Cornwall required additional evidence that his wife's family operated as a powerful political machine, he needed look no further than the Provençelles' response to the imprisonment of Thomas of Savoy in 1255 by his neighbors in Asti. Thomas, who had been at the family Christmas party in Paris the year before, was a strong advocate of Edmund's candidacy for the Sicilian throne, mostly because he saw it as a way to acquire new territory in Italy. The former count of Flanders, whose wife had died in 1244, leaving him a very rich man, had been in the process of trying to take over Asti, about thirty miles southeast of Turin, when his forces were overcome and he was taken prisoner and held for ransom.

The news of his capture spread quickly to the courts of Europe and the family took immediate action. In England, Henry and Eleanor shut down trade with northern Italy, and forcibly detained all merchants and citizens from Asti and Turin who happened to be visiting at the time. In France, Marguerite had Louis follow suit, an action that resulted in hundreds of arrests. She then demanded a payment of ten thousand pounds, in addition to the release of her relative, as a condition of freedom. Beatrice of Savoy, the sisters' mother, ordered her soldiers to close the roads between Switzerland and Provence and took numerous prisoners. Sanchia even persuaded Richard to do his part by forwarding the money needed to underwrite a rescue attempt. Faced with the poverty brought on by the imposition of what were, in effect, international economic sanctions, the citizens of Asti realized their mistake, and let Uncle Thomas go.

With both the pope and Eleanor's family firmly in support of the Sicilian project, the king and queen of England had acquired an air of confidence and international respectability that stung Richard's pride. The proposition had obviously been discussed at length and he, the most important private individual in England, had been excluded from the deliberations. Henry and Eleanor were trying to replicate their Gascon success in Sicily. Once again, the plan was to use the military stick to promote a diplomatic carrot. Manfred had a daughter, and this daughter could be married to Edmund, as the king of Castile's sister had been married to Edward. It was telling that John Mansel, the very same ambassador who had negotiated Edward's marriage, was sent in secret to Manfred in May 1257 with a similar assignment.

Perhaps most discomfiting to Richard was the grand ceremony held at Westminster, presided over by a special representative of the pope, at which Edmund knelt and was presented with an impressive ring symbolizing the boy's investiture with Sicily. On this occasion Henry also knelt before the altar, and, in the presence of the most illustrious members of the English aristocracy, swore by St. Edward to send an army to defeat Manfred in his son's name. "The king's heart was now elated with pride and full of exultation . . . as if his son Edmund were already crowned king; in fact, he in public called his son Edmund, king of Sicily," said Matthew Paris. The earl of Cornwall, a man who ached for his own crown the way a bourgeois hungered for a title, suddenly faced the unsupportable prospect of seeing his nephew assume a throne that could have been his.

Richard could not stop Henry and Eleanor, but he could hold them up and make trouble. This was a project that called for money—vast quantities of money—and money was an asset that Henry conspicuously lacked. Stirring up opposition was a tactic that had worked for Richard in the past, and it worked for him now. But only because of his wife.

Christmas 1255, the year after the great family gathering in Paris, was a wretched holiday for Sanchia. Her husband was barely speaking to his brother. "My own flesh and blood attack me; already has my brother Earl Richard been excited against me," Henry is reported to have sighed at the family party at Winchester. The earl of Cornwall's anger and frustration was not directed solely at his brother. He also blamed Sanchia and her family for advancing his nephew Edmund's interests over his own.

After more than a decade of marriage, Sanchia felt her husband's disappointment keenly. She was a very rich woman, but wealth had not brought happiness. She had given Richard a son but Edmund was still too young to be of interest to a gruff man of forty-six. Besides, Edmund was usually at Windsor with Eleanor's younger children, as was the custom at the time. Sanchia visited often, of course, but Richard much preferred to be with Henry, his twenty-year-old son by his first wife. Indeed, he preferred Henry's company, or work, to anything else, including Sanchia, which perhaps explains why the countess of Cornwall did not bear any more children.

Religion provided solace. Sanchia named her son after St. Edmund the Confessor; she read the lives of the saints and took religious instruction from Matthew Paris, who was a trusted familiar of both the earl of Cornwall and his wife. She had gone with Richard when he visited the pope in 1250. Together, they had built and dedicated a church at Hailes (about thirty miles northwest of Oxford) at great expense the following year, the consequence of a vow the earl of Cornwall had taken when he thought he was going to die during a storm aboard ship while returning from Gascony. This dedication had been the highlight of Sanchia's English existence, a melding of piety and spectacle, ten thousand marks spent in good works. But it had not translated into warmer conjugal relations, and her connection at the end of 1255 to her husband had never been colder. She must have prayed that Christmas for guidance.

Rarely has providence acted so quickly to reward devotion. Within a month, on January 28, 1256, the reigning sovereign of Germany, William of Holland, who had taken advantage of Conrad's death in 1254 to seize the title of king of the Romans for himself, died while attempting to pacify some of his northern subjects. Apparently, he ventured out too far on a frozen lake and his horse fell through the ice. "The enraged rider [William] dug his sharp spurs into the animal's sides till they reached his entrails, and the noble, fiery beast struggled to rise and free himself, but without success." The rest of his knights, fearing a similar accident, retreated. Helpless to defend himself, William scrambled to shore and tried to bribe his opponents to let him go, but they preferred to hack him into pieces. The post of king of the Romans was suddenly, conveniently, available.

Ordinarily, leaping to become king of a principality that had just proven its belligerence by slaughtering its previous leader would have given the earl of Cornwall pause. But Richard, who had already squandered one such opportunity through what he now considered to be excessive caution, began at once to promote his candidacy for the title. William of Holland had been dead barely a week when the earl of Cornwall hired a prestigious intermediary for two hundred pounds to act as a behind-the-scenes advocate. Richard next informed Henry of his campaign and the king demonstrated his enthusiastic support for his brother's undertaking by dispatching a member of his own household to Rome to petition the pope for official approval of the plan. King of the Romans was an elected office; seven regional German despots—Count Palatine of the Rhine, the archbishop of Cologne, the count of Bohemia, the archbishop of Mainz, the archbishop of Trèves, the duke of Saxony, and the marquis of Brandenburg—were responsible for choosing the German monarch. Luckily, a simple majority was all that was required to elect a new leader, so Richard only had to bribe four of them.

Count Palatine, who came on board early, was rewarded with the promise of the hand of one of Henry's own daughters in marriage, complete with a dowry of 12,000 marks (which Henry expected Richard to provide). The archbishop of Cologne, who held out until December, received 8,000 marks on the fifteenth of that month; the archbishop of Mainz found out how much the archbishop of Cologne had been given and demanded the same. He got it.

It was at this point that Richard's nomination, which had been uncontested, ran into an unforeseen obstacle: an honest man. The archbishop of Trèves rebuffed the earl of Cornwall's graft and proposed a new, equally credible nominee: Alfonso X of Castile. The counts of Saxony and Brandenburg joined him in opposing Richard's candidacy.

Alfonso's nomination posed a serious threat to Richard's election. The pope preferred Alfonso; Church policy demanded that the former Holy Roman Empire be weakened by separating Germany from Sicily so that the Papal States would not be squeezed in between as they had been during the reign of Frederick II. If Henry III's son Edmund ruled Sicily and Edmund's uncle Richard ruled Germany, then England effectively ruled the empire, a situation the pope feared. Only the assurances of Sanchia's uncles, who wanted to preserve their Sicilian plan and needed a complaisant king in Germany, convinced the pope to approve Richard's election over Alfonso's.

Similarly, Louis IX preferred Alfonso's candidacy to that of Richard of Cornwall's. To halt the encroachment of English influence outside their borders, he and Marguerite had hastened to marry their eldest son, Louis, to Alfonso's daughter in November 1255, after Edward had married Eleanor of Castile. To have France hedged in by English control of both Germany and

Sicily was a situation that Blanche of Castile would never have tolerated. France was the most powerful kingdom in Europe; Louis could have stopped Richard's election at any time. His mother would not have hesitated.

But Blanche was dead and Marguerite was queen, and Marguerite, Eleanor, Beatrice of Savoy, and all of the uncles rallied behind Sanchia and threw their support to Richard. When the swing elector, Ottocar of Bohemia, agreed to support Richard, Louis did not object. On December 26, 1256, at the Christmas court in London, Richard had the satisfaction, "in the presence of all there assembled," to receive the news that the electors "had, by unanimous consent, duly elected Earl Richard king of Germany . . . The archbishop of Cologne . . . had by these special messengers, sent testimonial letters, bearing evidence to the unanimity of the election . . . and they declared that no one had ever been elected to that dignity so spontaneously, so unanimously, and with such few obstacles." In fact, Saxony and Brandenburg never acknowledged Richard as king, Ottocar of Bohemia changed his mind two months later and voted a second time for Alfonso, and Frankfurt was so opposed to Richard's election that his name had to be proclaimed outside the city walls. But after 28,000 marks, which is what the crown of Germany ultimately cost Richard in bribes, the archbishop of Cologne can perhaps be forgiven for shading the truth a little.

Still, all the money in the earl of Cornwall's considerable coffers would not have purchased him this honor without his wife and her family. The offer of the German monarchy was conditional upon his backing Edmund's kingship in Sicily, and Richard acknowledged this debt to Sanchia and Eleanor by sending messengers to the French and papal courts with assurances of his support.

Richard's being named king meant that Sanchia was now to be queen— but of what a kingdom! Germany was cold, brutal, and fractured; its people coarse, its culture and language, such as it was, foreign and impenetrable. Sanchia counted no German nobleman or woman among her acquaintance, and, although Richard had done business with some of the German merchants, neither she nor her husband had ever visited within that bleak, dispiriting locale that they were now to call home. For to rule, by definition, meant to live, at least for a time, among their subjects, a prospect from which she recoiled. If Provence occupied the center of European aristocratic society, of genteel manners, erudite troubadours, and charming company, and England was a remote outpost on the fringes of civilization, Germany represented a murderous, barbaric wilderness.

She need not have worried. Richard had no intention of urging his authority on those provinces that might be hostile to his person. He had acquired his title for the prestige of being addressed as "Your Majesty" and to be consulted as his brother's equal in international affairs of state. He had no intention of risking his life by undue exposure to his subjects.

The coronation was held in Aachen, in western Germany, a town that fell within the archbishop of Cologne's sphere of influence. Richard, Sanchia, Richard's son Henry, little Edmund, and enough followers to make an impressive showing at the ceremony sailed from Yarmouth on April 29, 1257. It took "forty-eight large ships and two little ones" to accommodate the retinue.

Before he left, Richard made a formal farewell at a great parliament held in London. The king had used this occasion to present his son Edmund, "dressed in the Apulian fashion," to shame his barons into providing the funds necessary to fulfill his obligation to the pope. Henry "added that, by the advice and goodwill of the pope and the English church, he had, for the sake of obtaining the kingdom of Sicily, bound himself, under penalty of losing his kingdom, to the payment of a hundred and forty thousand marks, exclusive of interest, which daily increased, although without being apparent." Tellingly, this time Richard did not speak out against his brother's request for funds and the barons "were at length compelled to give a promise of relieving the king's pressing necessities." Henry got 52,000 marks, not as much as he had asked for, but certainly more than he had obtained previously. Henry and Eleanor's advocacy of Richard's election had bought the earl of Cornwall's—or, rather, the king of the Romans'—unquestioned support, and this had an effect on the baronage.

Sanchia and her husband reached Aachen on May 11, and the coronation was held on May 27. The archbishop of Cologne himself conducted the ceremony. Richard had taken the precaution of bringing a large sum of money with him, which he dispensed liberally to the population, so that quite a crowd was on hand to gawk at the spectacle. No detail was too small to merit the earl's attention; earlier he had presented the archbishop with "a most handsome mitre, ornamented with precious stones, and fastened with pieces of gold; and when the archbishop had fitted it on his head, he exclaimed: 'Earl Richard has enriched me and my church with a handsome gift; . . . He has mitred me, and I will crown him.'"

The festivities lasted for two days. With Alfonso X still contesting the election results, Richard strove to make the occasion as opulent as possible in order to legitimize his reign. There was such an abundance of meat, fish, wine, and other delicacies at the coronation feast, and he, Sanchia, and the rest of the entourage were outfitted so magnificently, that the population of Aachen and the invited German dignitaries, unaccustomed to such entertainments, were flabbergasted. The parochial nature of this audience suited the earl of Cornwall's purposes. Henry and Eleanor had offered to attend, but Richard had dissuaded them; he feared their presence might distract attention that the new king felt ought, under the circumstances, to be directed solely at him. One of his first official acts as king was to write home, addressing himself to his nephew, Prince Edward, and the mayor and citizens of London. In his letter, Richard stated that "three thousand knights, thirty dukes and counts, two archbishops and ten bishops were present [at his coronation];" he made sure to sign it with his new title, *"Dei gratia Rex Romanorum"* ("By God's Grace King of the Romans"). On the second day, he knighted his son Henry, henceforward known as Henry of Almain, with equal splendor. Then he made plans to travel up the Rhine to Cologne, ostensibly to overtake the forces of the archbishop of Trèves, who, with the rest of eastern Germany, still refused to recognize Richard's election.

Before the royal party began this trip, Sanchia, too, wrote a brief letter home, where she reiterated that all had gone well at the coronation. Strangely, she did not write to her sister Eleanor. Perhaps Richard's letter sufficed as official notification to the English crown of the health and well-being of the new king and queen of the Romans, and the wife did not want to begin her reign by trespassing on her husband's territory. Or perhaps it was simply that the new queen wrote to the person in England with whom she felt the deepest sympathy. Sanchia's note was addressed to her local churchman, the prior of Wallingford.

For the next fifteen months, Richard and Sanchia traveled in the area around Mainz. It was all very ceremonial, and Richard was in his element. He loved receiving the homage of his subjects, and crowed in his letters home that all of the most important noblemen in the region had knelt at his feet. The king and queen of the Romans spent the winter as far south as possible while still remaining in Germany, and then returned in the spring to Aachen, where Richard once again played the role of the fair and generous monarch, building a new town hall, which was dutifully dubbed "King Richard's *curia*" in his honor.

For Sanchia, however, this expedition was lonely and wearisome. Richard was much involved with administrative business, of which she had no part. Almost everyone who had accompanied them from England to witness the coronation, including Richard's son Henry of Almain, went home by October, and she was left friendless. She clung to nine-year-old Edmund, and asked to go home.

Richard also wished to return, but for different reasons. The political climate in England had deteriorated greatly in the short time he and Sanchia had been away. Henry's favoritism towards his Lusignan half-brothers, and his continual demands for money from his barons to finance the Sicilian business, had provoked a baronial revolt. There had been a parliament held at Oxford to which the barons had come armed with soldiers; Henry of Almain had been in attendance. All present, including the king, had been made to swear an oath to uphold the Charter of Liberties, to which the barons had added some new provisions. King Henry and his son Edward had taken this oath, but the king's half-brothers had not, and as a result, they had been banished from the kingdom by the angry barons. Henry of Almain had tried to stall, saying that he could not take the oath without first consulting his father, but the barons would have none of it. "He was told plainly and publicly, that even if his father himself would not acquiesce in the plan of the barons, he [Richard] should not keep possession of one furrow of land in England," Matthew Paris wrote.

The prospect of losing all of his property in England was enough to cause the king of the Romans to abandon Germany in a hurry. He, Sanchia, Edmund, and a small contingent of knights landed in Dover in January 1259, and were met by Henry, Eleanor, and Uncle Boniface. Richard had initially blustered about his being a foreign power and therefore not obliged to take the new oath but he changed his mind quickly. On January 23 he stood up in front of the baronage, which had come in a menacing fashion en masse to Canterbury where he was staying, and swore to uphold the Oxford provisions.

Richard and Sanchia stayed in England for the next year and a half, during which time the tension between King Henry and his barons eased, due in no small part to the efforts of his brother. By June 1260 Richard had determined that his property was safe enough to leave England for a short period. This time, he was lured by the prospect of becoming emperor. The pope had promised Richard this honor over Alfonso X's strenuous objections if he would come to Rome to be crowned. Sanchia resigned herself to another trip through Germany, before proceeding on to her coronation as empress.

But there would be no coronation; the king and queen of the Romans never made it to Rome. Germany was not so welcoming to Richard this second time as before. Alfonso's claim to the kingdom had gained strength in Richard's absence. There were enemies all around them; what had been meant as a triumphal procession through the kingdom took on the appearance of stealth as the company, guarded by knights, was forced to proceed with extreme caution, avoiding the larger cities. By September, Richard and Sanchia had made it only as far as Worms. There the king of the Romans took fright and turned back quickly. He and Sanchia were back in England by October 24. "It was almost a flight," medievalist N. Denholm-Young observed.

This second, frightening trip to Germany took its toll on Sanchia's health. It must have been terrible to have lived with the possibility of ambush, to have felt so uncertain of one's surroundings, to have had to rely upon retainers whom she didn't know and couldn't trust. Her reign had brought her nothing but misery. She crept back to the family castle at Berkhamsted, about halfway between Oxford and London, and became an invalid. There is no record of Sanchia's specific ailment, but by December she was so ill that she could not travel. She had Richard go without her to Windsor to celebrate Christmas with Henry and Eleanor.

She stayed at Berkhamsted throughout the spring and summer of 1261, growing steadily weaker. Richard, who was not a man to stay with an ailing woman, went about his business, which involved traveling back and forth between London and Oxford. There was quite a demand for his services, as the English baronage was once more on the verge of armed revolt. Henry's Lusignan half-brothers were back in England, and they had brought foreign knights with them to support the king. Even worse, Henry had appealed to the pope to absolve him of the oath forced on him by the Oxford parliament. Prince Edward, heir to the throne, had joined with Simon de Montfort and the disgruntled barons against his father the king. Richard did his best to support his brother by bringing his considerable negotiating skills to bear on the situation, and succeeded in reuniting Prince Edward and his father.

By this time Sanchia no longer took an interest in political events. In October, her illness had reached a critical stage, and Richard came back to

Berkhamsted one last time to visit her. On November 5 he was told she was dying. Unlike his brother Henry, who in similar circumstances would never have abandoned Eleanor, Richard decided to go to London the next morning anyway in order to transact some routine administrative business involving Germany.

And so Sanchia was alone but for eleven-year-old Edmund and her maidservants when she died on November 9, 1261. So anxious was Richard to have her gone that he had the executors of her estate begin giving away her property on the first of November, before she was dead.

Nor did her husband bother to return for her funeral, which was conducted at the church at Hailes, the festive dedication of which had been the source of such pleasure to Sanchia a decade before. She was buried on November 15 in the presence of Uncle Peter and Uncle Boniface. Other clergymen were present as well; presumably, the prior of Wallingford was in attendance. Eleanor was not able to attend her sister's funeral. The king and queen of England's political woes had by this time forced them to take refuge in London. But Eleanor had Mass read for Sanchia at the Tower of London, and arranged for a memorial service in her honor at Westminster.

The circumstances of Sanchia's death mirrored that of her life. A queen in name only, such political influence as she had was by her association with one of the most powerful families in Europe. Her husband, who could not have achieved his most cherished dream without her, saw only her inadequacies. She was not respected, as was Marguerite; or ambitious, like Eleanor; or even determined, as her youngest sister, Beatrice, would prove to be. She was simple, pious, and a devoted mother; but this was not enough, she knew. She strove to meet her husband's expectations and in the process sacrificed herself.

She was only thirty-three years old when she died. The ruins of the abbey of Hailes where she is buried have survived the ages. The faded outline of the coat of arms of Provence can still be seen on the walls.

Beatrice

Banquet with minstrels playing.

CHAPTER XVIII

ROYAL SIBLING RIVALRY

Beatrice of Provence was of course aware that her mother and older sisters were plotting to deprive her of her Provençal inheritance. Since her return from the Holy Land, Marguerite had made no secret of her animosity. Eleanor and Henry continued to press Charles to return the castles Beatrice of Savoy had promised them as security against an earlier loan, and both Eleanor and Marguerite, Beatrice knew, still had hopes of worming the ten thousand livres they'd each been promised upon their father's death out of Beatrice's estate and into their own. In Beatrice's opinion, though, her mother was the worst of the lot. Not only had Beatrice of Savoy formed what amounted to a rebel base within Provence at her castle at Forcalquier, which was a lightning rod for all the discontented barons in the county, she had now launched a diplomatic initiative aimed at influencing Louis to intervene against his own brother on her behalf. To that end, the French queen's mother had tagged along with the crusading party upon its return from Egypt and was now comfortably ensconced, with no apparent timetable for leaving, in one of the king's own castles at Nesle, just outside Paris. In addition to having a view of the Seine, these new quarters allowed Beatrice of Savoy unlimited access to the king's court, and she used every audience to either press her case with Louis or conspire with Marguerite.

Beatrice of Provence was twenty-two years old in 1254, the mother of two girls, Blanche and Beatrix, and a brand-new infant son, Charles. She had every intention of having more children, and had a vested interest in seeing her progeny rule Provence. Her family's opposition to her legitimate inheritance, which had been upheld by the pope himself, infuriated her. Where someone like Sanchia would surely have buckled under the pressure, Beatrice only held her head higher and waited for the chance to exact her revenge.

Luckily, in Charles, Beatrice had a more than willing partner. Charles, too, chafed under the restraints imposed upon him by his older brother and envied Louis his wise and saintly reputation and international standing. Charles felt himself to be every bit the man his brother was—and perhaps more. "This Charles was wise, prudent in counsel and valiant in arms, and harsh, and much feared and redoubted by all," wrote the Italian chronicler Giovanni Villani. "Steadfast in carrying out every great undertaking, firm in every adversity . . . speaking little and acting much, scarcely smiling, chaste as a monk, catholic, harsh in judgment . . . but greedy in acquiring land and lordship and money, from whencesoever it came."

But Charles's relations with his eldest brother were marked by a fondness on Louis's part, a relic of childhood, upon which the count of Provence knew he could rely. However much Charles might push his own agenda, Louis would never disown him, although, at least on one occasion, the older brother had had to remind the younger that "there was only one king of France." Eventually, though, Charles knew that if he angled properly, Louis would give in, and he would get his way.

Charles had a very ambitious plan for his and Beatrice's advancement. It had been difficult to turn down the pope's offer of Sicily in 1252, but the proposal had come too soon: even if Charles had managed to get Louis to agree, the count of Provence simply had not had the money necessary to launch a successful conquest. His relative poverty was a condition that Charles needed to rectify. With money, he could buy off his mother-in-law and begin the process of consolidating power in Provence, certainly a prerequisite to any larger scheme. For although Charles, at Louis's behest, had reluctantly refused the pope's invitation to take Sicily, he never actually gave up on the idea of becoming monarch of that rich kingdom, or of using Sicily as the springboard to acquire an empire that would rival that of his brother. This goal remained ever present in the background, a possibility to be considered once other pursuits had been settled to his satisfaction. It was simply a matter of recognizing opportunity when it made its appearance.

★ ★ ★

It made its appearance in 1253 when Flanders, Thomas of Savoy's old stomping ground, suddenly erupted in civil war. Joan of Flanders, Thomas's wife, had died in 1244, and the county had gone to her sister Margaret. Margaret had been married twice, and had children by both marriages. She much preferred the children of her second marriage, however, and tried to disinherit her sons by her first husband. The sons from her first husband were quite naturally upset and used the occasion of Louis's being away on crusade to try to take over Flanders and neighboring Hainault.

Margaret's need for military help coincided nicely with Charles of Anjou's need for money. Chivalrously, he offered to defend her rule in Flanders, but only if he could have Hainault. Having no other choice, she agreed. Charles then raised an army and occupied Hainault. Once firmly in charge, he levied heavy fines on his new subjects to support his military operations.

It was at this point that Louis came home from crusade. The citizens of Hainault, unhappy with their new count, immediately appealed to the king to rescue them from his younger brother's rule. Louis made peace in 1255 by giving Flanders to Margaret's sons by her second marriage and Hainault to her sons by her first marriage. This solution suited everyone but Charles, who protested that Hainault belonged to him. It was a ploy for money—Charles had no authentic claim to the county—and it worked. Louis, seeking to avoid the embarrassment of an open rift with his brother, allowed Charles to extort a whopping 160,000 livres tournois from Margaret, 40,000 of which had to be paid up front. To put this sum into perspective, Charles was paid more to evacuate Hainault than Henry III got for giving up Normandy, Anjou, and Poitou. Thus did the count of Provence find his financial problems solved.

His elder brother was also instrumental in facilitating a settlement between Charles and his mother-in-law over the contentious issue of exactly who owned what in Provence. By 1257, Beatrice of Savoy, who had been opposing her son-in-law's rule almost from the day he had married her youngest daughter in 1246, seems to have reconsidered her position. She had just turned fifty; possibly she was weary of the long struggle and wished to retire gracefully. Whatever the reason, she demanded and secured a sizable sum as compensation for her voluntary abdication. In exchange for an annual stipend of six thousand livres tournois, plus five thousand livres tournois in damages for out-of-pocket expenses and general mental hardship, Beatrice of Savoy agreed to turn over all of her holdings in Provence to Charles and to relocate permanently from the county. She further promised to refrain from harassing any of his agents, should she ever meet up with any of them in the future, and she made Charles swear not to retaliate against any of her former supporters. To get this agreement, Louis had to guarantee his mother-in-law payment of her annual income out of the royal treasury, as Beatrice of Savoy adamantly refused to rely on Charles for her money.

As for Henry and Eleanor's castles, even the crown of England seemed tired of the whole affair and agreed without too much difficulty to assign right of ownership to Charles in return for four thousand marks. Four thousand marks was nothing to a man who had just netted 160,000 livres, so Charles paid promptly. In January 1257, in the presence of Louis, he and Beatrice of Savoy swore clause by clause to uphold the treaty. It had taken more than a decade, but Charles of Anjou and Beatrice of Provence were finally in control of her inheritance.

If her mother's settlement represented a setback to Marguerite's interests in Provence, the queen of France did not manifest signs of discouragement. If anything, she stepped up her efforts to recover her claim to the county. The very next year she used the engagement of her second son, Philip, to the king of Aragon's daughter to reintroduce the subject of the unfairness of her father's will with her cousin King James I of Aragon. After some negotiation, the king of Aragon graciously agreed to assign his rights in Provence to his daughter's new mother-in-law. This agreement was made outright in Marguerite's name, although Louis was of course informed of the arrangement. This meant that if Beatrice died childless, Provence would legally revert to Marguerite. It wasn't perfect, but it was a start; in any event, this understanding with the king of Aragon indicates that, at least in Marguerite's mind, the issue was not yet closed.

Beatrice by this time had six children, including two sons, Philip and Robert, in addition to little Charles, as extra insurance that her line would survive. Yet she and Charles knew better than to disregard Marguerite's intentions. The queen of France was a powerful enemy.

With Beatrice of Savoy finally out of the way, the obvious course of action was to return to Provence and consolidate power, and this Charles and Beatrice did. They spent most of their time in Aix-en-Provence, which Charles used as the administrative capital of the county, and at their fortress at Tarascon. In fact, the count and countess had been actively engaged in quieting the rebellion fomented by her mother since their return from the Holy Land in 1251. Charles's approach involved abolishing the traditional local town councils and administrators and replacing them with his own officials (although in some cases he kept the councils but had its members appointed by his bailiffs instead of elected by the townspeople as had been the case in the past). To ensure that the new clerks and judges remained loyal to his rule, Charles made it a policy to appoint outsiders, particularly churchmen from northern and western France, to these positions. Ordinarily, such a policy would have caused confusion, but Charles and Beatrice benefited greatly from the superior administrative system they had inherited along with the county from Raymond Berenger V. Tolls and fees were collected with admirable efficiency; the system even survived the loss of its original architect, Romeo de Villeneuve, when Charles had him sacked as well.

After Beatrice of Savoy's capitulation, Charles's regime turned increasingly autocratic. The count of Provence was known for his stern ways and quick, harsh judgments. Gone were the relaxed, merry days when the troubadours had overrun Raymond Berenger V's court—"in jongleurs, minstrels, or jesters he [Charles] never took delight," Villani reported. The count ruled any questioning of his authority as an act of treason and behaved accordingly. He banished two important barons for supporting rebellion and confiscated their property. The commune of Marseille, used to independence, was a perennial problem. Through the 1250s the town reluctantly recognized Charles's suzerainty but frequently fought his officials. The count of Provence took care of this once and for all in 1263 by capturing, trying, and executing twelve of the port's leading citizens.

This new emphasis on centralization worked to the count's military, political, and monetary advantage. It allowed Charles to squeeze as much as possible from the Provençal salt monopoly, and to encourage those industries, like shipbuilding, that would prove most useful in the future. From 1252 through 1256 the count of Provence sent a specially selected team of lawyers, accountants, and government officials, led by his purser, to the far reaches of his domain with the aim of ferreting out every conceivable source of income or right of ownership or homage that had ever been claimed by any count at any time in the long history of the province. The result was additional fees, tolls, and military service.

Thus, by degrees, was Provence shaped into a unified political and economic system responsive to the needs and desires of its demanding leader. As a result, Charles has been credited with providing Provence with a degree of security not seen since Charlemagne. Part of this was, of course, due to Charles's policies, but the count also benefited in no small measure from the changed international climate. Throughout his administration, Raymond Berenger V had had to contend with the hostile intentions of his powerful neighbor, Raymond VII of Toulouse. This intimidating aggressor, however, was dead by the time Charles took over. The count of Anjou's neighbor in Toulouse was his brother Alphonse.

As for Beatrice, the new, respectful atmosphere in Provence suited her temperament well. She was treated as a great lady by her subjects, particularly the sycophantic functionaries who surrounded Charles and were always underfoot at the castle. With the exception of her eldest son, Charles, who was lame, her children were all healthy and no one could fault her fertility; from 1250 to 1261 she bore a child every two years. Her husband, who understood that his legitimacy as count was dependent upon his wife's goodwill, made sure to maintain satisfactory domestic relations with her, taking her with him when he traveled, and making her presents of expensive robes and jewelry. By the time Christmas 1259 rolled around, Beatrice had become quite accustomed to deference and held every bit as high an opinion of her person as Charles did of his. This attitude did not go unnoticed by her sister Marguerite.

Christmas 1259 saw another illustrious Provençal family party in Paris. Henry and Eleanor had crossed the Channel for the purpose of signing an official peace treaty with Louis. This agreement, which had its genesis at the family party five years earlier, marked an historic event. For the first time, in exchange for a monetary settlement, Henry III would publicly renounce England's claim to the lands conquered by his much more able grandfather Henry II. He would keep Gascony, but only as a fief of the crown of France. As a result, part of the ceremony involved Henry's paying homage to Louis by going down on one knee and placing his hands between those of the king of France. As that gesture promised to be somewhat theatrical in nature, the occasion was well attended. The king and queen of England were still quite popular in Paris. The memory of Henry's generosity on his previous visit caused the citizenry to spill out into the streets to gawk and cheer.

Although Richard was back in England from his first tour of Germany by this time, he did not attend the festivities. Henry could not appoint his brother, who was now a separate foreign power, as regent, but he needed the king of the Roman's diplomatic skills in England during his absence to help keep the baronage quiescent. But it is possible that Sanchia once again made the journey alone, to be with her mother and sisters, who were all present for the occasion.

Marguerite was thus able to use this gathering to launch a new offensive against her sister Beatrice in her private war to regain Provence. At the formal banquet arranged to consummate the ceremonies, she seated the countess of Provence at an inferior table, explaining that protocol demanded that Beatrice sit separately from the rest of the family on the dais because she alone among the sisters was not a queen.

It was an act of public humiliation highly reminiscent of Blanche of Castile's treatment of Isabella of Angoulême those many years ago in Poitou, when the White Queen had made the former queen of England wait for an audience. Marguerite had witnessed that snub and registered its effectiveness. Blanche, by this action, had provoked Isabella and her husband, Hugh of La Marche, to rebel, which in turn had given the French army an excuse to invade and conquer Poitou. Isabella had gone from a pretentiously important but relatively powerful provincial noblewoman to a disgraced nun in two years. And now, not quite twenty years later, Marguerite had just witnessed Isabella's son Henry III renounce all claim to the county Isabella had dominated before Blanche's ignominious treatment of her prerogative had caused her to behave rashly. Perhaps that is what gave the queen of France the idea.

It almost worked. Beatrice, did, indeed, experience great anger at the provocation. "And this was largely by reason of the contempt and disdain which a little while before had been shown to her by her three elder sisters, which were all queens, making her sit a degree lower than they, for which cause, with great grief, she had made complaint thereof to Charles, her husband," wrote Villani. The countess of Provence's pride was stung. She wanted, like Isabella, to get even. She wanted to see her sister brought down.

But Charles of Anjou was no Hugh of La Marche. He only laughed. Why rebel against a credulous older brother who could be manipulated without the bother and expense of raising an army? "Be at peace," he told his wife, "for I will shortly make thee a greater queen than them."

Eleanor

King Henry III sails for France.

CHAPTER XIX

PRELUDE TO WAR

By Christmas 1259, Eleanor was so consumed by her own problems that she probably barely noticed Marguerite's deliberate snubbing of Beatrice at the festivities crowning the signing of the Treaty of Paris. In Eleanor's world, the French queen's behavior toward her younger sister was to provocation what sewing needles were to swords. To experience true humiliation, Eleanor must have thought, come to England. The English baronage was by 1259 so antagonistic to the crown that Henry and Eleanor had been quite relieved to have had the excuse to leave the kingdom for Paris. Nor were they in a hurry to return. In fact, Eleanor had had to take the precaution of bringing over quite a bit of jewelry with her to Paris, just in case she and Henry needed to purchase the services of some foreign knights in order to ensure a secure landing in Dover upon their return.

If the queen of England wondered how the political situation in her own kingdom had managed to deteriorate so badly in the five years following her husband's triumph in Gascony, she was under no illusions as to who was responsible for her predicament. She laid the blame securely at the feet of Henry's greedy half-brothers from Lusignan, the sons of his mother, Isabella, by Hugh of La Marche. Eleanor had warned Henry innumerable times that his favoritism toward these men, which took the form of ostentatiously granting them some of the most important castles and livings in England (castles and livings, which, by coincidence, Eleanor had wanted to bestow upon members of *her* family) was causing hostility among his barons. Anxious to curtail the influence of this other side of Henry's family, Eleanor and Peter of Savoy had even joined forces the previous year with the native English barons, who, with Richard out of the country touring Germany, had been led by Simon de Montfort. The result had been a satisfyingly dramatic moment at the great parliament held at Oxford in 1258, when the baronage had voted overwhelmingly to strip the Lusignans of their assets and Simon de Montfort had growled, "Yield your castles or your head," to Henry's half-brothers, who had prudently chosen to flee.

But the expulsion of the Lusignans from England had come at the highly unsatisfactory price of government reform. Simon de Montfort, schooled by medieval visionaries like Adam Marsh, had acquired some alarmingly unconventional ideas. Specifically, he and many of the other barons believed that the native aristocracy should, in the interest of the general welfare, have some say in managing the kingdom. It was at this same Oxford parliament that Simon de Montfort and his cohorts had established a council of barons who were responsible for advising the king on matters of policy. For the immediate future, Henry was not to make a decision on any issue of substance without first referring the matter to this council. The act by which this council was established had become known as the Oxford Provisions, and it was to abide by these Provisions that Henry and all of his supporters, including Eleanor, Edward, Richard, Richard's son Henry of Almain, the archbishop of Canterbury, and Peter of Savoy had been required to swear an oath. It is impossible that there was anyone present at that parliament who did not understand that the Oxford Provisions represented, in essence, a replay of the restraints imposed upon Henry's father King John, all those years ago, restraints that had resulted in civil war.

Of course, Eleanor was aware that the reforms adopted at Oxford had been provoked not just by the partiality shown to her husband's half-brothers, but by her and Henry's aggressive pursuit of Edmund's Sicilian crown. This venture had been marked by a series of unforeseen obstacles, among them Thomas of Savoy's capture and subsequent imprisonment by his enemies in Asti, which had frustrated plans for the English invasion. Henry and Eleanor had expected Uncle Thomas to organize and lead an army into battle for Edmund, and this he obviously could not do while confined to a Swiss dungeon. Eleanor and her mother and sisters had banded together to free him, but Thomas's release had not had the salutary effect on the Sicilian project that the English crown had hoped. It seems that Thomas's captors had taken advantage of his incarceration to punish their former tormentor for his past sins and as a result Thomas had had rather a bad time of it in prison. Eleanor had been quite shocked at her uncle's appearance when he visited England in 1258 after his release; it did not bode well for her plans that he had to be carried into meetings on a stretcher. When Thomas died the following year, Edmund's candidacy for the throne of Sicily effectively died with him.

But the debt had not. The pope, who had advanced a large sum of money in anticipation of Edmund's conquest, had become increasingly insistent that Henry fulfill his financial obligations to the papacy. There was money coming from Louis in accordance with the new peace treaty, but this was spread out over time and not sufficient in itself to satisfy the debt. Henry and Eleanor, thwarted by the English barons' refusal to honor liabilities contracted under a foreign policy on which they had not been consulted, had had to resort to their usual chicanery to try to raise funds. It was these methods that had prompted the call for political reform and the hated Oxford Provisions. Eleanor and her family were held especially responsible for the kingdom's woes, as the chronicle of Bury St Edmunds, written at the time, reported, an indication of the influence the queen wielded in England during this period:

> At this time the great men of the land were exasperated with the queen, and also with the king's Poitevin brothers and the queen's Savoyard kinsmen, because wherever they held sway they behaved unbearably, like tyrants. The magnates, therefore, met at Oxford after Easter and made public certain provisions ostensibly to preserve the dignity of the Church and Crown and the well-being of the whole kingdom . . . The magnates bound themselves to each other under solemn oath to risk death if necessary in defense of the provisions and to hunt down those who would not observe them.

Eleanor had also to contend with the bad feelings that had sprung up between her eldest son, Edward, and herself as a result of the expulsion of the Lusignans. Edward was every bit as fond of his half-uncles as Henry was—he had made one of them his second in command in Gascony—and he knew his mother and her family had abetted the decision to force them into exile. Edward was by now twenty years old, the head of his own household, and rebellious. He had moved away from his parents and his great-uncles on his mother's side and instead fallen in with a group of young men, among them his cousins Henry of Almain and the sons of Simon de Montfort. Eleanor did not approve of Edward's set; in her opinion, Simon de

Montfort had entirely too much influence on this younger generation, and she blamed the older man for Edward's disaffection. Rumors that the heir to the throne had allied himself with Simon de Montfort and the reformers against his own father had been the cause of a highly unpleasant, unresolved row between the queen and her son before Eleanor and Henry had left for France.

There was more to do in France than just the business of the peace treaty; Henry and Eleanor, with Marguerite's help, were in the final stages of arranging the marriage of their daughter Beatrice to the son of the duke of Brittany. That Marguerite was involved in this negotiation is indicated by a letter Henry wrote to her soon after the fact detailing further specifics of the dowry. "Pray urge the king of Navarre to make over the lands he promised to John of Britanny in Champagne," Henry wrote. The wedding was set for early January 1260. Eleanor and Henry were lingering in France at the abbey church of St. Denis, a little to the north of the royal palace, awaiting the date of the wedding, when a messenger arrived with the sudden, terrible news that Marguerite's eldest son, Louis, the heir to the French throne, had succumbed to illness and died.

Crown Prince Louis was only fifteen when he perished and Marguerite was distraught; even Louis IX, not much given to sentimentality except as it applied to events of a strictly religious nature, called his eldest-born "most dear and lovable to us." Henry and Eleanor quickly changed their daughter's wedding plans so that they could remain in Paris for the funeral, Henry electing to help carry the boy's casket on the first leg of the journey to Royaumont, where he would be buried. The king and queen of England had lost their three-year-old daughter Katharine in 1257, and sympathized strongly with Marguerite and Louis. Eleanor, in particular, had been devastated by her youngest daughter's death. Katharine apparently had been mentally retarded— Matthew Paris called her "dumb, and fit for nothing, though possessing great beauty"—and this infirmity had made her mother all the more protective. When she died, "the queen was so overcome with grief that it brought on a disease, which was thought to be incurable, as she could obtain no relief either from medical skill or human consolation." Now Marguerite had lost her son, and her sister hastened to her side. It is a measure of just how close these two families had become that the king and queen of France, despite their great grief, nonetheless attended Beatrice's wedding the following week.

How much Louis and Marguerite's shocking loss of their child affected Henry and Eleanor's relationship with their own son is impossible to say. But there was a reconciliation of sorts with Edward upon their return to England.

* * *

Eleanor demonstrated prescience in having brought all that jewelry with her on this visit to France—she and Henry did, in fact, require the services of foreign knights upon their return, both to ensure their safety and to demonstrate that the crown still had resources available to it that the native baronage lacked. A significant proportion of these knights came from Flanders, and their leader was distantly related to the queen. She and Henry also hired a French force, led by the count of St Pol, an exceedingly fierce and experienced knight. St Pol reveled in warfare to such a degree that the money he earned from this occupation seemed almost (but not quite) superfluous. As it was, even with Eleanor's rings, the king and queen of England did not have quite enough cash on hand to satisfy the mercenaries' demands, so Louis sped up some of the payments due under the Treaty of Paris, and Marguerite arranged a loan. It was still not enough, so Eleanor borrowed from some northern French merchants under her own name, and the foreign troops' loyalty was secured for a period of three months.

Thus equipped, the royal party finally sailed for England in April 1260, surrounded by a small but potent army. The show of strength worked; the baronage did not choose to confront the king and queen upon their return. Instead, influenced by his uncle Richard and great-uncle Boniface, Edward stood before a hastily convened parliament in London and swore publicly that he had never meant to disobey his father or mother. The chroniclers specifically mention Eleanor as being included in the reconciliation.

But Edward's apology was a token gesture, intended for appeasement, not surrender. He was still allied with Simon de Montfort, who, if anything, had gained respect and power during Henry and Eleanor's absence. "Simon de Montfort emerged as the leader of the baronage," the chronicle of Bury St Edmunds reported for the year 1260. Simon's prestige transcended provincial English politics; he was a man of international repute and an intimate of Louis IX. The earl of Leicester had the easy assurance of an individual who understood that his capabilities far exceeded those of his sovereign. When Henry complained to the council established by the Oxford Provisions that Simon had behaved improperly toward him, the earl could not hide his contempt as he answered the charges. Simon, not without reason, viewed the policies of the English crown as feckless and dangerous to the prosperity of the kingdom. It disgusted him that at a time when his good friend Louis IX was engaged in implementing a program of active reforms aimed at promoting justice and fairness throughout France, Henry III's administration, crippled by the enormous debt due to the pope for the Sicilian business, survived on corruption and greed.

It was around this time that the earl of Leicester's political aspirations took on a new and dangerous dimension. Simon had long since judged that England would be better served if he, and not Henry, ruled it; the difference was that he now felt compelled to act upon this opinion. Even in a world characterized by the most blatant opportunism, and regardless of the potential benefits to the kingdom, Simon's plan—to substitute himself for a living, legitimate, consecrated sovereign—stood well outside the bounds of accepted behavior. The earl of Leicester's rationale for this exploit is complex. Certainly he, like many other barons, experienced intense frustration over what he considered to be Henry and Eleanor's determination to pursue policies damaging to the kingdom's interest, and considered that he alone, by virtue of his stature among the baronage, was in a position to do something about it. Overweening ambition was not a quality new to Simon; the earl of Leicester had spent a lifetime more or less specializing in audacity, and this personality trait had served him well. Additionally, there is no question that contributing to Simon's decision to act was the conviction that he could win.

Even so, the situation had to be handled delicately. Although he was married to the king's sister, Simon was not himself of princely lineage and it would be difficult to justify usurping the crown's prerogative. That was one reason the earl of Leicester made such efforts to enlist Edward's support for his reforms. The heir to the throne lent an aura of royal legitimacy to Simon's grab for power.

Faced with the fact of Simon de Montfort's growing domination, Henry and Eleanor were left with two choices. They could (as Richard advised) adopt a policy of conciliation, effectively ceding control of the kingdom for the short term, hoping that support for the earl would erode on its own—not likely, given present trends. Or, they could act before Simon had a chance to completely consolidate his authority by forcing a confrontation. By Christmas 1260, Henry had come to a decision. The king resolved to squelch the rising challenge posed to his authority by employing a daring preemptive strike: like his father John, he would petition the pope to void the hateful Oxford Provisions and back up this exploit with force if necessary.

There is no way to determine how much of this plan originated with Eleanor, but there is no doubt that it was conceived with her wholehearted approbation and probably at her urging. It was not in Eleanor's temperament to compromise on matters pertaining to her children or her power base. She had proved herself a fighter over and over again in her career: sailing to Gascony over her husband's proscription; intriguing against the Lusignans; establishing precautionary ties with foreign mercenaries. Eleanor never lost faith in herself or her projects—even at this late date she had not given up on Edmund's Sicilian kingship even though the pope had officially withdrawn her son's name from consideration. She seemed to believe that controlling events was by and large an act of will. If she and Henry held firm and pressured the baronage, it would all come out right in the end. It always had in the past.

The first step was to disavow the oath to abide by the Oxford Provisions. John Mansel, whose fortunes were by this time inextricably linked with those of the English crown—he would be one of the first to go if the reformers gained unilateral control, he knew—huddled with Henry and Eleanor in January 1261, and determined that the best course of action would be to send Mansel's nephew (who, for confusion's sake, was also called John Mansel) to Rome to obtain the necessary documents. Although this was done under a cloak of secrecy, the conspirators could not be sure that word would not leak out. Anticipating the barons' furious reaction, in February 1261, Henry and Eleanor prudently relocated to the Tower of London, the most secure facility in the city. Henry took the further precaution of ordering everyone in London over the age of twelve to swear fealty to the king, and to agree to fight for their sovereign against his enemies the barons, should the occasion arise. Money was offered as an additional inducement. "All who would fight for the king were to come at once, and they would be supported at his expense," reported a chronicler. Only those barons upon whom Henry knew he could rely were allowed into London. The rest gathered ominously, "from all quarters, with large bodies of troops," outside the city gates.

Under the circumstances, it was clear that Henry was going to need all the help he could get, so the king, with the queen's reluctant agreement, summoned his exiled half-brothers to come to his aid. Eleanor loathed the Lusignans, but she had to admit that they were excellent warriors. Even better, they could be relied upon to bring soldiers and other knights friendly to the crown's cause with them. Still, she extracted a promise from Henry that none of these men would return without apologizing to her first, and promising not to work against her interests in the future, and to this condition Henry agreed. The king also sent for St Pol and the other foreign knights who had escorted him back from France the year before. Edward, who was off on athletic holiday trying his prowess on the French tournament circuit, was informed of the impending confrontation by his Lusignan uncles, and hastened back to England in their company.

Thus it was that by the spring of 1261, England saw the return not only of the heir to the throne, but also of Henry's fearsome, formerly exiled half-brothers, and an armed cadre of foreign mercenaries under the command of the vigorous St Pol, hired specifically to prop up the monarchy. These were accompanied by perhaps the most potent and provocative weapon of all: a bull from the pope dated April 13, 1261, absolving the king and queen of England and all of their supporters from their oath to abide by the Provisions of Oxford.

With momentum shifting in their direction, Henry and Eleanor were emboldened to leave the Tower in John Mansel's control at the end of April and journey to their castle at Winchester in order to greet Edward and their other expected guests. Eleanor in particular made a great show of receiving St Pol and his knights when they arrived later in May, riding out to meet them without Henry, distributing more rings and gifts, and escorting them personally to her husband's court. Edward was reunited with the king and queen and this time the reconciliation was genuine; Edward understood that his powers, as much as those of his parents', were in danger of being perma-nently reduced by Simon de Montfort's policies. Once again, Eleanor's role was central to the proceedings: "From that time Edward the king's son, flat-tered by his mother, held to his father's side and favoured aliens as kinsfolk," reported a London chronicler.

The barons backed down in the face of the crown's aggressive policies. With his support eroding, Simon de Montfort agreed to arbitration and quit the kingdom for France, where he remained in voluntary exile. For the next two years, power teetered ominously, first toward the royalists, then toward the reformers, without falling definitively on either side. But the crown was visibly reinvigorated by the events of 1261. The despised council, most heinous of the conditions imposed by the 1258 parliament at Oxford, was disbanded. Free of the obligation to subject his every decision to the igno-minious process of baronial review, the king was able to secure his hold on the political structure by appointing officials, mostly local sheriffs, supportive of the monarchy. Nor were the reformers able, despite their efforts, to re-verse the papal decree relating to the oath. When the old pope died later that year, the new pope, Urban IV, showed himself to be firmly in the royalist camp. In a bull dated February 25, 1262, addressed to the archbishop of Canterbury, the pope wrote: "You should publicly proclaim the king and queen and their children to have been absolved from the bond of the oath," and "enjoined you [Boniface] to coerce all who might oppose by excommunication of their persons and sentences of interdict upon their lands, without any appeal." Henry was thus able, with a tinge of triumph, to declare the Oxford Provisions officially null and void.

Eleanor, not without justification, interpreted these events as a vindication of her methods. The solution to their problems, she continued to insist, lay not in compromise, but in the need to resist, by the most vigorous means if necessary, the demands of the opposition. In this, Eleanor gravely misjudged the temperament of the kingdom. The barons' appetite for power had been sharpened by their short taste of success. The queen's attitude did not bode well for arbitration or for her well-being.

Arbitration nonetheless proceeded in a meandering way, with various fits and starts, throughout 1262 and into 1263. A number of mediators attempted to intervene on different issues. Richard was asked to adjudicate on the question of whether Henry was within his rights to replace sheriffs loyal to the barons with sheriffs loyal to the crown (Richard ruled he was). Queen Marguerite, who knew and was sympathetic to both parties, and who had quite a bit to say on the subject of unfair inheritances, was asked to negotiate a settlement between Henry and his sister Eleanor on the by-now very sore subject of Eleanor's estate, which the countess of Leicester, supported by her husband, claimed Henry had mishandled. In a document dated March 14, 1261, written in French, Henry wrote: "We and the earl and countess of Leicester have agreed to refer our differences to the king of France, and if he will not undertake the arbitration, we pray him to refer it to the queen of France." Simon and his wife had held up negotiations on the Treaty of Paris on this issue, refusing to compromise until the very last minute, and still sought additional remuneration. All of these complaints and grievances were mixed up with the general idea of government reform, which made them even more difficult to settle.

By July 1262 the royalist faction was so firmly in control that Henry felt able to leave the kingdom to go to France to confront Simon de Montfort. Louis and Marguerite, who had come to understand that there would be no long-term peace in England until the king addressed his differences with the earl of Leicester, had earlier agreed to mediate and were persistent in their efforts to arrange a meeting on neutral territory between the two. For their part, Henry and Eleanor knew that it was dangerous to allow Simon de

Montfort, who could be extremely persuasive, to remain unchecked in France. They could not take the chance that the earl, through sheer magnetism and unanswered repetition of grievances, would captivate Louis and Marguerite and turn the king and queen of France against them. The support of the French crown was by now essential to the health of Henry and Eleanor's regime; if the king and queen of England needed mercenaries they would have to have Louis's approval to recruit in France; if they needed money it was Louis or Marguerite who could provide the loan. Accordingly, the crown of England agreed to accept French hospitality and removed with a large party, including prince Edmund, John Mansel, and Peter of Savoy, to one of Louis's own castles very near the royal court at Vincennes to begin a series of hearings on the principal areas of conflict. Also invited to participate was the queens' mother, Beatrice of Savoy, who had succeeded in reconciling the earl and the king after their bitter quarrel over Simon's marriage to Henry's sister some twenty years before.

These parleys were an unmitigated disaster. Despite Louis and Marguerite's patient counsel, and Beatrice of Savoy's mollifying presence, there was far too much bitterness between the earl and the king to affect even a veneer of reconciliation, and the proceedings devolved into a litany of recriminations and counter-recriminations. Then, in September, Henry and most of his entourage fell victim to serious illness. Only the queen escaped the epidemic. Many of the party died. Edmund was so sick that he had to be rushed back to England to convalesce; John Mansel, whose oratory skills reputedly matched those of Simon de Montfort, and who was entrusted with handling the briefs for Henry's defense, could not get out of bed. Henry was himself so ill that he believed he was dying, and made out his will, meticulously endowing his wife with an extremely generous settlement. Arbitration was, by necessity, suspended.

Not that it mattered; reconciliation demands that at least one side be willing to compromise and this neither Henry nor Simon was willing to do. Simon, in fact, was still so committed to the government reforms articulated by the 1258 parliament at Oxford, that he used this period in France as a holding mechanism to divert attention from his real scheme, which was to convince the pope to retract the decision to absolve Henry and Eleanor and Edward of their oath to abide by the Provisions. Toward this end, the earl's agents in Rome were busy bribing cardinals and in October 1262, they seem to have scored a partial success. Taking advantage of Henry's weakness—the king of England had recovered but only enough to take short walks before collapsing, so there was no question of his yet undertaking the arduous journey back to England—Simon de Montfort stole back to London under a veil of secrecy, and, in an electric moment before a hastily convened parliament of barons, triumphantly unfurled a parchment in which he claimed the pope had reversed his earlier decision on the oath.

It was a brilliant piece of theatrics, particularly as the pope had never signed such a document. It marked a turning point in English history. The intoxicating ideas behind the reforms of 1258 (these were, after all, the seeds of representative government in Britain and, later, America) had grabbed hold of the English imagination and the entire kingdom had become highly politicized. The necessity of consolidating support against the king had forced the barons to turn to second- and third-level country gentry and government servants, a heretofore ignored segment of the population, and in this class the reformers found a willing partner. Seasoned provincial administrators much preferred to work under the aegis of a local authority than a royal appointee, who likely as not was unfamiliar with county customs and methods, and they had been upset by Henry's blanket replacement of the sheriffs.

Moreover, by a twist of fate, a number of influential older barons died just at this time and were replaced by their twenty-year-old hotheaded sons, who were not experienced enough to dread civil war and who itched for the powers that had been snatched away from them by the pope's renunciation of the Oxford oath. This combination of trends provided fertile ground for revolution.

But grand ideas are not enough; a political movement needs a leader and this Simon de Montfort provided in one devastating stroke with his astonishing pronouncement in October. By his action, the earl reminded everyone that he had neither forgotten them nor abandoned their just cause; that he alone among them wielded influence abroad in the most prestigious courts; and, most important, that the elusive, seductive quality of leadership was innate and not restricted to those who sewed ermine to their cloaks. The reputed bull provided hope, and hope quickly sparked enthusiasm and optimism. The crown's advantage, so prevalent as to be suffocating just three months before, evaporated at that instant. As the chronicler of Dover reported: "And when he [Simon] had had the letters read, though against the wish of the justiciar, he returned at once [to Paris], leaving behind him many who were ready to support him."

From this time on events moved rapidly and no act of will on Eleanor's part was going to change them.

CHAPTER XX

A QUEEN IN CRISIS

lthough Simon slipped back to Paris quickly, Henry and Eleanor were nonetheless aware of his clandestine visit to England. A short while after his return, Henry, doubting Simon's motives and worried that the earl had caused mischief in his absence, officially gave up on mediation. The royal party, much reduced by illness, began the slow journey home. It took the better part of two months, as the fifty-five-year-old king had resolved to stop and visit a shrine in Reims along the way, to give thanks for his and Edmund's recovery. It wasn't until December that he and Eleanor sailed for England. Even then, Henry was still so feeble that the couple did not attempt to reach London immediately, but spent Christmas 1262 at their residence in Canterbury.

Meanwhile, in November, armed resistance to the crown had begun in Wales, domicile of some of the most powerful and independent barons in the kingdom. Incensed at Henry's renunciation of the oath, Llywelyn, one of the principal barons, formed an army and began taking over other people's castles, including those belonging to Edward. The king, who was too weak to confront this internal revolt, sent an urgent appeal to his son, who was in Gascony administering his province. "These things should cause you grave concern," Henry wrote to his firstborn. "This is no time for laziness or boyish wantonness. It is a disgrace to you that Llywelyn spurns the truce that he promised to maintain with us, for I am growing old, while you are in the flower of early manhood; and yet, instigated by some men of my realm, he dares to do it."

Edward, accompanied by mercenaries, rushed home in February 1263 to defend his property. Although he made some inroads in Wales, the damage was done. The royal regime had started to give off an odor of torpor and impotence, which encouraged further ingress by its enemies. "The king had lost his strength, Edward had not yet found his friends; the one was growing old, the other was still too young," observed Oxford historian Sir Maurice Powicke.

But Simon de Montfort was just right. In April 1263, the earl of Leicester, heeding a call from some of the younger, more bellicose magnates, returned to England from France to lead a rebellion. Simon de Montfort's sons and Richard's son, Henry of Almain, were prominent members of this group. (Henry of Almain's participation in the early stages of the rebellion caused the king of the Romans, who had once again forsaken the needs of his acquired kingdom in order to protect his property at home, no small embarrassment.) Congregating at Oxford in May, Simon and his supporters decided unilaterally to reinstate the oath to abide by the Provisions. All who refused to swear would be chased from England and have their property confiscated. The assembled noblemen vowed to defend the Provisions to the death. A squad of vigilantes was deputized to begin the process of enforcing the ultimatum and weeding out the opposition.

There wasn't any doubt about whom the earl of Leicester and his companions were targeting for exile. Mixed into the reformers' lofty words and noble vision of representative government was the decidedly less altruistic ambition of ridding the kingdom of well-placed foreigners. (Everybody at the Oxford meeting conveniently forgot that Simon de Montfort, being French, was himself a well-placed foreigner.) And there was no group of foreigners more visible, who had received more preferential treatment or greater honors, than the cluster of expatriate Savoyard and Provençal friends and relatives who comprised Eleanor's power base in England. Simon de Montfort was under no illusions as to the identity of his true adversary in the coming struggle. "About this time, Simon de Montfort, the leader of the barons, plundered the property of the king's adherents, especially of those foreigners who were allied by blood to the queen, and were introduced into England by her," noted an English chronicler. When the earl launched his army he attacked not the king, but the queen.

Simon's was a small but potent force and they succeeded, through lightning strikes, at intimidating a large percentage of royalists. They began in Hereford by abducting a Savoyard bishop out of his cathedral, plundering his lands and tossing him into the dungeon of one of their sympathizers; from there they attacked a castle in Gloucester. It was clear that they were making their way to London. Simon sent messengers on ahead, demanding that Henry renew his oath to abide by the Provisions, and threatening the citizenry of London if they did not support the rebel cause. The leading men of the city, who feared Simon and his band far more than their aging sovereign, agreed to side with the barons and renewed their pledge to abide by the Provisions.

Henry, Eleanor, Richard, and Edward (who had brought his foreign knights with him) withdrew to the Tower of London to consult. The room divided between those of the family (namely Richard) who favored a peaceful settlement with the earl (which in this case meant capitulation) and those (Eleanor and Edward) who preferred to fight it out. Henry acceded to his wife and son and a daring plot was devised. On June 29 Edward and some of his men went to the Temple, which was where the royal family and much of the nobility, as well as the great merchants of the city, stored their treasure for safekeeping, ostensibly on an errand to retrieve some of his mother's jewels. Once inside, however, the young men produced mallets from within the folds of their cloaks, which they used to smash open the locks on the strongboxes containing the stockpiles of money, and made off with a thousand pounds. Edward and his mercenaries then made a dash for the royal castle at Windsor, in order to cut off and engage Simon's forces before the rebels could reach London. Simultaneously, Edmund was dispatched to the castle at Dover, to hold the port for the crown so that reinforcements could be shipped in from France. John Mansel, who knew he had been targeted by the rebels for imprisonment, also started for Dover, shepherding a number of Savoyard and Provençal wives who feared for their safety. All planned to flee the kingdom by sea.

The rebels, who had no intention of letting a figure of Mansel's standing get away, sent Henry of Almain to ambush the royal adviser, who had escaped to Boulogne. But Eleanor, who by this time had a sophisticated spy apparatus in place, was informed of the scheme and moved quickly. It was Henry of Almain, therefore, and not John Mansel, who was ambushed, arrested, and thrown into a French dungeon by one of the queen's men. Edward and his knights reached Windsor; Edmund secured Dover; and John Mansel, accompanied by Uncle Boniface (who had also come to the conclusion that this might be a good time to leave), together with the nervous wives, all got away to France. The whole party went straight to the royal court to inform Louis and Marguerite, with considerable vehemence, of these latest developments.

The barons howled for Henry of Almain's release. His arrest spurred on the rebel army to new victories, which in turn brought in fresh recruits. Richard, desperate for his beloved son's well-being, begged his brother to let him go and to make peace with the rebels. The king, trapped in the Tower of London, confused and irresolute, lost his nerve. On July 4, 1263, he sent a delegation to accede to Simon's demands. On July 10 he freed Henry of Almain and sent word to Edmund to relinquish the castle at Dover to the rebels.

Eleanor was furious. Why surrender when Edward held Windsor? How could he give up Dover without a fight? "The king, fearing that he would be close pressed in the Tower of London by the army of the barons, made peace for a time with them by the agency of some timid people, and promised to observe the provisions made at Oxford, but the queen, instigated by woman's malice, did all in her power to prevent his doing so." Finding her husband incapacitated by fear, Eleanor took control. On July 13 she left Henry and the safety of the Tower and took a small boat up the Thames. It was her intention to make her way to Edward at Windsor to press her eldest to continue to resist Simon de Montfort's entry into London despite his father's submission. It was a bold move, completely in character, a demonstration of the type of courage for which her son Edward would later be renowned.

She got as far as London Bridge before being spotted by pedestrians. London was jittery. Simon de Montfort and his army were expected at any time and, even though the citizens had reiterated the oath to abide by the Oxford Provisions, the city was not sure that Simon's band would not try to punish them for originally supporting the crown. Word spread quickly that the queen, whom everyone knew was the source of the opposition to the reformers, and who was therefore, in the Londoners' opinion, responsible for the approaching danger, was trying to escape. "A mob of the lower orders of the city assembled on a bridge under which she would have to pass," reported a chronicler. The hostile citizens "received her on her approach with mingled insults and curses, and by throwing mud and stones into the vessel." The ship was small and could not withstand a prolonged attack; it was not clear that the queen's party could pass under the bridge without risking serious harm. Eleanor suddenly realized that she was trapped, and that her life and those of the people with her were in jeopardy.

She was saved by the mayor of London, who, whatever his politics, understood instinctively that it would not do to stand around idly while the queen of England was assassinated by a mob. There is a report that Eleanor tried to return to the Tower and that Henry wouldn't let her in, but this seems unlikely. In any event, the mayor escorted the queen and her party to the bishop of London, who vouched for her safety and gave up his own quarters to her company. And that was where Eleanor was when Simon de Montfort triumphantly entered the city less than a week later and took over England.

Because Henry had publicly accepted all of the rebels' terms, the reformers allowed the king and queen to retire to Westminster unmolested. But their ordeal had only begun. With great fanfare, the baronial council was reinstated, and began issuing orders. One of Simon's men was appointed custodian of Henry's great seal, and used it in the king's name. On July 20 the great seal was affixed to a decree that enraged the helpless king and queen: it summoned all of the knights who owed service to Henry to gather on the first of August in preparation for an attack on the castle at Windsor. Since Edward was still holding Windsor, the presence of the seal on the document was tantamount to the king's commanding an assault against his eldest son. Edward seethed but could do nothing but surrender the fortress and dismiss the foreign knights, who were escorted by a baronial army to the coast. The humiliation Edward and his mother endured during this period cost the earl of Leicester any chance of coaxing a member of the royal family to change sides and cooperate with the rebels. The days of Simon de Montfort's influence over Edward were over.

Back in France, Louis and Marguerite were appalled by the stories told by Mansel and the others; when these were followed by an account of Eleanor's scare at London Bridge they resolved to help their beleaguered relatives. A necessary first step must be to liberate the pair from their persecutors. Louis and Henry, who were in secret communication, accomplished this rather cleverly. According to the Treaty of Paris, Henry held Gascony as a fief of the French king, so Louis simply ordered him, as his vassal, to be in Boulogne on September 23, 1262, and to bring his family and some of his barons with him.

Simon de Montfort could not afford to ignore Louis's summons. If he and Henry did not appear in Boulogne on the appointed date, Louis might feel the need to defend the honor of the king his vassal by raising an army and invading England. But more than that, Simon, whose confidence in his own abilities never flagged, seems to have been convinced that he could persuade Louis and Marguerite, who, after all, were close friends and had sympathized with and aided the earl and his wife many times in the past, of the legitimacy of his actions. Accordingly, he and the reformers agreed to allow Henry and Eleanor to leave London for France in the company of a few baronial representatives, one of whom would be Simon himself. Their only stipulation was that Henry, Eleanor, Edward, and Edmund must return in time for the October parliament.

It is not clear exactly what sort of hearing Simon expected in Boulogne, but it is safe to say that the proceedings did not go as he planned. The earl was treated to an angry family confrontation led by Marguerite, Eleanor, and Beatrice of Savoy. Also arrayed against Simon and the two churchmen he had brought along for moral support were Uncle Peter, Uncle Boniface, and John Mansel. It did not help Simon's case when John Mansel pointed out that all of his property, which had been appropriated by the reformers, had gone to one of the earl of Leicester's four sons.

Although Eleanor gave full vent to her feelings at these meetings, and had the satisfaction of seeing her mother, sister, and uncles rise to her defense, she saw that Simon de Montfort's eloquence was having an effect upon Louis and some of the French noblemen, and was clever enough to understand that the danger was not over. She, Henry, Edward, and Edmund had promised to return to England for the October parliament, which meant that they had only a few weeks to make their case in Boulogne. There was not sufficient time to raise an army of foreign mercenaries to accompany the king to London as they had before.

Eleanor enlisted Marguerite's aid, and the French queen wrote to Louis's brother Alphonse of Poitiers, to see what he could do. Did he perhaps have some ships (and by implication some men) that Henry and Eleanor might borrow sometime about the middle of October? Alphonse, who clearly did not want to get involved in a messy family situation like this one, answered that he was afraid he didn't. The two queens then conferred and decided that it was not advisable for the entire family to return to England. As a result, when Henry and Edward left to attend the October parliament, Eleanor and Edmund stayed on in France, both to ensure that the French court stayed sympathetic to Henry's cause and, more important, to raise an army for the purpose of invading England to secure redress for the crown's grievances. By this time, Eleanor didn't care what she had promised the barons. The queen of England had no intention of allowing the earl of Leicester to sue for peace or orate his way out of the punishment she felt due him for his insult to herself and her family. To the queen, armed confrontation was the only solution.

It seems that Henry, urged on by Edward, at last agreed with her. The sympathy the beleaguered king had received in France, coupled with the general condemnation of Simon's actions, bolstered his spirits and he returned to England emboldened to fight for his rights. When it became clear that the barons present at the October parliament were not prepared to restore the royal prerogative, Henry took the initiative and he and Edward decamped for the castle at Windsor. There they were joined by a group of armed supporters.

This evidence of an undercurrent of sympathy for Edward and the king evidently gave Simon de Montfort pause. Although the earl and the rebellious barons still held London, Simon had gained the endorsement of only the younger, more unstable magnates; he was uncertain of the depth of royalist sentiment in the country. After having been forced to give up Windsor at the end of July, Edward had been free to move around the kingdom and had used this period to shore up support. The crown prince was by all accounts an attractive young man, possessed of a winning personality, and by the October parliament he had come to an understanding with some of the barons of Wales (although not Llywelyn). Edward had also gone to work on his childhood friend, Henry of Almain, and Richard's son had suddenly remembered how dearly he loved his cousin and changed sides. The bitterness with which Simon took this defection is measured by his response to Henry of Almain's assuring him that, despite his change of heart, he would "never bear arms" against the earl. "My lord Henry," Simon returned, "my regard was not given to your arms but to the constancy which I hoped to find especially in you. Go and take your arms with you. I do not fear them."

But he must have feared something, because in November 1263 the earl suddenly capitulated on the subject of arbitration and agreed with Henry III to submit their disagreement one last time to Louis's judgment. He further swore to abide by the French king's ruling, whatever it might be. Letters to this effect were signed by all the relevant parties and sent by messenger to France. Both sides employed the same language: "Know that we have laid our dispute formally in the hands of the lord Louis, illustrious king of the French, on the provisions, ordinances, statutes, and all other obligations of Oxford, and upon all the disputes and disagreements which we have and have had, down to the feast of All Saints' last [November 1, 1263], with the barons of our realm and they with us [Henry's version], with our lord the illustrious king of England, and he with us [the barons' version], by occasion of the aforesaid provisions, ordinances, statutes, and obligations of Oxford." Louis agreed to undertake a final arbitration and for the next two months, while the belligerents waited for a judgment from France on the legality of the Oxford Provisions, the kingdom of England teetered in the peculiar, disquieting limbo of not quite peace nor yet quite war.

Then, on January 23, 1264, Louis handed down his final decision. It was published at Amiens and Henry and Eleanor were both present; Simon de Montfort was not, having broken his leg while riding, which prevented his traveling at the time. Louis decreed:

> In the name of the Father, and of the son, and of the Holy Spirit, by our award or ordinance we quash and invalidate all these provisions, ordinances, and obligations, or whatever else they may be called, and whatever has arisen from them or has been occasioned by them; especially since it is apparent that the pope, by his letters, has already declared them quashed and invalid, and we decree that both the king and the barons, with all others who agreed to the present compromise, and who in any way had bound themselves to observe them, shall now entirely acquit and absolve themselves from them.

The French king went on to rule that all of the crown's property, and those of their supporters, including castles, had to be returned and that Henry "shall freely be allowed to appoint, institute, dismiss, and remove at his own free will" everyone from the justiciar down to the sheriffs. Any foreigner who had fled must be allowed to return safely, and to have their property restored, and that Henry had the right to employ whatever foreign diplomats or soldiers or relatives he wanted.

This decision, which became known as "the Mise of Amiens," represented nothing less than a complete vindication of the crown's position. Every action taken by Simon de Montfort and his barons was repudiated and dismissed in the coldest of terms. The earl of Leicester had lost.

Once again, how much Eleanor and her family were responsible for influencing Louis is impossible to say. Certainly, the outcome of the Mise of Amiens justified Eleanor's decision to stay in France, together with Peter and Boniface of Savoy and John Mansel, and argue the case herself. And argue she did, as the chronicler of Tewkesbury, who laid the blame for the barons' defeat at Eleanor's feet, pointed out. Louis, he wrote, had been "deceived and beguiled by the serpentlike fraud and speech of a woman; the queen of England."

Louis was indeed deceived, but not by Eleanor. He had handed down his judgment in the interests of peace. Instead, he provoked a war.

Simon de Montfort's supporters in England were stunned. Apparently, when they had agreed to accept the judgment of the French king it hadn't occurred to them that they might lose. There was an immediate, hostile reaction to the award, particularly among the second-level gentry and country administrators, who'd had no say in the decision to allow Louis to rule on the matter in the first place. They weren't about to surrender all of their hard-earned political and economic gains just because some meddling foreign king said they should. The city of London and the members of the Cinque ports, a confederation of coastal towns stretching from Hastings to Margate, which included the main port at Dover, also vowed to fight for the earl and the Oxford Provisions and went so far as to refuse Henry reentry into the kingdom. Fighting broke out in Wales where Llewlyn, in combination with two of Simon de Montfort's sons, took advantage of the crown's absence in Amiens to plunder the property of those barons who had swung their support to Edward.

Henry, Eleanor, and Edward, still in Amiens, braced themselves for a fight, and split up into their now familiar roles. Henry and Edward sailed for England in February to organize and lead an army of those barons who supported Louis's award and the crown against Simon de Montfort. Eleanor stayed in France with Peter of Savoy and John Mansel, to arrange for an additional battalion of foreign mercenaries who would launch a supplementary invasion from the coast. Before he left, Henry gave his wife and these two trusted counselors the authority to sell the crown jewels (which he had sent to Marguerite for safekeeping in 1261 and which the queen of France had lodged in the Temple in Paris) and to use the monies still owed him by Louis under the Treaty of Paris to purchase men, ships, and supplies.

Henry arrived in England and, denied London, established his military headquarters at Oxford, from which he summoned all of the knights of the realm who owed him service. Edward went first to Wales to muster his supporters and chase away the earl of Leicester's sons before rendezvousing with his father at Oxford. Richard of Cornwall and his son Henry of Almain, now in the royalist camp, as well as the king's Lusignan half-brothers, also hurried to Henry's side. By March 8 a formidable force had gathered around the king, and the royal standard, a fearsome dragon embroidered in gold thread on a pennant of crimson silk with a long, fiery tongue that undulated menacingly in the wind, was smuggled in from Westminster Abbey to fly at the head of the procession that rode off to battle. England was officially at war with itself.

The king's side won an early and important battle. At Edward's urging, Henry rode his army to Northampton, held by Simon de Montfort's second son, Simon the younger. The Northampton townsfolk were evidently ambivalent about fighting against their legitimate sovereign, for the town walls were breached almost immediately. The castle was overrun so quickly that the younger Montfort did not have time to escape, and was taken prisoner. Encouraged, the royalists spread their forces to the north and northwest, securing their flank.

The defeat at Northampton was a serious blow to the rebel cause. Military actions are as much about the perception of vigor as they are about troops and arms, and by early April momentum had shifted to the king's faction. The earl, a veteran of countless campaigns, schooled in armed tactics so thoroughly that warfare ran through his veins like blood, understood that he would have to strike quickly. Still hobbling from his broken leg, he gathered his supporters in London. Keenly aware that the royalist forces outnumbered his own, and that many of his commanders, while young and enthusiastic, were untried, he was obliged to enlist the citizenry of London in the struggle. Like Henry, he demanded allegiance from every Londoner over the age of twelve. He inflamed their passions and incited lawlessness. Then he marched them out of the city to battle, an untested and unlikely fighting unit.

Henry's focus had meanwhile shifted from the north and west of England to the Cinque ports on the eastern coast, still held by the rebels, and which were vital to the successful landing of the mercenary army that Eleanor had been charged with assembling. Simon marched south to meet him. By May 11 the two armies had converged in Sussex about five miles from the Channel. There was the requisite attempt to mediate by three bishops sympathetic to the earl's agenda (thoroughly scorned by the royalist forces), followed by the issuance of a formal challenge to the rebels in Henry's name.

The process begun six years before at the great parliament at Oxford was finally to be decided, not in the courts of English judges, nor in the great halls of foreign princes, but in the muddy cow pastures of a sleepy little town called Lewes.

The battle began very early on the morning of May 14. Simon, desperate for any advantage, had mustered his army in the middle of the night, marched them as quickly and noiselessly as possible through the forest, and secured the only high ground in the area, a hillock just outside the town walls. There he camped and, in a gratifyingly romantic ceremony just before dawn, knighted several of his younger officers. He then gave them their assignments and an inspiring speech, likening their efforts to those of soldiers upon crusade, and sounded the call to arms.

He caught by surprise the royalist forces who, aware of the superiority of their numbers, had spent the previous evening drinking to their expected victory. "Thus didde these gaye and wayward menne/With wine inflame their heades—/And Sir Symon in mighte, had ascended the height,/Ere theye had left their beddes," wrote a later wag. Still, Edward roused his men quickly to meet the challenge. Simon had sent his unseasoned London unit over the hill first, and when these greenhorn foot soldiers saw Edward and his noble cavalry arrayed against them they hastily turned tail and fled back from whence they had come. Edward and his horsemen gave chase, intent upon annihilating the enemy. The Londoners panicked, spread out in disorderly ranks, and managed to cover quite a bit of territory, so it took Edward and his men some time to track them all down.

It was a fatal error. An army only maintains superiority of numbers if everybody is on the battlefield at the same time. When Edward rode off after the decoy London troop, he left his father and Richard, neither of whom was known for military prowess, to fight off Simon's main advance. Henry was said to have fought valiantly—apparently, two horses were killed under him and he remounted each time—but the king of the Romans lost his nerve entirely and was found hiding in a windmill. By the time Edward came back, there was nothing to do but surrender. "This year on the 14th of May . . . there was a deadly battle between King Henry and Symon de Munfort and the barons," wrote a monk from Lewes, who seems to have been an eyewitness. "And so it was that the greatest part of the King's army was utterly over thrown between prime and noon. Firstly, the king was much beaten by swords and maces . . . so that he escaped with difficulty, and his brother Rickard, King of Germany, was soon captured. Edward, the King's son, delivered over in hostage to Symon de Munfort, and many of the greatest men of England who held with the King, wounded in their heads and bodies even to death, the number of which dead is reckoned at 2,700, more or less. All of these things took place at Lewes, at the Mill of the Hide."

The Battle of Lewes was decisive. As of the evening of May 14, 1264, Simon de Montfort ruled England.

Eleanor, waiting in France, soon heard the wretched news: the king's forces utterly routed; thousands dead or wounded; her husband and eldest son captured and held prisoner by the rebels; Simon de Montfort and a small group of barons in control of the government. The chronicle of Bury St Edmunds reported that "the queen of England, who was abroad, grieved to hear the course events had taken." Eleanor, naturally optimistic, particularly where military action was concerned, would have put her faith in the strength of the king's support and the numerical superiority of his troops. She could not have anticipated a failure of this magnitude.

There was no time to lament or second-guess, however. Eleanor flew to Louis and Marguerite in Paris to plead for her husband's rights. They joined her in an appeal to the pope to use his influence on Simon de Montfort to release Henry and Edward and to ensure that the hostages came to no harm. The pontiff, astounded by the barons' revolt, sent one of his most senior and trusted advisers to England, the man who would succeed him as pope the very next year, to negotiate a peaceful settlement between the king and the earl. The papal legate was supplied with official papers threatening Simon de Montfort and his supporters with excommunication and interdict if they did not come to terms.

The pope's intervention on her side represented progress, but another negotiated settlement, which could then be ignored or broken, was not what Eleanor was seeking. What the queen wanted was an invasion. She had already been in the process of organizing a foreign regiment to supplement the king's forces when the disaster at Lewes had struck; now she renewed her efforts on a much larger scale. She knew that the only way to rescue Henry and Edward was to assemble a mercenary army of such strength and ferocity as to overwhelm the forces of the earl of Leicester. The king's Lusignan half-brothers had escaped after the battle of Lewes, and Eleanor put aside her hatred of these men to work with them and Peter of Savoy to build up the necessary force.

Money was, as always, an issue. Eleanor was inspired in the stratagems she employed to raise funds. Louis was once again persuaded to forward monies due under the Treaty of Paris, and when these were not sufficient, Eleanor undertook to sell him back the rights to three English bishoprics for an additional five thousand pounds, on condition that Henry could repurchase the properties when he was restored to the throne. She hawked the crown jewels, which Marguerite had had stored at the Temple of Paris, for one thousand pounds and then borrowed money in her own name from Florentine bankers; she even turned to Henry of Castile, Edward's wife's brother, for a loan of 2,500 marks, which was guaranteed by Peter of Savoy. Uncle Peter also borrowed against properties in his own name to help Eleanor finance her military effort.

Funds in hand, Eleanor turned to the business of acquiring ships and soldiers. She exercised her son's rights in Gascony, ordering the knights who owed him military service there to convene in Flanders with men and arms, and even convinced her irascible uncle, Gaston de Béarn, to come to her aid. Henry's half-brothers brought forces from Poitou, St Pol arrived with his contingent, and the fighting men from Flanders also answered her call. The whole family (except for Beatrice of Provence and Charles of Anjou, who were suspected of favoring the baronial cause for their own purposes) rallied behind Eleanor and did all they could to augment her forces. Marguerite added her support by again trying to induce Alphonse of Poitiers to help, this time by asking him to apprehend all of the English ships moored at his ports with the intention of subverting them for Eleanor's use. He refused, but did arrest some of the baronial supporters in his territories. Eleanor's mother made a special trip to Savoy to raise troops and supplies and Peter of Savoy paid for the travel and employment expenses of a large contingent of Savoyard knights who owed him service. All converged at the port of Damme in Flanders in August 1264. All were under Eleanor's command, and that of Peter of Savoy. The chronicle of Bury St Edmund relates that the queen "collected an enormous army." England readied itself for an invasion.

But the ships never sailed. There seem to have been a number of reasons for the failure to embark. Some chroniclers claim that winds were against the queen's fleet, and that by the time they had changed, her money had run out; others, like that of Bury St Edmund, suggest that, "As, however, the sea and coasts were strongly guarded by an English army by order of the king and barons, the enemy was afraid to sail." The papal legate, who was optimistic for a peaceful solution, argued strongly against it, and Eleanor would have moved against his advice at her peril; she could not afford to lose the goodwill of the pope. But most significant was Henry's own position on this issue: the king begged Louis by letter to frustrate efforts to free him by force. Henry feared that the kingdom would be harmed and he and Edward blamed for Eleanor's action, and that the repercussions would be serious. Edward and Richard's son Henry of Almain "are hostages for the fulfillment of the mise [the peace agreement forced on Henry by Simon de Montfort after the battle of Lewes]," the king of England wrote to the king of France in August 1264. "If you are so indifferent to our ruin and the ruin of our realm as to allow an expedition to be prepared in France with the object of releasing them, you will put them in inestimable peril; for if we and our friends disturb the peace their safety may, under the law of nations, rightly be at stake."

This last argument would have had weight with the queen. If she attacked, she risked the safety of her husband and eldest son; she could not ensure that even if her armies won that the hostages would not be killed in retaliation before she could reach them. She would not know where they were, or how to get to them before it was too late. And that was if she won.

And so, for the first time in her life, Eleanor hesitated. August turned to September and then to October and still she did not proceed. Whatever sign she was waiting for never appeared, because at the end of October the three months' service she had purchased with her hard-won funds ran out. It was hardly consolation that it was at about this time that the papal legate, too, gave up, and issued the previously threatened sentences of excommunication and interdict on the kingdom. The queen of England, whose courage and strivings to free her husband and son caused one chronicler to liken her to a heroine of ancient times, who had "sweated" in her devotion to them, could only watch, helpless, as the powerful army she had assembled packed up and drifted away.

In the immediate aftermath of the Battle of Lewes, Simon de Montfort moved quickly to consolidate his gains. His victory had been stunningly complete. He had captured not only the king and his eldest son, but Richard of Cornwall and Henry of Almain as well. The lives of the two younger men were pledged as hostages to an imposed peace, thereby ensuring the cooperation of their respective fathers in the new baronial government, which the earl made haste to organize. Once again, a council was established and the king's great seal used to legitimize its proclamations. The Oxford Provisions were reinstated. Aliens were forbidden to hold political office. Parliamentary representation was expanded to include heads of local religious houses, knights, burgesses, officials from various districts, and free citizens from the Cinque Ports, a sign of the depth of support for Simon's reforms among the country gentry and local administrators.

On August 12 the king, Edward, and Henry of Almain were all brought to Canterbury to swear fealty to the new government. The earl of Leicester threatened to depose Henry III and to imprison Edward if they did not agree to abide by the rulings of the new council, and to accept the council for the rest of Henry's reign and also for a significant period, to be negotiated at a later date, of Edward's. Having no choice, both men agreed.

The ceremony at Canterbury ushered in a surreal period of outward tranquillity. The rebels, observed the chronicle of Bury St Edmunds, "captured the king of England. They did not, however, guard him like an ordinary prisoner, but treated him courteously as their lord . . . Edward gave himself as a hostage for the liberation of his men. They all swore to observe the Provisions of Oxford in future. Thereafter the king went wherever the barons went, and of his own free will did whatever they had decided should be done."

It was not free will; it was house arrest, a bizarre pretense at normalcy. Edward, Henry of Almain, and Richard were confined at Richard's castle at Wallingford, which the king of the Romans had been forced to surrender to Simon de Montfort. (Sanchia's son, Edmund, was there as well, with his father.) They lived in comfort but without freedom of movement. Edward, in particular, had to endure the continual presence of his cousin, Henry de Montfort, Simon's eldest son, who was instructed by his father to dog the heir to the throne's every footstep: "With him to wend about, to follow him up and down." The king himself was lodged with the earl and his sister, the countess of Leicester, and moved from castle to castle when they moved, which was often, rather like a favored pet lapdog.

But harmony was only a veneer. There were many still loyal to the crown, especially to Edward. In November a daring rescue was planned. A group of armed supporters attacked the castle at Wallingford with the aim of freeing Edward. They were egged on by Eleanor, who had sent a secret message to them at Bristol relaying the information that the castle at Wallingford was not heavily guarded and could be overthrown. The attackers rode across England and broke through the outer wall of Wallingford; they were only turned away at the last minute when the prince's jailers brought him out and threatened to throw their prisoner off the roof if his rescuers did not depart. This incident demonstrates that Eleanor's fear that a large, concerted military invasion might precipitate recriminations was, after all, correct. Edward's captors seemed to have no scruples about killing him if provoked. The outcome of this exploit undoubtedly reached the queen and was perhaps the reason invasion plans were ultimately abandoned. After the bungled rescue attempt, Simon had Edward and the other hostages removed to a remote accommodation at Kenilworth in northern England, and from there to Hereford, which would have been even more difficult for Eleanor's forces to get to in time.

But it is harder to run a kingdom than it looks, particularly if the majority of your supporters in the baronage are young, passionate, and callow, and you yourself, despite the noblest of intentions with regard to representative government, are inclined to avarice. A split developed quickly between Simon de Montfort and Gilbert de Clare, the twenty-two-year-old scion of Gloucester. It was Gilbert who had taken the king of the Romans and Henry of Almain prisoner on the battlefield of Lewes, which, according to custom, meant that he had a right to their lands. Simon, however, kept these for himself. "The Earl of Leicester was not content with keeping the King of England a captive, but took the royal castles in his own power, disposing of the whole realm according to his will," wrote a chronicler. "And his chief offense was that he claimed the entire possession of the revenues of the realm, the ransom of the captives, and other profits, which according to the convention ought to have been equally divided between them . . . it increased Gilbert's indignation that the said Simon, when asked by him to return to him the King of Almaine and certain other captives taken in the battle by Gilbert and his men, replied with brevity or levity. For which cause the old friendship was turned into hate . . . And Gilbert went over to the party of the nobler knights of the March [Wales], whom Earl Simon had ordered by public edict to leave the realm, and joined them in alliance."

Word of this rift evidently got to France, possibly through Henry of Almain, whom Simon, in his eagerness to demonstrate the legitimacy and goodwill of his regime, was using as a courier to the court of Louis and Marguerite. Eleanor's party moved quickly to exploit the quarrel. A new, much more scaled-back plan was devised, which depended on secrecy, speed, and intrigue rather than overwhelming force. Eleanor moved to Gascony in February 1265, where she had the authority, through Edward, to command ships and men. Also in February, Henry's Lusignan half-brother William of Valence was sighted moving through Poitou with a troop of approximately

120 fighting men and their horses and supplies, some of which had come from the Gascon port of Bordeaux. Louis himself issued the order for their safe passage through France. The knights made their way across the Channel and landed quietly in Wales in May 1265, where they immediately linked up with Gilbert de Clare and the other Welsh barons who had remained loyal to Edward.

Edward himself was at Hereford, not too far from Wales, in the company of his keeper, Henry de Montfort, and a number of other young men whose job it was to guard the prince. One of these young men was Gilbert de Clare's brother Thomas. One of Gilbert's men got in touch with Thomas, who surreptitiously forwarded a message to Edward.

It was quiet out there in the country. There wasn't a great deal to do, and the young men guarding Edward were all rather bored. So when Edward suggested on May 28 that they amuse themselves by going outside the castle walls and having a race, there was unanimous agreement. To make the event even more diverting, Edward bet that his horse would be the fastest, and to make sure he tried out several, running in heats with his captors, which tired out their horses. At length, he took a fresh horse and the race commenced. However, instead of following the course laid out in advance, Edward, followed by Thomas de Clare, rode as fast as he could away from everyone else. He was right: his horse was faster. Another chronicler, Robert of Gloucester, later celebrated Edward's flight in song:

> *Away went this good knight. When he was out of hand,*
> *"Lordings," he said, "have now a good day,*
> *And greet well my father the king; and I shall, if I may,*
> *Both see him well betime and out of ward him do."*
> *What need of a long tale? He escaped so,*
> *And to the castle of Wigmore his way soon he nome.*
> *There was joy and bliss enow, when he was thither come.*

From Wigmore, Edward rode to Shropshire in the north, where he met Gilbert de Clare, and the two came to an agreement to restore Henry to the throne.

Simon was actually at Hereford with the king when Edward made his escape; one can only guess at the conversation he had with his son when the latter returned to the castle without his prisoner. For the first time, the earl of Leicester displayed confusion in his actions. He left Hereford, taking

Henry with him, to try to reach his ally Llywelyn in Wales, and for a month he marched his soldiers around trying to rally support. During this period Edward, Gilbert de Clare, and William of Valence succeeded in taking over much of the territory north and west of Hereford, adding to their army as they went along. "Thus released from his imprisonment, Edward assembled a large army, as numbers flocked to join him, and the counties of Hereford, Worcester, Salop, and Chester, entered into an alliance with him, the towns and villages, cities and castles, pouring forth their inhabitants to join his standard." Llywelyn, no fool, felt the shift in momentum and refused to help his old ally, so Simon was forced to march back to Hereford having succeeded only in exhausting his own troops.

His only hope was to gather reinforcements around him quickly, and so he sent an urgent message to his son Simon, who was all the way south in Sussex, to hurry and meet him in Hereford with a large army. Unfortunately, Simon the younger was not nearly as good a soldier as his father. He got the message, but took his time. He was in Kenilworth on July 31, 1265, only to find Edward and his army waiting for him. The younger Simon's army was routed and his barons captured.

Meanwhile, Simon de Montfort had left Hereford, and was trying to get to Kenilworth as well. But he had Henry with him, and Henry was old and feeble, and so the earl had to stop often to feed the king and let him rest. By August 4 they had made it only as far as Evesham. There they were soon surrounded by Edward and his troops. Even faced with certain defeat, the earl of Leicester adopted a stoic pose. From his vantage point at the top of the tower of the Evesham abbey church Simon watched as Edward's men advanced from all sides in an organized, disciplined fashion. "They learned that from me," was his comment.

The battle of Evesham has been called a massacre. Certainly Simon's forces were greatly outnumbered and Edward attacked with understandable savagery. Almost everyone who fought on the side of the earl died. Henry was himself in terrible danger; according to the Melrose Chronicle: "It seems then that the barons wished that the King should die with them, if it were necessary that they should die in the battle in which the King was engaged; their plan was that he should be unknown to his own adherents and should fall under the heavy weight of their blows." Simon and a small group of barons, including his sons Henry and Peter, surrounded Henry and fought with their backs to him. They put a helmet on the king's head so that he was not immediately recognizable. Henry himself seems to have been confused and bewildered by this. "Being unable to fight like the others he kept calling out at the top of his voice, 'I am Henry, the old King of England,' . . . and he cried to the men who were hitting at him, 'Do not hit me, I am too old to fight,'" reported the chronicle. He was wounded and nearly cut down when he was saved at the last minute by one of Edward's men, who removed Henry's helmet and recognized him. "Discovering by his countenance that he really was King, he was taken out of the battle."

The whole offensive took less than two hours, and when it was over Simon de Montfort and two of his sons lay dead. In vengeance, a knight who had originally fought by the earl's side at Lewes, but had since reverted to the royalist cause, cut off his head and sent it as a trophy to the wife of one of Edward's supporters. Simon's hands and feet were also amputated. On Edward's order the mutilated remains of the man who had dared to reform the government of the kingdom of England and who, at the height of his success, had wielded absolute power over his countrymen, were buried by the monks of Evesham. "Thus ended the labors of that noble man Earl Simon, who gave up not only his property, but also his person, to defend the poor from oppression, and for the maintenance of justice and the rights of the kingdom."

Edward had rescued his father and saved his birthright. Henry III was king again. Eleanor could come home.

Dismemberment of Simon de Montfort at Evesham.

Beatrice

The Battle of Charles of Anjou against Conradin.

CHAPTER XXI

FOUR QUEENS

Beatrice of Provence would not have been human if she did not experience a certain, secret satisfaction at the outbreak of the English civil war and the consequent abasement of her sister Eleanor. After all, the queen of England, in combination with Marguerite, had made a point of emphasizing the countess of Provence's lower social rank for years. Thus it was that Beatrice and Charles of Anjou were notable exceptions to the general Provençal-Savoyard family rush to defend Eleanor and restore the king and queen of England to the throne. Both of these younger siblings recognized that the crisis in England could be used to their advantage, and they were quick to pursue the opportunity.

As disturbing and dramatic as was the revolt of the baronage, by the pope's standards, the hostilities in England were by no means the most important conflict in Europe. That honor was reserved for the increasingly distressing situation in Italy, where Manfred was in the process of consolidating power. The pope's preoccupation with the Sicilian succession was a function of geography: Manfred's ambitions in central and northern Italy, which by 1262 had become obvious, were a direct threat to papal interests and property. As a matter of physical safety, the pope had already to remove himself and his court from Rome to Viterbo. A pope who cannot claim Rome is not much of a pope.

Manfred was proving himself to be a subtle and enterprising opponent. He never actively sought the title of king of the Romans; his forces were based in Sicily and he knew that he did not have the resources to conquer and hold faraway Germany. (That is why, upon his half-brother Conrad's death, the kingdom of Germany went first to William of Holland and then to Richard.) Instead, Manfred concentrated on cementing his control of Sicily, and then using that kingdom as a springboard from which to absorb the rest of Italy.

It was a bold plan, particularly as Manfred was a usurper to the throne of Sicily—upon Conrad's death, the crown ought to have gone to Conrad's son, Conradin. But Conradin was a toddler in Germany when his father died, and Manfred successfully dodged the issue of his nephew's inheritance by offering to resign his rule as soon as the boy came of age. To then rid himself completely of this inconvenient relative, Manfred concocted a rumor that Conradin had fallen seriously ill and was perhaps dying. The concerned uncle sent ambassadors to Conradin's mother in Germany to discover the true state of the boy's health; these ambassadors were instructed to poison the child. But according to Villani, Conradin's mother was a match for Manfred, and hid her child from the treacherous emissaries.

> The ambassadors found the boy whom his mother guarded most carefully, and with him she kept many other boys of gentle birth clothed in his garments; and when the said ambassadors asked for Conradin, his mother being in dread of Manfred, showed to them one of the said children, and they with rich presents, offered him gifts and reverence, among the which gifts were poisoned comfits from Apulia, and the boy having eaten of them, straightway died. They, believing Conradin to be dead by poison, departed from Germany, and when they had returned to Venice, they caused sails of black cloth to be made to their galley and all the rigging to be black, and they were attired in black, and when they were come into Apulia, they made a show of great grief, as they had been instructed by Manfred.

After a similarly affecting period of public mourning, Manfred had himself crowned king of Sicily in 1258.

The new king spent the next few years expanding and legitimizing his rule. He moved first into Tuscany then went on to win a particularly brutal battle against Florence. Lombardy and Sardinia also fell to Manfred and his lieutenants. By 1260 almost all of Italy, with the exception of Rome, was under Manfred's control. By May 1261 the papacy had lost Rome as well; Alexander IV, the exhausted old pope, died in exile in Viterbo, conscious that his policy to unseat Manfred had failed miserably.

Success breeds allies; Manfred sought to capitalize on his military victories by turning his considerable talents to the realm of diplomacy. In 1262 he scored a major coup by marrying his daughter Constance to Peter, the son of James I, king of Aragon. Eleanor must have been chagrined; in an earlier, more idealistic time, she had intended Constance to be Edmund's bride. It is a measure of Manfred's solid entrenchment in Italy that the highly religious James I was willing to overlook the fact that his son's future father-in-law was an excommunicate bastard when agreeing to the marriage terms.

The new pope, Urban IV, protested the wedding, but in vain. Manfred was now poised to succeed to his father's position and declare himself emperor. He might even, through martial strength, force the pope to recognize him as such. If that happened, the Church stood to lose its influence in Italy permanently, and with it the source of all of its wealth and power. No wonder, then, that the most pressing item on the pope's agenda in 1262 was the question of where and how to recruit a prince capable of defeating Manfred.

The problem was, the Church had already run through most of the available candidates. The obvious choice was Richard, who was already king of the Romans, but Richard had been unable even to journey safely across his own kingdom, let alone attack Manfred. The pope had then considered Alfonso X of Castile, but Alfonso was busy contesting Richard's reign in Germany. The king of Castile had gotten himself elected king of the Romans a couple of months after Richard (one of Richard's electors changed his vote and swung his support to Alfonso). Alfonso kept meaning to travel to his new kingdom and combat Richard personally, but somehow he never found the time to actually visit Germany. A king who could not marshal enough forces to confront a man as obviously physically timid as Richard was not the sort of leader destined to take on a Manfred. Similarly, by 1262 Edmund's candidature was also out of the question—what with all that business about taking oaths and the hiring of foreign mercenaries to control the baronage, anyone could see that the king of England was not in a position to launch an attack on Sicily.

Actually, there was never any doubt about who was the right man for the job. Whoever it was, it was imperative that he come from France. France was the only kingdom left with the power and resources to destroy Manfred.

Louis IX himself, the pope understood, would never consent to raise an army against Sicily in his own name. The king of France still nourished the hope of returning to his crusade in the Holy Land. He would not permit an assault against a Christian country like Sicily to distract him from his primary goal. Louis's brother Alphonse of Poitiers, the next prince in line, had been enfeebled by a stroke, so he was out. That left Charles of Anjou.

There is no question of Charles's desire for the post. "He had the kind of thirst associated with dropsy, that deep craving, so that the more he drank, the more his stomach burned and drove him back to drink," wrote the Italian chronicler Saba Malaspina. The acquisition of the kingdom of Sicily is clearly what the count of Provence had in mind when he hinted to his wife as early as 1259: "Be at peace, for I will shortly make thee a greater queen than them." With regard to this dignity, husband and wife were of one accord: Beatrice, too, lusted for the honor.

But the matter had still to be raised with Louis, and this required deftness. It was essential that the king of France give his consent to the enterprise; only Louis could command the service of the French knights that Charles would need to staff his army. Only Louis had funds sufficient to purchase ships and supplies; Charles's income, even given the financial gains from his exploit in Flanders, could not support an army of the size and strength necessary to defeat Manfred. Charles could not, however, broach Louis openly on this subject. The count of Anjou knew his brother well: if the king of France caught even a hint of ambition or self-interest in Charles's request, he would deny the suit. Ambition and self-interest were sins. The antagonism of the queen of France to her younger sister's husband had also to be considered; if Marguerite were given advance warning of the project she would oppose Charles's candidature with all her might. Charles and Beatrice had therefore to affect a noble disinterest in the outcome of the affair. Charles must wait until the pope had demonstrated to his older brother, by the appropriate religious and legal arguments, what everybody else in Christendom already knew: the count of Anjou was the most qualified, most realistic, in fact, the only, man for the job. Only then would Charles consider the pope's offer, and allow himself to be persuaded as a favor to the Church, against his natural modesty and rectitude, to accept the kingship of Sicily.

The pope, who was himself French, understood this and played his part well. He sent his personal secretary, Albert of Parma, a man expert in Church law, to Paris to argue the case. Albert had been working on the problem of the Sicilian succession for a decade. It was he who had first offered the kingdom to Richard of Cornwall in 1252; he who, upon receiving Richard's refusal, went to meet Eleanor at New Year's where Edmund's candidacy had been mooted; he who then went on to offer the crown to Charles of Anjou the first time, only to have Louis forbid his younger brother's accepting the honor. In a letter to the pope written in 1262 from the royal court in Paris, Albert listed all of Louis's objections to the scheme, and Albert's subsequent rejoinders. As Charles and Beatrice had expected, the king of France had serious moral reservations about his younger brother being offered the crown of Sicily. Louis was concerned that Conradin's rights of inheritance be respected (by this time it was known that the child's mother had foiled the uncle's plot); there were also Edmund's interests to be considered. But after ten years, Albert was well-versed in all the arguments, pro and con, legitimate and specious, pertaining to the rights of this particular inheritance, and he turned aside every objection of the king's with a carefully annunciated analysis of papal law. More than that, Albert made it clear that any future crusade to the Holy Land was out of the question until Manfred was brought to heel. This arrow hit its mark. At the end of the discussion, the king of France acceded, and allowed the throne of Sicily to be offered to Charles.

Even then, Charles had to wait for his prize; Manfred, alerted to the danger, tried to appease the pope by offering to lead an army to retake Constantinople, which had fallen to the Greeks. Louis insisted that this proposal be taken seriously, and encouraged Urban IV to readmit the excommunicated Manfred into the Church. The pope was forced to humor Louis for another year, until it became clear that Manfred had only made the suggestion to stall for time. It wasn't until May 1263 that Louis finally allowed the pope to offer the crown of Sicily to Charles; a formal request arrived in Paris, where Charles was staying, on June 17. To keep up the pretense that the honor was being forced upon a reluctant hero, on June 20, Urban IV also wrote to Alphonse of Poitiers, asking the count to use his influence with his younger brother to convince him to accept the position.

The pope's offer came with a written agreement, full of restrictions. Charles was never to aspire to take over northern or central Italy or to reinstate the empire. He was never to hold any office in Italy other than the kingship of Sicily. He was not allowed to make ecclesiastic appointments, or benefit from the earnings of a vacant Church position. He could be deposed by the pope at any time and had to agree in advance not to fight the sentence. He had to take over what was left of Henry's debt *and* pay a yearly stipend of ten thousand gold pieces (later reduced to eight thousand). Louis added the postscript that Charles must satisfy Marguerite's demands with respect to her Provençal inheritance. The queen of France had been out-maneuvered by Beatrice and her husband; by the time Marguerite was aware of the intrigue, Charles's appointment was an established fact. She must have protested vehemently, because both Urban IV and Louis IX agreed that Charles should make restitution to Marguerite before taking on Sicily.

Charles agreed to everything without a demur. This alone was indication of the depth of his desire.

The signed treaty was sent back promptly to the pope, who now resided in Orvieto. With this gesture, Charles accepted the kingship of Sicily. For his part, the pope gave his new champion the wherewithal to conduct his military campaign by bestowing on Charles the ability to tax the Church in France and Provence for a portion of their revenues for three years. Louis helped by supporting Charles in his efforts to induce James I not to interfere in either Sicily or Marseille, which had formerly given Charles trouble. To ensure that the king of Aragon kept his word, Louis agreed to the marriage of his son Philip, now heir to the throne, to one of James I's daughters.

Charles was now the unanimously accepted European choice to battle Manfred for Sicily. Curiously, the onerous conditions by which he achieved this goal did not seem to bother the count of Anjou and Provence. In fact, the pope could have saved his ink. The new king of Sicily had no intention of adhering to any of the provisions of the agreement.

At the end of 1264, soon after Charles accepted the pope's terms, his old nemesis, Beatrice of Savoy, died suddenly at the age of fifty-eight. For Marguerite and Eleanor, this was a wrenching loss. Their mother had been an active participant in their lives, and the source of much sound advice and comfort. Adding to their grief was the fact that neither was with the older woman when she passed away; as soon as the English civil war had broken out, Beatrice had left Marguerite's court in Paris to return to Savoy in order to recruit personally a troop of knights and foot soldiers to add to Eleanor's planned invasion. She died before the battle of Evesham, in ignorance as to the outcome of the conflict.

Not only her daughters but all of Savoy mourned the passing of this energetic, able, and determined woman. Although not a queen herself, Beatrice of Savoy was an accomplished diplomat who had influenced the policies of kings for nearly a quarter century, and, through her daughters, the fate of all Europe. Matthew Paris once remarked of her that she "shed a halo of light over the whole extent of Christendom."

The younger Beatrice's reaction to her mother's death was not recorded, although it was likely more complex. Beatrice of Savoy had stood in her youngest daughter's way for many years; she had also made known her preference for her elder daughters, and this must have hurt. As for Charles, the unexpected demise of his mother-in-law was a piece of unqualified good fortune. The count of Provence was aware that any army he raised to challenge Manfred would require the permission of his wife's family in order to cross the Alps on their way to southern Italy. Beatrice of Savoy's implacable enmity might have thwarted any chance he had to access the Savoyard pass at Mont Cenis, the most reliable approach at the time. As it was, her death encouraged the prospective king of Sicily to begin preparations for the attack on Manfred's forces in earnest.

The first order of business was obviously to raise a large army. To his dismay, Charles quickly discovered that Louis expected the count of Provence to furnish a military force independently. The French king felt that he had done quite enough by agreeing to the enterprise in the first place, and had no intention of taking soldiers and funds away from his own expected future crusade in order to augment his younger brother's Italian expedition. Alphonse of Poitiers also refused to provide outright aid, although under pressure from the pope, he was eventually induced to grant a loan.

Beatrice of Provence intervened. It was as though she had been waiting her whole life for this moment. All of her competitive spirit, her desire to be recognized, the inherent faith she had in herself burst forth. She rode all over Provence calling forth her knights. She charmed, cajoled, exhorted, and bribed her subjects to support her husband's cause. Then she took her campaign to Paris, where she and Charles spent Easter 1265 at court with Louis and Marguerite. Beatrice worked on the knights and younger sons of the French and Flemish aristocracy as Eleanor had the year before, bestowing rings and gifts in exchange for military service. "And his lady . . . when she heard of the election of the Count Charles, her husband, to the intent that she might become queen, pledged all her jewels and invited all the bachelors-at-arms of France and of Provence to rally round her standard and to make her queen . . . for which cause she sought after and obtained the best barons of France for her service, and those who did most in the emprise," reported Villani. "Beatrice, to aid him [Charles] in the gratification of her ambition, sold all her jewels and personal ornaments, and expended her private treasure in collecting round her standard, not only her own vassals, but the chivalric youth of France, who were attracted to her service not less by her personal solicitations than by her rich gifts," agreed the chronicler Angelo da Costanzo.

Beatrice's energy was infectious. She had watched her mother for years and knew how to persuade, to reward, to threaten, to cajole. In the end, a full quarter of Charles's army came from Provence. The count and countess lured their officers with the promise of high position and captured riches. Even the belligerent citizens of the port town of Marseille, who had for years sought to assert their independence of Charles's rule, were quick to grasp the potential economic benefits and trade advantages of a conquered Sicily, and gave their enthusiastic support to the project. Many of the scions of France's great families also answered the count and countess's call. The French aristocracy saw in this ambitious, capable couple a chance to redeem the kingdom's military reputation, which had been blotted by Louis's earlier crusade. The younger noblemen in particular, who were trained in the art of chivalry and the romance of war, had difficulty fully appreciating the merits of a king who wore the royal equivalent of sackcloth, had himself scourged regularly, and watered his wine. Charles, an obvious man of action, presented a much more palatable figure to this group. The count and countess filled out the remainder of their army with knights from the counties of Anjou and Flanders.

There was still the problem of money—the sacrifice of Beatrice's jewels was not, in the end, enough to completely finance the operation—but Charles solved this by borrowing freely from Florentine and Roman bankers. Some of these loans were secured by a papal guarantee. (So strapped for funds was the Church and so desperate for Charles's help was the pope that he was forced to pawn the gold plate belonging to the papal chapel to meet his protégé's needs.) Charles falsely implied that those loans not secured by the Church would be taken care of by Louis. The count of Provence managed to scrape together nearly 150,000 livres tournois in this way, just enough to finance his troops for the obligatory three-month engagement.

By the spring of 1265 all was in readiness. Charles had determined that the best way to proceed was for him to sail to Rome with a small expeditionary force and have the brunt of the army follow by land. On May 10, 1265, at almost exactly the same time that William of Valence, Henry's Lusignan half-brother, and his band of knights were landing covertly in Wales to begin the process of reclaiming England from Simon de Montfort, Charles of Anjou set sail from Marseille to defeat Manfred.

This naval excursion represented a calculated risk. To ward off Manfred's hegemony, the city of Rome had decided to elect Charles as their senator, and it was the count of Provence's intention to accept the honor in person. But ships were expensive and he couldn't afford to send his whole army by sea. So he gambled on speed and surprise. If Charles and a small force could take and hold Rome, the proposed future king of Sicily would secure an important foothold in enemy territory from which to launch a blistering offensive when the main battalion caught up with its commander. "Good care frustrates ill fortune," Charles is said to have noted before he sailed.

But Manfred was also prepared. He had some eighty ships trolling the coast to intercept invaders. There followed a farcical string of events typical of medieval seafaring. A few days out of Marseille, Charles's ships encountered a violent storm that scattered the fleet and rendered Manfred's defense futile. Three ships, including the one carrying Charles, were forced to dock at a Pisan port for repairs. Upon being informed of this serendipitous occurrence, Manfred's deputy in Pisa, Count Guido Novello, hurried to marshal his most experienced land troops to capture Charles. But the citizens of Pisa, taking advantage of their overseer's urgency, closed the gates of the city and refused to let Count Guido out until he had granted them some long-sought concessions. According to Villani, by the time Guido finally got his men to the shore, his prey had vanished: "And on account of the said interval and delay, when Count Guido had departed from Pisa and reached the port, Count Charles, the storm being somewhat abated, had with great care refitted his galleys and put out to sea, having departed but a little time before from the port . . . and thus, as it pleased God, passing afterwards hard by the fleet of king Manfred, sailing over the high seas, he arrived with his armada safe and sound at the mouth of the Roman Tiber . . . the which coming was held to be very marvelous and sudden, and by King Manfred and his people could scarce be believed."

This escapade served to enhance Charles's mystique, and he was warmly welcomed in Rome and "was received by the Romans with great honor, inasmuch as they loved not the lordship of Manfred." The count of Provence immediately accepted the position as senator of Rome, essentially the leader of the city. It had taken him less than a month to violate his contract with the pope, which had expressly forbidden him to hold any position in Italy other than that of monarch of Sicily.

Having established himself in Rome, Charles settled in to await the arrival of the remainder of his forces. With only enough money to pay for a few months' worth of his knights' time, and not knowing how long it would take him to secure Rome, he had left orders for the army to gather in Lyon in October 1265, and from there to make their way across the Alpine passes, through Asti and down into central Italy.

His orders were obeyed; in the fall of 1265, thousands of soldiers descended on Lyon in preparation for the march to Italy. Charles and Beatrice had managed to assemble an impressive fighting unit. "The French came in great numbers to help Charles, brother of the king of France, who was at Rome," wrote the chronicler Salimbene. "I myself saw them arriving when I traveled from Faenza to San Proculo to preach on the feast of St. John the Evangelist." The chroniclers estimated that there were six thousand horsemen, six hundred mounted crossbowmen, and perhaps as many as twenty thousand infantry. Villani claimed that Beatrice, "wife to the said Charles, and with her knights," accompanied the army on its journey to Rome; "they took the way of Burgundy and of Savoy," the chronicler averred.

As it happened, Beatrice and Charles had no difficulty in securing the requisite permission from her family to cross the Alps at Mont Cenis. Although the Savoyards had originally supported Edmund's claim to the Sicilian throne, by the fall of 1265 it was recognized that this was not practical, and the Savoyards were nothing if not practical. Philippe of Savoy, the youngest uncle, saw no reason why he shouldn't get something out of the Sicilian business, and joined his niece on her journey to Rome; it may have been under this condition that the family issued guides and a safe conduct to Beatrice and her forces.

In the Middle Ages, traveling through the Alpine passes was treacherous enough in the summer months; to make the attempt in late fall was madness, yet this is what Beatrice and her army did. Others who made a similar journey before and after her left descriptions. A chronicler who once crossed at the Mont Cenis pass in May observed that the mountains were of a "most excessive and stupendious [sic] height . . . so exceeding high, that if my horse had happened to stumble, he had fallen downe with me foure or five times as deepe in some places as Paules tower in London is high . . . the waies were exceeding uneasie. For they were wonderfull hard, all stony and full of windings and intricate turnings, whereof I thinke there were at the least 200 before I came to the foot." Usually the path was so narrow and winding and the weather so fierce that the guides had to maintain a strong grip on both a traveler and his horse in order to keep one or the other from falling over the side of the mountain. A wayfarer from the sixteenth century, who crossed the same pass in November, described his ordeal:

> It was very perilous going up . . . because of the snow, although I had a good strong palfrey and a strong man held me by my coat for fear my horse might fall . . . without which I should have been very frightened, for I was going along a narrow ridge which dropped off the edge three time the height of the belfry at Douai, or so it seemed. When we got up on the mountain the distance of a league, we found a house, and there I got off my horse and walked on foot, leading my horse by the bridle for fear it might fall into some abyss . . . for the path is only about three feet wide when filled with snow, and there the snow is hard, but on the side a horse would never get out . . . But the wind was so strong that it seemed all was lost; the snow blinded me and I could hardly stand against it.

The fall of 1265 was a mild one; once again, the count and countess of Provence's luck held. "In the year they [Charles's army] came a great miracle took place, because there was neither cold weather, nor frost, nor ice, nor snow, nor rain and mud—so that the roads were in fine shape, safe and excellent, as if it were May," wrote Salimbene. Still, no matter how balmy the weather in central and southern Italy, there must have been snow and frost and ice in the Alps in November, and it is a measure of Beatrice's determination that she prevailed.

It took nearly six weeks for the army to wend its way to Rome. "So that it was not till the beginning of the month of December, in the said year 1265, that they arrived . . . and when they were come to the city of Rome, Count Charles was very joyful, and received them with great gladness and honor," wrote Villani. As soon as Beatrice was reunited with Charles, preparations for the coronation began in earnest.

The new king and queen of Sicily were crowned on January 6, 1266, in Saint Peter's Church in Rome. By this time there was a new pope, Clement IV—Manfred had outlasted two pontiffs to date—but Clement, like his predecessor, was too timid to venture into Rome, so he sent five cardinals to conduct the ceremony in his stead. Villani reports that Charles and his lady were crowned with "great honor," which meant all the usual trappings. Beatrice would have worn a jeweled crown and robe of gold cloth trimmed with ermine. Music, dancing, and a great feast necessarily followed the ceremony; certainly the presence of the army ensured an adequate supply of guests. Chivalry demanded that the festivities last two or three days. Although Charles was known for parsimony, he would not have scrimped on this occasion; as he had learned from his mother, Blanche, the more opulent the celebration, the more legitimate the enterprise in the eyes of the world. And Charles, who had yet to fight Manfred for his throne, needed all the validity he could get.

As for Beatrice, the coronation represented the culmination of a long, hard-fought campaign to garner respect from siblings already noted for worldly accomplishment. Ironically, her crown did not convey superiority, only equality; Beatrice had not gained, she had only caught up. But perhaps equality was an end in itself in a family that had now produced four queens.

As soon as the coronation festivities had concluded, Charles marched his army out of Rome in search of Manfred. He had only a month within which to engage the enemy decisively; after that, his money would run out and his troops would disperse. Manfred tried to negotiate by sending ambassadors empowered to make certain concessions in the interest of a truce, but Charles rejected them: "I will have nothing but battle," he said, "and in that battle, either he shall slay me, or I him." Beatrice stayed behind in Rome with a small force to hold the city, much as Marguerite had once held Damietta for her husband.

Manfred hastily called for his troops to gather together at Capua to repel the invaders, but a large number of his men were stationed north and east of Rome, under the command of his nephew, and Manfred couldn't be sure when these would arrive. At first his strategy was to stay put and try to outlast his opponent while he waited for his nephew's reinforcements, but as Charles's army moved quickly and relentlessly southward, Manfred's subjects, unaware of his strategy and thinking themselves abandoned, surrendered easily. Castle after castle fell to the French. By February 10, 1266, Charles was already at Cassino. Aware of his antagonist's position at Capua, the French commander quickly veered inland toward Benevento, with the intention of isolating Manfred from further support and surprising him with an attack from the east. Manfred, informed of Charles's movements by spies, understood that if he did not move he would be surrounded so he, too, marched toward Benevento in the hope that he could take the town first and surprise Charles instead.

And that is what he did. Benevento lay at the foot of a mountain and Charles, who was low on supplies, had marched his troops double-time up and over, through difficult terrain, in order to conserve on food. His men were tired and hungry, "for the day before they arrived [at Benevento], through want of victual, many of the troops had to feed on cabbages, and their horses on the stalks, without any other bread, or grain for the horses; and they had no more money to spend," reported Villani. As they trudged their way down the rocky mountain pass, the French army was greeted with the dismaying sight of Manfred's imposing legions swarming around Benevento, safely encamped behind a rising river, which formed a natural barrier. In that position, the enemy was nearly impregnable. If Manfred chose to have his troops stand steadfast behind the river, Charles faced defeat, "for had he [Manfred] tarried one or two days, King Charles and his host would have perished or been captive without stroke of sword, through lack of provisions for them and for their horses."

But Manfred did not wait. He could see that the French soldiers were weary and dispirited, and he resolved to strike quickly. Besides, he had a new weapon—a troop of 1,200 German mercenary horsemen, very large men on very large horses. They wore heavy, technically superior armor and had a reputation for invincibility, a sort of tank on horseback. Manfred stationed the Germans behind his highly trained Saracen archers; behind the Germans were his paid Italian cavalrymen, who were considered less able. He himself held back with a reserve of about a thousand Sicilian knights, whom he intended to use at the last moment, to demoralize the French completely.

Charles saw the opposition crossing the river while his army was still coming down the mountain and grimly organized his troops into three waves to meet the challenge. To combat Manfred's Saracen archers, the French had crossbowmen; to counteract the German menace, Charles arrayed a troop of perhaps nine hundred knights and squires from Provence. He himself commanded the third line, mounted knights and soldiers from France. The warriors from Flanders were held in reserve.

The battle began. The French sustained heavy losses. "There began the fierce battle between the two first troops of the Germans and of the French, and the assault of the Germans was so strong that they evilly entreated the French troop, and forced them to give much ground and they themselves took ground," wrote Villani. Charles, seeing his second line waver and break, rushed in with his Provençal and Flemish troops; he left nothing in reserve. "Wherefore the battle was fierce and hard, and endured for a long space, no one knowing who was getting the advantage, because the Germans by their valor and strength, smiting with their swords, did much hurt to the French."

Although he did not know it, Charles also had a secret weapon: gravity. As a result of Manfred's impatience, the heavy German mercenaries had to ride uphill to fight the French. This made their horses tire. Moreover, while their armor was absolutely impregnable when attacked from the front, the manufacturer had neglected to provide protection for their armpits. Every time a German raised his arm to swing his sword at an opponent, the flesh under his arms was exposed. A perceptive French knight noticed this defect and alerted his companions: "To your daggers! To your daggers!" he cried. "And this was done, by the which thing in a short time the Germans were evilly entreated and much beaten down, and well-nigh turned to flight." The collapse of the supposedly invincible German line provoked panic among Manfred's Italian troops; many turned and fled. Manfred, knowing the battle was lost, acted with magnificent courage. He rallied those officers still with him and plunged into battle "without the royal insignia, so as not to be recognized as king, but like any other noble, striking bravely into the thickest of the fight," wrote Villani. "Nevertheless, his followers endured but a little while, for they were already turning; and straightway they were routed and King Manfred slain in the midst of his enemies, it was said by a French esquire, but it was not known for certain."

Charles had won the day. His troops pursued the fleeing Italian soldiers past Benevento, and then took the city. The victorious king of Sicily showed no mercy. Many of Manfred's officers were taken prisoner and shipped to Provence to die in captivity. Manfred's widow and his children were captured a few days later and suffered the same fate in an Italian prison. Only Manfred's lot remained unknown. Then, three days after the battle, an Italian foot soldier wandered into Benevento with a corpse slung on a mule, calling, "Who buys Manfred? Who buys Manfred?" The body was brought to Charles who had the captured officer of highest rank identify the remains as Manfred's: "Alas, alas, my lord," wept the lieutenant. Impressed with Manfred's valiancy at the end, Charles had a monument of sorts erected to his opponent. "Forasmuch as he was excommunicated, King Charles would not have him laid in a holy place; but at the foot of the bridge of Benevento he was buried, and upon his grave each one of the host threw a stone; whence there arose a great heap of stones," said Villani.

It was over. Charles had done it. He sent word to Beatrice, who joined him in Benevento. From there, the new king and queen of Sicily, accompanied by an elaborate retinue, proceeded to Naples to begin officially administering their kingdom. The couple had planned long for this day and their delight could be sensed in the grand fashion by which they entered the city: Charles, regally erect on his charger; Beatrice, carried aloft on a velvet couch.

Charles would go on to break every covenant in his contract with the pope, conquering city after city in central and northern Italy in a blatant attempt to acquire an empire that would rival that of any ruler in Christendom. In January 1267 Charles invaded Tuscany. By April he had Florence. "King Charles will be the lord of the greatest part of the world. It belongs to him and it is fitting for him," went a line in a song composed by a medieval troubadour. In 1268 the king of Sicily fought off his gravest threat: fifteen-year-old Conradin led a large German army down to Tagliacozzo, near Rome, and engaged Charles in battle. Conradin's forces gained an early success, but his troops were undisciplined and many scattered in search of plunder before Charles had been fully defeated. Charles, who had been hiding with a reserve, surprised the disorganized enemy and carried the day. To ensure that no other German champion appeared again to contest his rule, Charles made an example of the young Conradin by publicly beheading him in Naples, an act so despicable that it shocked even his supporters.

Although her ambition matched the king's, Beatrice never shared in Charles's successes. In July 1267 she died at Nocera, about 150 miles south of Rome, while her husband was engaged in an attack on a castle in Tuscany. Her illness was unnamed, but most likely she succumbed to fever and dysentery. The oppressive summer climate of southern Italy, with its attendant alien bacterial infections, claimed Beatrice's life as it had claimed so many other royal victims in the past. Charles had her body shipped to Provence and laid to rest beside that of her father in the expensive chapel that Marguerite had paid to have erected in Aix.

Beatrice was only thirty-five years old when she died, the mother of five. She had enjoyed her title for just eighteen months. She sacrificed her life to this ambition.

She never did get to sit at the front table with Marguerite and Eleanor.

Marguerite

Translation of the relics of Saint Louis.

CHAPTER XXII

THE LAST CRUSADE

Sadly, there is no indication at all that Marguerite mourned her youngest sister's death. The queen of France's sense of injustice at the terms of her father's will, coupled with Charles and Beatrice's betrayal of Louis during the crusade, seems to have prejudiced the siblings' relationship even in death. Moreover, there is little doubt that Charles's ascension to the throne of Sicily was a source of extreme vexation to Marguerite. If the count of Anjou hadn't settled her claims to her Provençal inheritance before, when he needed her and her husband's support for his campaign, what chance did she have now that he was himself the sovereign of a rich kingdom and celebrated by all of Europe for his conquest?

Charles's behavior as king of Sicily only confirmed Marguerite's suspicions of her brother-in-law's unscrupulousness. His first act upon her sister's death had been to flout the provisions of Raymond Berenger V's will, which had expressly stated that Provence was to be invested in Beatrice's oldest child, by usurping his eldest son's prerogative and keeping the title (and county) for himself. Marguerite protested sharply to Louis, but the king of France hesitated. Charles's profound, almost extravagant success in Italy seems to have caught Louis IX by surprise. On the surface, of course, the king of France could only applaud the new king of Sicily's achievement, particularly as he had labored in his task at the urgent entreaty of the pope. Still, it is not an altogether satisfying experience to be outshone so spectacularly in military affairs by one's younger brother. "He

[Charles] was a fine warrior, and he wiped out the shame which the French had received beyond the sea under St. Louis," wrote Salimbene.

Charles's decisive conclusion of the problem of the Sicilian succession did, however, remove the last obstacle to an ambition that Louis had been nursing for years, and which he now made haste to realize. In March 1267, a year after Manfred's destruction at Benevento, when it was clear that his brother was in firm command of his new kingdom, the king of France called a meeting of all of his barons. Attendance was mandatory. Joinville, who was suffering from a fever, "begged his Majesty to let me off this journey. However, he sent me word that he insisted on my coming, because there were good physicians in Paris who well knew how to cure such ailments."

Louis kept the purpose of this meeting secret from everyone, including Marguerite. "I found no one, neither the queen nor any other, who could tell me why I had been summoned by the king," wrote Joinville. But the aristocracy seems to have guessed. While attending a mass at Saint Chapelle, Joinville overheard the following conversation between two knights:

"'Never believe me again,' said one, 'if the king doesn't take the cross here in this chapel.' 'If he does,' replied the other, 'it will be one of the saddest days France has ever seen. For if we don't take the cross ourselves, we shall lose the king's favor; and if we do, we shall be out of favor with God, because we shall not be taking it for His sake, but for fear of displeasing the king.'"

The knights were right: not only Louis, but three of his sons, including his eldest, Philip, heir to the throne, and Jean Tristan, the child born in Damietta in 1250, when Marguerite had been forced to bribe the Pisan and Genoese sailors to remain in order to hold the city, joined their father in pledging themselves to a crusade. Louis and Marguerite's twenty-five-year-old daughter, Isabelle, and her husband, the king of Navarre, also took the cross.

Joinville, who had been so supportive of Louis seventeen years before in the Holy Land, was horrified. He refused, despite intense pressure from the king himself, to participate, and was scathing in his condemnation of those who encouraged Louis in his obsession:

I considered that all those who had advised the king to go on this expedition committed mortal sin. For at that time the state of the country was such that there was perfect peace throughout the kingdom, and between France and her neighbors, while ever since King Louis went away the state of the kingdom has done nothing but go from bad to worse.

It was besides a great sin on the part of those who advised the king to go, seeing that he was physically so weak that he could neither bear to be drawn in a coach, nor to ride—so weak, in fact, that he let me carry him in my arms from the Comte d'Auxerre's house, where I went to take leave of him, to the abbey of the Franciscans. And yet, weak as he was, if he had remained in France he might have lived for some time longer, and have done much good, and carried out many fine projects.

Marguerite's qualms and dread echoed these sentiments. She'd been on the last crusade. If it had all gone so awry the first time, when Louis was young and strong, what would happen now when he was fifty-three and infirm? The queen of France had no faith in her husband's military capabilities; were three of her sons and one of her daughters now to be sacrificed to this madness? She tried to dissuade Louis, but the king was adamant, and preparations for the crusade accelerated as Louis fixed an embarkation date of May 1270.

Once again, a considerable effort was made at recruitment. Louis used the occasion of his son Philip's knighting on June 5, 1267, a deliberately elaborate and therefore well-attended affair, to encourage his many guests to join him on his new mission to save the Holy Land. He even had a papal legate preach a sermon immediately after the ceremony exhorting all of those present to take the cross. Fifty-two of France's finest young men were knighted alongside Philip; significantly, each of them received the gift of a war horse from the king. For once Louis put aside his own asceticism in his attempts to persuade the erudite French nobility: "He even allowed himself to be splendidly dressed," medieval historian Jean Richard observed. The king offered other inducements as well; those who agreed to a one-year contract (dating from the day the excursion landed overseas) were to be well paid, even eating at the king's expense. Additionally, in many instances, Louis underwrote the entire cost of the journey and guaranteed to replace any horse lost in the line of duty. In this way, the king of France seems to have managed to scrounge together an army of respectable size, although not apparently of the magnitude of his former effort. There seems to have been a general lack of enthusiasm all around: even the vigorous St Pol had to be bribed 1,200 livres over and above his contracted salary of 2,000 livres before agreeing to sign up.

Charles's support was imperative. Louis needed ships and men from Sicily; his brother's personal participation would lend the affair an aura of capability. But Charles was evidently as reluctant about a crusade to the Holy Land as the rest of the French nobility. Rather, the king of Sicily, seeking to expand his holdings, planned to invade Constantinople. By 1267 he had entered into several diplomatic agreements designed to forward this goal, including the exchange of friendly ambassadors with the Mamlūks, the very Muslims Louis was now proposing to attack. Charles was hard-pressed to refuse his brother, however, so when Louis sent messengers asking the king of Sicily to put off his own war in favor of the crusade, Charles reluctantly complied. But it is clear that he wasn't happy about it.

Having secured his base, Louis applied himself once again to the question of international recruitment. Marguerite watched helplessly as her husband, convinced of the sacredness of his motives and the invincibility of his plan, issued an appeal to her sister's family in England.

The England to which Eleanor had returned at the end of October 1265 was by no means peaceful. Although the battle of Evesham had destroyed the rebellion's leaders, there were still pockets of fierce resistance that needed to be eliminated. The unstable political situation was further exacerbated by the policy of vengeful retaliation, which the victorious royalists pursued. At a hastily convened parliament in Winchester in September, those barons who had fought with Edward demanded and received a wholesale transfer of property from their former opponents. "At this parliament . . . he deprived of their inheritances all those who had stood by Earl Simon against their lord the king, and soon afterwards gave their lands to those who had faithfully adhered to the king, recompensing each one according to his deserts," wrote a chronicler.

The royal family did especially well at this parliament. Edward was awarded the castle at Dover and Edmund, perhaps to console him for the loss of Sicily, received Simon de Montfort's vast earldom of Leicester, the most prestigious and lucrative property in the kingdom. The city of London was fined the crippling sum of twenty thousand marks, which Henry intended to use to buy back those three English bishoprics that Eleanor, in her desperation, had pledged to Louis. The queen was not forgotten. She received her share of the reclaimed lands. In a particularly divisive gesture, the king made a point of awarding her London Bridge. The result of all of this high-handed revenge was predictable: "The disinherited parties thereupon assembled together and indulged in pillage and incendiarism in all directions." Civil disorder ensued and violence settled over the land, conditions that had not been present during Simon de Montfort's regime.

Eleanor returned—but she did not rule. Confusing tragedies such as England had just experienced demand a scapegoat, and Eleanor made a convenient villain. Neither rebels nor royalists could forget that the queen of England had assembled a formidable invasion force on the opposite shore, which she had only been prevented from launching at the very last moment by the urgent supplication of the papal legate. She was also irredeemably identified with, and held responsible for, the obvious partiality of the crown for foreigners. The war had not put to rest this divisive issue; there remained the widespread perception that the queen had callously enriched her relatives and countrymen to the detriment of the kingdom. Eleanor made an immediate, symbolic effort to rehabilitate her image by bringing along a new legate dedicated to establishing a lasting peace with her on her return. If she believed that this gesture would reassure her subjects, she was mistaken. She was never forgiven. Of course, accepting London Bridge didn't help much, either.

It took a further three years to quell the last traces of the revolt. Guy de Montfort, Simon's third son, recovered from the terrible wounds he had sustained at Evesham and escaped to France; he was joined soon after by his elder brother Simon; clearly the Montforts still had friends in England. Those rebels remaining believed that the two would return at the head of a great army, which stiffened resolve. By May 1267 Henry and Eleanor were forced once again to employ St Pol and his knights for a short period to supplement native royalist forces. In fact, Guy and Simon went to fight for Charles in Sicily, another indication that Charles and Beatrice had supported the rebel cause against that of Henry and Eleanor in the civil war.

By 1268, however, peace was more or less established. Edward, who had been in his element during the fighting, found the subsequent quiet rather tedious. He tried to appease his lust for martial exercise by arranging tournaments, but they proved unsatisfactory. So when his uncle Louis announced he was going on crusade, Edward decided to go, too.

Louis was delighted. The king of France, said an English chronicler, "sent special messengers to Edward, the son of the king of England, begging him immediately to give him an interview; which request Edward at once complied with, and hastened across the Channel to meet the French king. The latter received him with a pleasant countenance, and after closely embracing him, explained the cause of his having sent for him as follows. The fact was, he said, that he wished to return to the Holy Land, and to have Edward as his companion in taming the barbarous fury of the Pagans."

Edward replied that, while he would ordinarily love to accompany Louis, at this time he was prevented from doing so as the recent civil war had unfortunately depleted his resources. "To this the king of France replied, 'I will,' said he, 'lend you thirty thousand marks of good and lawful money, or in fact, I will give you that amount, if you will only acquiesce in my wishes.' In fact, Edward was a man of lofty stature, of great courage and daring, and strong beyond measure; and the king of France considered himself fortunate if he could obtain such a companion. Edward, therefore, who had a no less desire than the king of France himself to enter on such an undertaking, consented to his wishes." Where Edward went, Henry of Almain went, and where they went, Edmund went, so all three of them took the cross on June 24, 1268, at Northampton.

Henry III was appalled. England had only just returned to a semblance of normality. The king himself was old and frail. He relied heavily on his eldest son for advice. There was no saying that order could be kept if Edward left, he argued. He asked him not to go, but Edward refused to listen.

Eleanor probably agreed with her husband but she was no longer in a position to demand obedience from her eldest son. Since his daring escape from Simon de Montfort and rescue of the king, the relationship between mother and son had changed. Edward's political influence dwarfed Eleanor's. The circle of powerful men that had once orbited the queen had vanished in the wake of the war. John Mansel had died before Eleanor's return to England; he did not live to see the monarchy restored. Uncle Peter succumbed in 1268; Uncle Boniface would follow in 1270. Edward did not turn to his mother for counsel. Rather, he did his best to exclude her from power. Deprived of her political base, Eleanor dared not oppose Edward's wishes or policies. She was much closer now to Edmund, who had been abroad with her during most of the civil war.

Plans for the crusade were set. To finance the expedition, the pope allowed the king of France to collect a tenth of the revenues of the Church in France; this was in addition to the tenth that Charles was already collecting for his Sicilian campaign. The local prelates tried to rebel. They did not wish to beggar themselves for another of the king's hapless crusades. A petition was dispatched to the pope, begging him to rescind the mandate; the petition was denied. Louis got his tenth.

The king of France and his forces were scheduled to embark from the port of Aigues-Mortes in May 1270. His brother Alphonse and his three sons and daughter would leave with the king. Edward would follow shortly thereafter. Charles and his fleet would sail separately from Sicily.

On March 14, 1270, Louis inaugurated his crusade by once again accepting the pilgrim's staff at St. Denis. The next day, he walked barefoot from the palace to Notre Dame. Then he set off at the head of a large army for Provence. It was all exactly as it had been more than twenty years before, with one notable exception.

This time, Marguerite stayed home.

There was a slight delay in Provence—some of the ships Louis had contracted for were not yet available—so the crusaders did not actually set sail until July 2, 1270. It wasn't until the army was actually underway that Louis revealed to his troops and officers that their destination was not Acre, as everybody expected, but Tunis.

Tunis was a very odd choice for someone who had dedicated his life to the protection and rescue of the Holy Land. And certainly, the Holy Land was in desperate need of rescuing at that moment. The Mamlūks, fearful of a combined French-Mongol attack, had turned on the native Christian community with a vengeance. All of those settlements that Louis had so carefully and expensively fortified on his last visit had been overrun and destroyed.

Muslim fears of a joint attack were not unjustified. Louis had in fact been in contact with the Mongols. It seems that one of their leaders had been very impressed with the red silk tent that doubled as a portable chapel, which Louis had sent him just before the last crusade. It was mentioned specifically in a letter that had arrived in Paris in 1262, asking if the French king cared to join forces against the Egyptians. The Mongols were particularly interested in ships. If Louis would be so kind as to bring a fleet with him, they would appreciate it. In the letter, the Mongol leader offered the French Jerusalem as incentive. Louis's response to this proposal is not known, but it is possible that the king of France chose Tunis with the Mongol offer in mind, as a base from which to protect his army from attack while he waited for the Mongols. This may have been what the chronicler Villani meant when he explained, "And believing it to be the better course they determined to go against the kingdom of Tunis, thinking that if it could be taken by the Christians they would be in a very central place whence they could more easily afterwards take the kingdom of Egypt, and could cut off and wholly impede the force of the Saracens."

But it is also possible that the king of France diverted the military campaign to Tunis as a result of Charles's influence. Mohammed, the emir of Tunis, had favored Manfred and Conradin in the Sicilian succession, and had given sanctuary to their supporters and other disgruntled Sicilians. Subsequently, the emir had encouraged rebellion to Charles's rule in Italy. Worse, by the new king of Sicily's standards, was that Mohammed was supposed to be paying him an annual stipend of 34,300 gold coins and since Charles's ascension he had fallen in arrears. Louis would have known of the debt.

The king of France told his confessor before he left that the reason he chose Tunis was because he believed that he could convert the emir to Christianity. There remains the still-unanswered question of who put the idea into Louis's head that somebody named "Mohammed" would be eagerly awaiting conversion to Christianity.

Whatever the reason, the crusaders sailed for Tunisia. Just this once the weather behaved, and Louis's fleet arrived altogether and unscathed on July 18. The port of Tunis was found to be undefended and was therefore taken quickly. Mohammed had been alerted to French intentions and had sent for reinforcements before retreating behind the walls of the capital city, some miles inland. Lacking fresh water, Louis moved away from the port and instead installed his army on a plain outside the city of Carthage, "the which Carthage, whereof some part had been rebuilt and fortified by the Saracens in defense of the port was very soon stormed by the Christians," wrote Villani. Louis did not move his army inside the city walls, but stayed camped out in the heat of August awaiting the arrival of Charles of Anjou. The crusaders were still fifteen miles from the city of Tunis.

Waiting is never pleasant; waiting in a confined space, even if it is out of doors, with hordes of unwashed compatriots in oppressive heat and humidity, was torture. It was also fatal. Almost as soon as the French arrived, Louis's soldiers fell ill. Salimbene called it plague, but most likely it was typhus. "And when the Christians would have entered into the city of Tunis, as it pleased God, by reason of the sins of the Christians, the air of those shores began to be greatly corrupted, and above all in the camp of the Christians, by reason that they were not accustomed to the air, and by reason of their hardships and the excessive crowding of men and animals," explained Villani. The army was decimated. Jean Tristan, whose twenty-year-old life was bookended by his father's two futile crusades, died in ten days. It took the papal legate and the cardinal of Alba a little longer, and with these died also "a large number of counts and barons and commoners," wrote Salimbene. "Not only the water but the very trees spread fever," asserted another chronicler. Crown Prince Philip also sickened.

As was to be expected of an older man in weakened condition, King Louis himself fell ill. He outlived Jean Tristan by three weeks. Just before he died, he called his eldest son to his bedside and left him instructions on how to be a good king. The advice was recorded by Joinville. It is a sincere, devout letter, which outlines principles which form the essence of good government. "Maintain the good customs of your realm and abolish the bad ones," the dying father admonished the son.

> Do not be greedy in your demands on your people, or impose heavy taxes on them except in a case of emergency . . . Take care to have around you people, whether clerics or laymen, who are wise, upright, and loyal, and free from covetousness. Talk with them often, but shun and fly from association with the wicked . . . In order to deal justly and equitably with your subjects, be straightforward and firm, turning neither to the right hand nor to the left, but always following what is just, and upholding the cause of the poor till the truth be made clear . . . You must give your attention to ensuring that your subjects live peaceably and uprightly under your rule . . . Take special care to have good bailiffs and provosts, and often inquire of them, as also of people attached to your household, how they conduct themselves . . .

Louis's reign was one of largely unrealized potential. The king of France was born with every advantage. He was diligently educated and admired. The first three decades of his life were spent in the protective care of an extremely competent mother, who bequeathed him the largest, strongest, most stable kingdom in Europe. The depth of the anguish that resulted from his first crusade, and his obvious desire to redeem himself through good works, was so poignant that his subjects generously forgave him the disaster and shame. The world respected his suffering and looked to him as to a moral compass. For a brief, exalted period he made good on the principles he so piously espoused. He made peace with his neighbors, fed the poor, dispensed justice to the best of his ability. He built the exquisite Sainte-Chapelle. But in the end he used all of that trust, goodwill, and deference not to improve his subjects' well-being about which he professed to care so much, but as an excuse to lead them to a ghastly, fetid plain in Tunisia with the intent of annihilating an alien culture for the greater glory of God.

By the end he was so weak he could barely speak. He died on August 25, 1270, in a tent, on a bed covered with ashes at his own request. His last words were "I will come into thy house . . . I will worship in thy holy temple. O Jerusalem! O Jerusalem!"

Well should Louis IX, king of France, sigh for Jerusalem. That saintly man twice led thousands of his countrymen to their deaths and bankrupted his kingdom, and he never even got to set foot in the city.

Shield with fleurs-de-lis and crown of King Louis IX of France.

★ ★ ★

Charles of Anjou arrived the very next day to find his brother dead. "And as the Christian army was groaning at the death of the king and the Saracens exulting, King Charles of Sicily, the king's brother, for whom he had sent before his death, arrived with a great army," reported Salimbene. Charles went first to the tent where his brother's body lay in state (and in the heat) and wailed with grief, prostrating himself at the corpse's feet. Then he recovered his composure and took stock of the situation. Louis's soldiers, although heartened by the arrival of the king of Sicily and his troops, were stricken and in disarray. For weeks Mohammed's forces, taking advantage of the crusaders' immobilization, had been tormenting the French with assassinations and small skirmishes. "They never dared come to a pitched battle with the Christians; but they came with ambushes and with artifices, and did them much hurt," noted Villani. Louis's army was used to large, organized battles and sieges and was unequipped to deal with the sort of guerrilla tactics employed by this amorphous enemy.

Charles took immediate command. He regrouped the French forces and wisely forbade individual initiatives, which decreased the incidents of ambush and improved morale. He packed up and marched the army forward toward Tunis. Getting away from the camp at Carthage ameliorated the unclean sanitary conditions and the soldiers' health improved. The king of Sicily was further aided by the weather; it rained soon after his arrival, which provided untainted drinking water. Prince Philip recovered sufficiently to be proclaimed king, and messengers were sent to France with the news of Louis's death. The crusaders began to believe that they could take Tunis after all.

But Charles had his own objectives. The king of Sicily did not want to fight. The march on Tunis was only a ploy to force Mohammed to come to terms. "The king of Tunis with his Saracens seeing themselves in evil case, and fearing to lose the city and the country round about, sought to make peace with King Charles . . . to which peace King Charles consented," wrote Villani. Charles struck a hard bargain and one highly advantageous to himself. The emir would become his vassal. All of Manfred's and Conradin's supporters would be expelled from Tunis. The annual tribute to Sicily would double and full restitution would be made for unpaid back payments. To compensate the crusaders for their troubles, Mohammed was to pay a further twenty thousand gold pieces (approximately five hundred thousand livres), of which Charles claimed a third.

Charles's self-interest in this agreement did not go unnoticed. If Tunis had been taken by force, medieval etiquette demanded that all who fought share in the product of the victory; by convincing Mohammed to surrender preemptively, Charles saved himself from having to divide the spoils. Some "blamed King Charles, saying that he did it through avarice, to the end he might henceforward, by reason of the said peace, always receive tribute from the king of Tunis for his own special benefit; for if the kingdom of Tunis had been conquered by all the host of the Christians, it would have afterwards pertained in part to the king of France, and to the king of England, and to the king of Navarre, and to the king of Sicily, and to the Church of Rome, and to divers other lords which were at the conquest," Villani explained. Certainly Edward, who arrived in Tunisia with Edmund and Henry of Almain on November 10, 1270, protested angrily when he found the terms concluded and himself and England excluded from benefiting financially.

But there was nothing Edward could do. The relief the French felt at being released from the obligations of Louis's crusade can be measured by the alacrity with which they accepted Charles's invitation to withdraw from Tunisia and accompany him to Sicily. The entire camp packed up and shipped out in a day. Edward, Edmund, and Henry simply turned their small fleet around and put to sea with everyone else on November 11 for the Sicilian port of Trapani.

There was a gale on the way back; the crusaders lost forty warships at the port of Trapani and King Philip and his wife only just escaped with their lives. This was taken as a further omen and it was decided that it would be best for everybody if they all went back to France by land. Yet even here tragedy and misfortune dogged their footsteps; the journey home through Italy resembled a funeral procession. Louis's daughter Isabelle lost her husband, the king of Navarre, to illness in Trapani in December 1270. She herself died the next year en route home. In January, King Philip's wife, the new queen of France, was thrown from her horse while trying to cross difficult terrain; she gave birth prematurely to a stillborn son who would have been heir to the throne, and herself died a few days later. Neither Alphonse of Poitiers nor his wife, Jeanne of Toulouse, ever made it back to France; they died, one day apart, in August 1271 near Genoa. The most virulent enemy of France could not have done a better job of decimating the French royal family than did Louis with his crusade.

Nor were the English spared. Edward, exceedingly frustrated at having arrived too late to participate in the operation in Tunis, alone among the crusaders decided to go on to Acre. Fearing he would be away from England for a few years, he sent Henry of Almain back with the French to administer Gascony in his absence. Henry passed through Viterbo to pay his respects to the pope. There he was betrayed. Guy de Montfort and his brother Simon, still seething over Henry's unfaithfulness to the English revolt, ambushed Richard of Cornwall's most-loved son while he was praying at church. According to the chroniclers, it is possible that Charles, for whom Guy worked, had something to do with it:

> Whilst the aforesaid lords were in Viterbo, there came to pass a scandalous and abominable thing, under the government of King Charles; for Henry . . . son of Richard of England, being in a church at Mass, at the hour when the sacrifice of the body of Christ was being celebrated, Guy, count of Montfort, which was vicar for King Charles in Tuscany, having no regard for reverence towards God, nor towards King Charles his lord, stabbed and slew with his own hand the said Henry in revenge for Count Simon of Montfort, his father, slain,

through his own fault, by the king of England. . . . The court was greatly disturbed, giving much blame therefore to King Charles, who ought not to have suffered this if he knew thereof, and if he did not know it he ought not to have let it go unavenged. But the said Count Guy, being provided with a company of men-at-arms on horse and on foot was not content only with having done the said murder . . . and took Henry by the hair, and dead as he was, he dragged him vilely without the church; and when he had done the said sacrilege and homicide, he departed from Viterbo, and came safe and sound into Maremma to the lands of Count Rosso, his father-in-law . . . For the which thing, Edward, after he became king, was never friendly towards King Charles, nor to his folk.

Marguerite, residing at the castle in Paris, had to wait until May 1271 for Philip and the rest of the survivors to straggle back to the capital. Although messengers had arrived previously with the news of Louis's death, it was only at this point that the queen mother discovered the magnitude of the loss that the crusade had wrought: her husband, son, daughter, son-in-law, daughter-in-law, prospective grandchild, and brother- and sister-in-law were all dead. Philip's first official act as king was to bury his father. A casket containing Louis's remains had accompanied him all the way from Tunis. The funeral procession wound its way mournfully through the streets of Paris. Louis IX was laid to rest at St. Denis, next to his eldest son. "As the scribe who, when producing a manuscript, illuminates it with gold and azure, so did our king illuminate his realm," Joinville eulogized. Marguerite's emotions on this occasion were not recorded.

No king of France ever led a crusade again.

The ripple effect of the Tunisian expedition continued. Also in May, Henry of Almain's coffin arrived in England. By all accounts, Richard of Cornwall, who had been informed of the savage murder only the previous month, was crushed by the loss of his son. The subsequent escape of Guy and Simon de Montfort from the Sicilian authorities added to his sorrow. Richard had his son's heart cut out and stored in a burial urn at Westminster; his body was interred on May 21, 1271, at the church at Hailes, next to Sanchia.

Richard was now sixty-two, and in failing health. The civil war had marked him, as it marked all of the royal family. His reputation was scarred by his performance at the battle of Lewes, where he had been discovered

cowering in a windmill. He had been forced to pay large sums to Simon de
Montfort, and, although his estates were returned to him after the war, it is
not clear if he ever recovered all of his property. He had been held at Kenilworth by Simon the younger during the battle of Evesham, and had gone
out of his way, after the war was over, to protect his overseer from the worst
of the king's and Edward's wrath. At Christmas 1266, Henry III, Eleanor,
and Richard were all at Northhampton when Simon the younger appeared
for an audience. "On his [Simon the younger's] arrival, the king of Germany
accompanied him into the king's presence, and there returned thanks to
Simon for having saved his life, stating that he should have been slain at
Kenilworth, at the time when Simon the father was killed, had he not been
rescued by the younger Simon; so enraged were the garrison of the castle at
the death of their lord. On account of this Simon was now admitted by the
king to the kiss of peace." How galling it must have been for Richard to
have this same man then turn around and murder his son.

Perhaps as a result of all of this melancholy, Richard had a stroke in
December 1271. His right side was paralyzed and he lost the ability to speak.
He died on April 2, 1272, and was buried next to Sanchia and Henry of
Almain at Hailes, although, as per his instructions, his heart was cut out and
buried at the Franciscan church at Oxford. Sanchia's child, Edmund, inher-
ited his father's title and property.

Richard left one further legacy, albeit unintended. Because he was such
a weak king, visiting Germany scarcely four times in fifteen years, a political
vacuum was created in the region during his reign. Upon his death a power
struggle ensued, and a new, much stronger leader, native to Germany this
time, emerged to take his place on the world stage. He came from what was
at the time a little-known family by the name of Habsburg.

Henry III was also ailing. He had fallen ill in January 1271, and his situation
was considered serious enough that he wrote to Edward in February asking
him to come home. Word of Louis IX's death had reached England, and
Henry and Eleanor knew that Louis's son Philip had decided to terminate
the crusade and return to Paris to assume his responsibilities as king. England
was still subject to periodic bursts of violence and Henry worried that if he
died the monarchy would again be compromised. But Edward was determined to honor his commitment to his uncle's crusade and sailed for Acre
instead. He would not return to England for another three years.

By the fall of 1272, Eleanor knew that Henry was dying. The king and queen were at Westminster. As Henry had predicted, the prospect of his demise had encouraged the citizenry of London, still angry over the harsh reparations forced on them after the civil war, to revolt. In an earlier time, Eleanor would have been an active participant in forming the crown's response, but now she was helpless. Even she knew that her involvement, particularly if Henry died, would only further inflame the city, so she left the task of pacification to the great barons who crowded around the king at the end, the "several earls and barons . . . as well as prelates [who] came there to be present at his last moments." Although there is no record of the queen's whereabouts at this time, it is unthinkable that Eleanor would not also have been at Henry's bedside as he grew weaker and weaker.

Henry III died on November 16, 1272. He was sixty-five years old and had reigned for fifty-six years. In that more than half-century he, in combination with his wife and her family, had tried to reinvent England as a great European power. In this attempt, he and Eleanor failed, and nearly lost everything. But there had also been achievements, most notably the establishment of a firm peace with France which would outlast his reign. For a man who possessed no real ability for leadership, whose talents lay principally in the realm of the aesthetic, who loved to live lavishly but had not the funds to do so, who was by turns generous, petulant, romantic, vindictive, pious, and partisan, Henry had done his best. He was buried with "all honor," according to an English chronicler. His body was laid in state and dressed in coronation robes; he wore his crown. His funeral was attended by all the great men of the kingdom. But for the absence of his two sons, it was all as Henry would have wished.

The king was buried in Westminster Abbey, which had been recently and gloriously renovated, in the tomb formerly containing the relics of Edward the Confessor. Somewhere between the wars and the oaths, the intrigues and the disappointments, Henry had found the time to express his great love of architecture in this one church; the artistic vision was his and his alone; he devoted years to its magnificent redesign. It still stands today, the great gift of the reign of a troubled king.

Thus, by the winter of 1272, of the great families of mid-thirteenth-century England, France, and Provence, only Marguerite, Eleanor, and Charles of Anjou remained. In one way or another, the last crusade of Louis IX had marked the end of a generation.

CHAPTER XXIII

ENDGAME

hilip III was twenty-five years old when he ascended to the throne of France. The new king had respected his father and wanted to abide by his principles. The problem was, he wasn't quite sure how to go about it. He wasn't the brightest of Marguerite's children; in addition, he lacked confidence and discipline. As a result, he was easily influenced by stronger personalities. Philip's admiration for his capable uncle Charles amounted almost to hero-worship. The situation was exacerbated by Philip's earlier training, which, as might be expected from a son of Louis IX, had centered primarily on religious instruction. Louis had bequeathed his son a set of lofty moral guidelines but not much practical experience with which to rule the largest, most powerful kingdom in Europe. On the whole, the new king much preferred to go hunting.

Marguerite was well aware of her son's limitations. After the sudden, unexpected death of her eldest son Louis in 1260, Marguerite, anticipating the political void that Philip's ascension would create, had followed the same path as her mother-in-law, Blanche of Castile. Taking her son aside in 1262 when he was seventeen, she asked him to swear an oath that he be guided by her judgment, and allow her to run the kingdom for him until he was thirty; that he obtain her permission before adding any advisers to the royal council; and, most important, that he not collude with his uncle Charles, or enter into any agreement contrary to her wishes with the then-count of Provence. Philip's response to her action was typical of his personality: he swore an oath before God to abide by everything

Marguerite had said, and then went and complained of her to his father. Louis, remembering only his own struggle to assert himself against parental authority and not the stability and experience his mother had provided to the kingdom during the early years of his reign, appealed to the pope to have the oath rescinded. (This was at approximately the same time that Henry and Eleanor were also trying to get their oaths agreeing to the Oxford Provisions rescinded; the pope was very busy that year overturning oaths.) The pope, who needed Louis's support for Charles's bid for the kingship of Sicily, was only too happy to oblige, and Marguerite's preemptive assay at power was summarily squelched.

Thus it came to pass that an indecisive, unsure young man assumed the throne after Louis's death with the predictable result. Lacking a vision of his own, Philip latched on to the designs of others, most particularly that of the ambitious Pierre de la Broce, who had been a minor official in his father's household. Pierre's vision was to accumulate as much power, prestige, and wealth for Pierre in as short a span of time as possible. The king's preoccupation with rewarding his new chief adviser left a gap in leadership, which various factions competed to fill; one of these was Marguerite's.

As ever, her focus was on Provence. Louis's death had in no way diminished his wife's determination to recover what she considered to be her property. French policy, with respect to the rest of Europe, was confused; her son's incompetence left her the flexibility to make one last strike against her opponent. She watched Charles carefully and waited for her opportunity.

Of course, he gave it to her. A man as intent as Charles was on acquiring an empire was bound to leave a little disaffection in his wake.

It started with Germany. Richard of Cornwall's death in 1272 had left the prestigious office of king of the Romans vacant. A number of candidates vied for the honor. Alfonso X of Castile wrote immediately to the pope, claiming that he had been the true choice of the German electors in 1259 and demanding that he finally be officially confirmed as king; but nobody wanted Alfonso, and the pope and the electors turned him down. Ottocar, the king of Bohemia, then announced his intention to pursue the position; being one of the electors, he knew he could count on at least one vote (his own). He was a much stronger candidate—too strong, in Charles's opinion; if Ottocar, who was rich and commanded a large army, was elected, Charles's influence in northern Italy might be contested. The king of Sicily could lose control of a key region. Charles would have liked to have put his own name forward for the title, but even he knew that the pope would never allow it. Charles was already senator of Rome and imperial vicar of Tuscany, in addition to being king of Sicily. To become king of the Romans and perhaps even emperor as well would make him more powerful than the pope, and this the pope would not permit.

So Charles went in search of someone who could be relied upon to do what Charles told him to do. Very soon he found him: his nephew, Philip III of France. During the summer of 1273, Charles wrote to the king of France suggesting that he announce his candidacy for the office, and promising him his full support. Philip thought this a capital idea and allowed his uncle to investigate the possibility with the pope. But the pope didn't want Philip any more than he'd wanted Charles, and for much the same reasons, so he turned him down as diplomatically as possible.

The absence of a strong outside candidate allowed the German electors to proffer one of their own statesmen for the post: Rudolph of Habsburg. Rudolph was intelligent, well-off, and familiar with German political problems, of which there were many. Richard of Cornwall's fourteen-year absentee administration had encouraged petty power struggles, which in turn had led to outbursts of violence. The electors wanted someone who could control the kingdom and provide stability and prosperity. The pope, too, was willing to support Rudolph. The Habsburg's relative anonymity worked in his favor. If no one had ever heard of him, the Church reasoned, it was unlikely that Rudolph would be powerful enough to cause the papacy problems. Accordingly, Rudolph of Habsburg was elected in October 1273, by a vote of six to one, Ottocar of Bohemia receiving the one opposing vote— his own.

The German election provided the opening for which Marguerite had been searching. Immediately after Rudolph's coronation in Aachen, the queen mother penned a flattering letter to the new king of the Romans, congratulating him on his ascension to the throne and asking for his help. As historically Provence had been a fief of the empire, she wrote, would he, as its new sovereign, undertake to rule on the subject of her inheritance?

This was clever of Marguerite, as the king of the Romans' suzerainty over Provence (and therefore over Charles, its count) was by no means a settled matter. By pretending that it was an established fact, Marguerite put the idea into Rudolph's mind. If the queen mother of France believed that the new king of the Romans held authority over Provence, well, then, perhaps he did. Certainly, he could use the support of this mighty neighbor to the west. If the price of Marguerite's friendship—and she was clearly offering friendship—was the bestowal of a county that he hadn't known he'd owned in the first place, and couldn't actually control, well, then, Rudolph could afford to be generous. He behaved just as Marguerite had hoped, promising to invest her with Provence.

Although Rudolph's response was encouraging, the French queen mother knew that the king of the Romans would not keep his word unless he was convinced that his own interests were served by the bequest. She sought to broker an understanding, buttressed by an alliance, which would be of obvious benefit to Rudolph. To do that, she would need help and so turned to her one remaining sister, the queen mother of England.

By the mid-1270s, Eleanor's political standing in England was not nearly as solid as was Marguerite's in France. Edward and his wife, Eleanor of Castile, had returned from their crusade in August 1274, and been crowned king and queen at a magnificent ceremony at Westminster Hall. "To the south of the old palace as many palaces were built on all sides as room could be found for, and in them tables were set, firmly fixed in the earth, for the refreshment of magnates and princes and nobles on the coronation day and for fifteen days afterwards; so that all men, poor and rich, coming to the ceremony, might be freely received, and no body sent away," enthused a chronicler. Edward's popularity had only increased in his absence. On the journey home, he had dined with the pope and been fêted by kings, just as his late uncle, Richard of Cornwall, had more than thirty years before; like Richard, as a result of this world tour, Edward was awarded a high degree of respect by his peers and was generally viewed as a statesman of great international presence. England had almost forgotten what it was like to have such a personable, erudite young man as ruler. In addition, his subjects rather liked Edward's being an athlete, and took pride in his military accomplishments. It was such a change from Henry.

Eleanor of Castile was also accorded an approval bordering on adulation. The new queen had been an active participant on the crusade. A story had filtered back to London that when a corps of elite Saracen swordsmen, sent by the Mamlūk sultan to assassinate Edward, had succeeded in stabbing him with a poisoned saber, Eleanor of Castile had saved her husband's life by sucking the toxin from his wound. Edward loved his wife very much and respected her judgment. He frequently employed her as a diplomatic envoy.

In this happy marital and political atmosphere there was no room for a disgraced fifty-one-year-old queen mother. Eleanor was all that remained of a regime that most of England preferred to forget; the ugliness of the years of civil war still clung to her like a soiled cloak she could not remove. She lived in semi-retirement, traveling between her various estates in Guildford, Marlborough, and Amesbury. Ironically, money, which had been the cause of so much strife for Eleanor during her years in power, was now no longer a problem. The deaths of Henry and Uncle Peter had left her rich.

Still, she roused herself to aid Marguerite in her scheme. The one royal arena left to Eleanor in which she still held influence was in the arranging of her grandchildren's marriages. Between them, she and Marguerite agreed that, to encourage Rudolph to honor his bequest, Rudolph's son Hartmann should become engaged to Edward's daughter Joanna. When Marguerite died, Provence would then go to Hartmann and Joanna. In 1278 Marguerite herself wrote to Edward to confirm the compact. In her letter she observed that, "The marriage of the son of the German king to your daughter . . . will provide an occasion for celebration."

Marguerite had a very special relationship with her nephew Edward. To Marguerite, Edward was everything Philip wasn't. Edward also very much admired his aunt, more so, it would seem, than his own mother. The French queen had been of unfailing support during the English civil war, and he knew that without her participation he might very well have been deprived of his birthright. Edward enthusiastically embraced Marguerite's proposal.

But Charles had learned of the plot. It is possible that King Philip himself informed his uncle of the particulars. Philip was by now under a new influence. In 1274 he had taken a second wife, Marie, daughter of the duke of Brabant. At nineteen, Marie was canny and adroit. Unlike Marguerite, who had been cowed into acquiescing to her mother-in-law's policies and domination, Marie's instinct was to attack those who stood in her way. As she was not particularly scrupulous about her methods, the new queen of France was enormously successful. She dispatched her husband's former confidante, Pierre de la Broce, with admirable efficiency. Soon after her arrival at court, letters were found implicating Pierre in treasonable activity; the counselor was tried, sentenced to death, and hanged six months later. Pierre went to the gallows protesting his innocence and swearing that the documents were forgeries. The letters themselves disappeared mysteriously after the trial. The entire affair was questionable enough to have Dante refer to it in Canto VI of *Purgatory:* "I saw that soul/torn from its body, so he said, by hate/and envy—not for any wrong he did:/Pierre de la Brosse, I mean. And while still here/on earth the Lady of Brabant [Marie] might well/take care lest she end up in fouler flock."

Marie was not interested in having a mother-in-law who meddled in French politics. At her urging, Philip, who was already stung by his mother's partiality to Edward, swung his allegiance to Uncle Charles.

Charles, faced with the possibility of an alliance between Germany and England against him, made haste to offer Rudolph a counterproposal, buttressed by a different set of marital arrangements. In exchange for Charles remaining count of Provence, Charles would arrange for his grandson, Charles Martel (eldest son of Charles's eldest son, Charles, prince of Salerno; the family was not imaginative when it came to naming boys) to marry one of Rudolph's daughters, Clementia. Charles Martel and Clementia would be given the kingdom of Arles outright once they came of age (Charles Martel was only seven at the time), except in this case Arles would not include Provence.

Marguerite's response is indicated by the flurry of letters she wrote to Edward, asking him to please use his influence with her son Philip to encourage him to support his mother's interests over those of his uncle's. Eleanor added her pleas to Marguerite's, writing in 1279:

> Know, sweet son, that we have understood that a marriage is in agitation between the son of the King of Sicily and the daughter of the King of Germany; and, if this alliance is made, we may well be disturbed in the right that we have to the fourth part of Provence, which thing would be great damage to us, and this damage would be both ours and yours. Wherefore we pray and require you, that you will specially write to the aforesaid king, that since Provence is held from the empire, and his dignity demands that he should have right done to us about it, he will regard the right that we have, and cause us to hold it. Of this thing we especially require you, and we commend you to God.

But Marguerite did not content herself with writing letters. In the fall of 1281, at the formidable age of sixty, she organized an alliance of noblemen opposed to Charles and convened a meeting in Troyes, about a hundred miles southeast of Paris. The meeting was attended by the duke of Burgundy, her uncle Philippe of Savoy, the archbishop of Lyons, and others.

Marguerite herself rode to Troyes and was in attendance. The conspirators decided that the marriage of Charles Martel and Clementia must be opposed by force. It was known that the king of Sicily intended to send a fleet to Marseille and up the Rhône the following spring to secure Arles for his grandson. Marguerite's alliance promised to meet again in May 1282 in Lyons—and to bring an army with them.

Again, Marguerite turned to England. She knew that her best chance of success lay with Edward: if the king of England undertook to provide and lead troops against Charles, the king of Sicily would face a formidable opponent. But Edward, who was by this time distracted by a military operation in Wales, and who feared to provoke war with France if he supported Marguerite's initiative against her son Philip's (and his wife Marie's) wishes, withdrew his support. Moreover Hartmann, the prospective bridegroom, chose this inopportune moment to die unexpectedly. These factors had a deflating effect upon the other belligerents in Marguerite's conspiracy. The promised army never materialized. In 1282 Charles's ships sailed up the Rhône uncontested.

But the resentment engendered by Charles's opportunism did not dissipate; it simply shifted to a different venue. It would be left to Marguerite's cousins, Peter and Constance, king and queen of Aragon, to orchestrate the king of Sicily's downfall.

Constance was Manfred's daughter. She had never forgiven Charles for her father's death, and always believed that the kingdom of Sicily by rights belonged to her. Her husband agreed with her. For some time, these two had been secretly fomenting insurrection to Charles's rule in Sicily through an agent who knew the island well. Peter and Constance had a large fleet waiting to strike as soon as the Sicilians revolted, which they did on March 29, 1282, in an incident known as "the Sicilian Vespers." By October Peter and Constance had taken Sicily. At a defining battle in June 1284, Charles and Beatrice's eldest son, Charles of Salerno, impulsively attacked Peter and Constance's rebel forces against his father's orders before Charles had a chance to return from Provence with reinforcements. The rebels won. Charles arrived with a fleet the next day. "Who loses a fool loses nothing. Why is he not dead for disobeying us?" Charles is reported to have snarled when told of his eldest son's capture.

The revolt in Sicily acted as a catalyst for other rebellions against Charles and marked the end of his empire. By Christmas 1284 he was on the run and his health was failing. He died on January 7, 1285, in Foggia and was buried in Naples. "And take note, that he died on the same day on which he had been crowned many years before," wrote Salimbene. "A certain holy woman had received great visions about his death . . . 'It seemed to me that I was in a large, very beautiful garden, where I saw a huge, terrible dragon,'" the chronicler reported the woman as saying. "'Terrified by its appearance, I began a headlong flight. The dragon, however, swiftly pursued me, crying out and begging in a human voice, wait for him, because he wished to talk to me. When I heard the human voice, I stopped to hear what he had to say. And turning, I said to him, "Who are you, and what do you want to tell me?" And he answered, "I am King Charles, who was living in this beautiful garden, but King Peter of Aragon has now expelled me with a piece of flesh." The dragon in the dream was speaking of the wife of Peter of Aragon, on behalf of whom he occupied Sicily in opposition to Charles.'"

There is no evidence that Marguerite actively aided Peter and Constance in this intrigue. But it was impossible that the queen mother of France did not know of it. Aragonese intentions to take Sicily were an open secret. As early as 1282, Philip III had warned his uncle that Peter and Constance had organized a massive fleet against him. What her son and everybody else knew, Marguerite knew. Of her approval of the conspiracy there can be no doubt. Whether her encouragement was only tacit, or something more tangible, may never be known.

EPILOGUE

Eleanor of Provence lived to be sixty-eight years old. By the time of her death on June 24, 1291, she had buried all three of her daughters, and several of her grandchildren. In July 1286 she had taken the veil and retired to a nunnery in Amesbury. Nunneries were the assisted-living facilities of the Middle Ages, and Eleanor had made sure that the prioress would take good care of her by quietly funding the establishment for years. She seems even to have provided the lumber for the building of her own compartment. Technically, those entering the Church were supposed to give up all of their worldly possessions, but Eleanor wangled a special decree to hang on to a significant portion of her property. It wasn't necessarily that the queen mother eschewed the proper religious feeling; it was just that, after a lifetime spent scrounging around for money, Eleanor wasn't about to part voluntarily with her various estates and annuities.

Toward the very end of her life she was involved in a last, futile bid to obtain sainthood for Henry. By 1290 it was clear that Louis was going to be canonized, and Eleanor, recognizing that the honor would forever erase the debacle of the French king's two failed crusades, and that as a result Louis's reputation would eclipse her husband's, mounted her own campaign to secure a similar status for Henry. It was the remnant of her lifelong quest to have the crown of England accorded the same respect internationally as that of France, and it failed, just as all of her other attempts toward this goal had failed. The French effort was far more advanced and well-organized; Eleanor could not even convince Edward to support her initiative on his father's behalf. They had a row in 1281 when Eleanor reported that she'd had a visit from a knight who swore that he had been blind but could now see as a result of visiting Henry's tomb. This was just the kind of miracle she needed to press her case in Rome. But Edward would have nothing to do with it, and warned his mother that the knight was a charlatan, and that was the end of Henry's sainthood.

Nothing was ever easy for Eleanor; she weathered disappointment after disappointment; even her death was anticlimactic. On November 28, 1290, seven months before her own demise, the queen mother and the rest of England were startled by the sudden, swift loss to illness of Edward's wife, Eleanor of Castile. Edward was distraught and in the agony of his sorrow he arranged a funeral of historic dimensions. Eleanor of Castile's body was carried in state from Lincoln to London, and Edward planned a series of exquisite crosses, reminiscent of those used to mark Louis IX's burial procession, to be erected along the way. The king then had his wife buried in Westminster Abbey, next to the tomb of his father. In an interesting footnote, after the ceremony, Edward turned for solace not to his mother or brother, but to his cousin Edmund of Cornwall, gentle Sanchia's son. Edmund was very religious and employed his time and money in works of charity. It seems that Sanchia's legacy of quiet devotion had been passed on to her only child.

Thus it was that Eleanor of Provence lived long enough to know that there would be no grand funeral for her at Westminster. Her son had already given away her burial spot, next to Henry, to his own wife. When the queen mother finally died, the nuns of Amesbury had to write to Edward, who was in Scotland, to find out what to do with her corpse. Edward told the prioress to store his mother's body until he returned to England for her funeral. He does not appear to have hurried. Eleanor of Provence wasn't buried until September 8, 1291; it must have taxed the nuns' ingenuity to find an appropriately cool nook in which to shield the queen mother's remains during those hot summer months. Her son Edmund was present at her funeral as well. The chroniclers tell us that the ceremony was handled "with great reverence" and that she was buried "in the presence of a great gathering of the most influential men of England and France." But it was still Amesbury and not Westminster. Her heart was cut out as per her instructions and later interred in a gold box in the Franciscan church in London.

It is hard to believe that this was the sort of end that Eleanor of Provence, who loved privilege and pomp and grandeur, and who ached for distinction, would have wanted. Nor is it necessarily what she deserved. Her reign was marked by strife, and she had certainly made mistakes, but through it all her energy was unflagging, her loyalties true, and her dreams large. She may have been buried a nun, but throughout her long life she was, in every sense, a queen.

And so, finally, only Marguerite was left.

Marguerite, too, outlived all but three of her children, including the king. After Charles of Anjou's death in 1284, Philip III decided to avenge his uncle's honor by attacking Peter of Aragon, and took a large army down to Spain the following year. Unfortunately, Philip had inherited his father's military capabilities. After losing a short skirmish, the king of France ordered his troops to retreat. Disease plagued the army on the long road home and Philip died on October 5, 1285, somewhere in the Pyrénées. "King Philip of France, seeing his fortune so changed and adverse, and his fleet, which was bringing victuals to his host, taken and burnt, was overcome with grief and melancholy in such wise that he fell grievously sick with fever and a flux, wherefore his barons took counsel to depart and return to Toulouse . . . And thus they departed about the first day of October, carrying their sick king in a litter, and they dispersed with but little order, each one getting away as best he could," reported Villani. "This enterprise against Aragon was attended with greater loss of men and more cost in horses and money, than the realm of France had almost ever suffered in times past; for afterwards the king which succeeded the said Philip, and the greater part of the barons, were always in debt and ill provided with money." As a result of this expedition, Philip was awarded the sobriquet le Hardi, or Philip the Bold. His body was brought back in state and he was buried with his father in the basilica of St. Denis. His son Philip, known as Philip the Fair, became king.

The death of her son in a manner so reminiscent of that of her husband seems finally to have convinced Marguerite to accept defeat with respect to Provence; in any event she did not interfere politically in her grandson's regime. She passed the last years of her life quietly, occupied mostly in charitable enterprises. After Charles of Anjou's death, Provence stayed in his and Beatrice's family, going first to Beatrice's son Charles of Salerno and later to one of her grandsons. The economic benefits of Charles's empire were such that his Provençal subjects remained loyal to his line of succession, but there would be no more gracious courts in the tradition of Raymond Berenger V; all of Charles's descendants preferred, or were forced by political necessity, to live abroad. With no grand patron available locally to provide the appropriately elegant and lucrative environment, the troubadours of Provence, once numerous, followed the royal court to Naples or simply drifted away. The Italy of Dante, Petrarch, and Boccaccio, not Provence, would serve as the backdrop to the great literary and cultural achievements of the next century.

Louis's canonization investigation, which had begun at Philip III's request the year after his father's death, proceeded into the 1290s. Two prelates established themselves at St. Denis "and remained there for some considerable time to make inquisition into the life, the works, and miracles of this saintly king," Joinville reported. All of the family and many important barons, including Joinville himself, were called upon to provide testimony. (Before he died, Charles of Anjou gave evidence to the effect that, in his opinion, all of Blanche of Castile's sons deserved sainthood, but the pope did not take the hint.) Louis's children were especially active in promoting their father's pious image. Marguerite's eldest daughter, Isabelle, queen of Navarre, who along with her husband had perished on her father's second crusade, was the inspiration for Joinville's *Life of Saint Louis*. "Our lady, the Queen your mother [Isabelle]—may God grant her grace—begged me most earnestly to have a book written for her containing the pious sayings and the good deeds of our King, Saint Louis," Joinville wrote in the dedication to his work. This unprecedented, coordinated effort to edit, mold, and control Louis's image had a lasting, positive effect on his reputation and contributed significantly to the 1298 decision in favor of sainthood.

Marguerite did not live to see her husband's body lifted from the grave by her grandchildren at the canonization ceremony, but perhaps that is just as well. Through all the long years of inquiry in Paris, she alone among his intimate acquaintances refused to testify in favor of Louis's sainthood. The thirteen-year-old girl who had arrived newly married, vulnerable, and shy on that summer day in Paris sixty years before died a venerated old woman on December 21, 1295, at the age of seventy-four. The chronicler of Reims called Marguerite "a very good and wise lady." She was buried by royal decree in the family vault at St. Denis.

Perhaps more than any of her sisters, Marguerite embodied the paradoxes of her age. She had reigned in Paris and survived in Egypt. If she had donned ermine and reveled in the splendor of a coronation, she had also experienced the anxiety of a sea voyage and the terror of a siege. She had wrestled with divided loyalties, adjudicated for fairness, and schemed for advantage. Her determination was inspiring.

Marguerite's grandson, Philip the Fair, arranged and attended her funeral, which was conducted with the grandeur and solemnity befitting a queen of France. In England, Edward mourned the death of his favorite aunt and ordered bells rung to mark her passing.

A NOTE ON MEDIEVAL MONEY

Like everything else about the Middle Ages, styles of money varied from place to place, and understanding the relationship between denominations can therefore be confusing. In fact, in the thirteenth century, there was only one type of coin in existence: a small, silver piece known in England as a penny and in France as a denier. In England, twelve pennies equaled a shilling (although there were no shillings minted, you simply counted out twelve pennies into someone's hand); in France twelve deniers equaled a sous (although, likewise, there were no sous in existence). There were, in England, 20 shillings or 240 pennies to a pound sterling; in France there were 20 sous or 240 deniers to a livre. Once again, there was no actual coin struck representing a pound or a livre; to pay off the debt of a pound the debtor handed the creditor a sack containing 240 pennies; in France, to pay off the debt of a livre, the sack would contain 240 deniers. In England, just to make the concept as complicated as possible, they also measured silver by a weight measure called the mark. A mark was two-thirds the weight of a pound sterling, so a mark of silver was the same as 160 pennies. But if the debt was in marks, you didn't have to supply pennies, a person could use any silver he or she happened to have lying around the house, like a silver plate, just so long as it weighed the right number of marks. When Henry and Eleanor promised to pay the pope 135,541 marks to fund Edmund's campaign for the kingship of Sicily, they were promising to pay approximately £90,812, or nearly three years' income, some of which, presumably, could have come in the form of the royal dining service. (Or, more to the point, they remitted other peoples' dinner plates, which is one of the reasons the baronage rebelled.)

Just like today, French money and English money differed sufficiently so as to require a rate of exchange. In France, the quality and fineness of a denier (and therefore of a livre composed of those deniers) varied so much that the coins were labeled by location, which is why some of the French sums mentioned in *Four Queens* were specified as livres tournois (minted in Tours, of high quality) and others as livres parisis (minted in Paris, of much lower quality). Whenever I used the generic term livres, as I did when noting the cost of Louis IX's crusade, I did so because the type of money used was not specified by a chronicler, and in those cases I generally assumed livres parisis. The exchange rate in 1265 between livres parisis and the pound sterling was 90 sous (or 1,080 deniers) to the pound. To make it easier, there were 4½ livres parisis to a pound sterling, and 3 livres parisis to a mark. The annual French royal income of 250,000 livres (most likely livres parisis) was therefore the equivalent of about £55,556, a much larger sum than was available to their English counterparts. Henry and Eleanor only had an average annual income of about £36,000.

Anyone who wants to go deeper into this subject should definitely read Peter Spufford's authoritative and comprehensive work, *Money and Its Use in Medieval Europe* (Cambridge University Press, 1988), and its complement, *The Handbook of Medieval Exchange.*

Thomas, Count of Savoy — **Marguerite of Geneva**
[Grandfather of the Four Queens]   [Grandmother of the Four Queens]
b. 1178–d. 1233   d.1258

THE UNCLES FROM SAVOY

Amadeus IV	**Humbert**	**Aymon**	**Guillaume**	**Thomas**	**Beatrice**	**Peter**	**Boniface**	**Philippe**	**Marguerite**
b. 1197–d. 1253	d. 1223	d.1237	Bishop-elect of Valence b. 1201–d. 1239	Count of Flanders b. 1203–d. 1259 married Joan of Flanders in 1237	[Mother of the Four Queens] b. 1207–d. 1265 married Raymond Berenger V, Count of Provence in 1219	Earl of Richmond b. 1208–d. 1268	Archbishop of Canterbury d. 1270	d. 1285	d. 1273

THE FOUR QUEENS

Marguerite	**Eleanor**	**Sanchia**	**Beatrice**
Queen of France b. 1221–d. 1296 married Louis IX, King of France in 1234	Queen of England b. 1223–d. 1291 married Henry III, King of England in 1236	Queen of the Romans [Germany] b. 1228–d. 1261 married Richard, Earl of Cornwall and King of the Romans in 1242	Queen of Sicily b. 1231–d.1267 married Charles, Count of Anjou and King of Sicily in 1246

IN FRANCE

Philip Augustus
King of France
[Louis IX's Grandfather]
b. 1165–d. 1223

Isabel of Hainault
Queen of France
[Louis IX's Grandmother]
b. 1170–d. 1190

Louis VIII
King of France
b. 1187–d. 1226

Blanche of Castile
Queen of France
b. 1188–d. 1252

LOUIS IX'S BROTHERS AND SISTERS

Loius IX
King of France
b. 1214–d. 1270
married Marguerite
of Provence
in 1234

Robert
Count of Artois
b. 1216–d. 1250
[killed on crusade
in Mansourah]

John
b. 1219–d. 1227

Alphonse
Count of Poitiers
b. 1220–d. 1271
married Jeanne
of Toulouse
in 1237

Philip Dagobert
b. 1222–d. 1235

Isabella
b. 1223–d. 1269

Charles
Count of Anjou and
King of Sicily
b. 1226–d. 1285
married Beatrice of
Provence in 1246

MARGUERITE'S CHILDREN

Blanche
b. 1240–d. 1243

Isabelle
Queen of
Navarre
b. 1242–d. 1271

Louis
b. 1244–d. 1260

Philip III
King of
France
b. 1245–
d. 1285

Jean Tristan
b. 1250–d. 1270

Peter
b. 1251–d. 1284

Blanche
b. 1253–d. 1323

Marguerite
b. 1254–d. 1271

Robert
b. 1256–d. 1318

Agnes
b. 1260–d. 1327

BEATRICE OF PROVENCE'S CHILDREN

Louis
b. 1248–d. 1249

Blanche
b. 1250–d. 1269

Beatrice
b. 1252–d. 1275

Charles II
King of Naples and
Count of Provence
b. 1254–d. 1309

Robert
b. 1258–d. 1265

Maria
b. 1261–d. 1300

IN ENGLAND

Henry II
King of England
[Grandfather of Henry III]
b. 1133–d. 1189

Eleanor of Aquitaine
Queen of England
[Grandmother of Henry III]
b. 1122–d. 1204

William
b. 1153–d. 1156

Henry
b. 1155–d. 1183

Matilda
b. 1156–d. 1189

Richard (the Lionheart)
b. 1157–d. 1199

Eleanor
Queen of Castile
b. 1162–d. 1215
married Alfonso, King of Castile
her daughter,

Blanche of Castile,
married Louis VIII, King of France

Joan
b. 1165–d. 1199

John
King of England
b. 1167–d. 1216
married Isabella of Angoulême
in 1200

HENRY III'S BROTHERS AND SISTERS

Henry III
King of England
b. 1207–d. 1272
married Eleanor of Provence
in 1236

Richard
Earl of Cornwall and
King of the Romans
b. 1209–d. 1272
married Isabella Marshal
her son,

Henry of Almain,
d. 1271
then Richard married
Sanchia of Provence in 1242
Her son was

Joan
b. 1210–d. 1238

Isabella
b. 1214–d. 1241
married Frederick II
Holy Roman Emperor in 1235
Her son was

Henry
b. 1237–d. 1252

Eleanor
b. 1215–d. 1275
married Simon de Montfort
Earl of Leicester in 1238

Edmund
Earl of Cornwall
b. 1249–d. 1300

ELEANOR'S CHILDREN

Edward I
King of England
b. 1239–d. 1307
married Eleanor
of Castile

Margaret
b. 1240–d. 1275
married
Alexander III,
King of Scots

Beatrice
b. 1243–d. 1275

Edmund
b. 1245–d. 1296

Katharine
b. 1253–d. 1257

BIBLIOGRAPHIC NOTE

Any work of medieval history requires the piecing together of diverse sources to produce a coherent narrative and *Four Queens* is no exception. Fortunately, an amazing amount of information has survived from the thirteenth century, including letters, edicts, tax rolls, and household accounts. But the enduring gift from the thirteenth century will always be the stories penned by the chroniclers.

The chroniclers were self-appointed historians, often members of religious houses, who took on the task of recording the events of the day for posterity. It is no hardship to read the chroniclers; for the most part they were people of enormous talent who felt compelled to write. Their voices are authentic, universal, and potent.

I came to this story through Matthew Paris, one of the most famous chroniclers of his time. Matthew Paris was an English monk who lived at the Benedictine monastery of St. Albans. He was born in 1200 and died in 1259. He began his chronicle in 1235, writing with a goose quill on parchment. He was an artist as well, and the pages of his journal are decorated with wonderful illustrations. Many of these have been published in *The Illustrated Chronicles of Matthew Paris: Observations of Thirteenth-Century Life,* translated and edited by Richard Vaughan. This book is readily available and serves as a useful introduction to the time period.

For those who want to go deeper, however, I highly recommend *Matthew Paris's English History, from the Year 1235 to 1273,* translated from the Latin by the Rev. J. A. Giles, D.C.L., Late Fellow of Corpus Christi College, Oxford. (Another monk undertook to continue the work after Matthew Paris's death, which is why the chronicle goes to 1273.) This work comes in three volumes and is much more comprehensive. Matthew Paris was a keen political observer and his journal is filled with stories of Henry and Eleanor's court and their numerous dealings with Richard of Cornwall, Simon de Montfort, the English aristocracy, and many of the other illustrious individuals who play roles in *Four Queens.* The author has a biting wit and a definite point of view, which must be taken into account when striving for objectivity, but the underlying information is reliable. It was while reading this set lying in bed one evening that I first stumbled across the story of the four sisters from Provence who all became queens and immediately became fascinated. I cannot recommend this work highly enough. Matthew Paris's is a voice that reaches out across seven hundred and fifty years.

Another chronicle upon which I relied for information about thirteenth-century England was *The Chronicle of Bury St Edmunds, 1212–1301,* edited and translated by Antonia Gransden. *The Chronicle of Bury St Edmunds* was not written by a single individual, but seems rather to have been the work of many monks over time. It is a much more declarative document, lacking the detail, flavor, and complexity of Matthew Paris's work, but it was very useful for confirming or supporting events described by other sources and in its way provides a picture and opinion of the time. If *The Chronicle of Bury St Edmunds,* which apparently prided itself on its brevity, went out of its way to mention that in 1260 Simon de Monfort was the acknowledged leader of the barons, then he probably was.

Letters and edicts were also an important source of information. Some of Eleanor's letters have been translated and reprinted in *Letters of the Queens of England,* edited by Anne Crawford (Sutton Publishing, 2002). An excellent source of material was a two-volume set entitled *Royal and Other Historical Letters Illustrative of the Reign of Henry III,* edited by Walter Waddington Shirley (London, Longman, 1862), which includes all the public letters available from the time, known as the Royal Letters. Although they are republished in the original Latin or French, they have been ordered by date (*very* helpful) and summarized in English. Similarly, *Documents of the Baronial Movement of Reform and Rebellion, 1258–1267,* selected by R. E. Treharne and edited by I. J. Sanders (Oxford: Clarendon Press, 1973), provides an in-depth look at the primary sources documenting the story of Simon de Montfort's spectacular rise and fall. Still another source of printed primary material upon which I relied was *Foedera, Conventiones, Litterae, et Cujuscunque Genens Acta Publica* (London, 1816), which sounds terribly difficult but was actually a treat, as it was here I found the report of Henry's marriage contract to Eleanor and his instructions to his emissaries about foregoing the dowry, for example, as well as many references to the Savoyards that supported evidence as to their whereabouts and influence.

Eleanor's complete correspondence, including letters to and from Marguerite, have been ordered by date and listed in Series SC 1 (Ancient correspondence of the Chancery and Exchequer), published by the Public Record Office in London. Photos of the letters are available on microfilm. Unfortunately, however, many of the originals, as might be expected from parchment so old, are torn, faded, and dirty, and therefore very difficult to decipher. As a result, there are a number of letters that have yet to be translated. It is a very big job and one I hope will be accomplished in the future.

I was luckier with Marguerite; a large number of her letters have been published in volume one of *Lettres de Rois, Reines et Autres Personnages des Cours de France et D'Angleterre,* edited by J. J. Champollion-Figeac (Paris: Imprimerie Royale, 1839). They, too, have been catalogued by date and appear in the original Latin, although they are also helpfully summarized in French. The volume and breadth of Marguerite's correspondence, particularly after Louis's death in 1270, were a potent indication of her influence (and literacy).

There are also excellent French chronicles to savor. Chief among these is Jean de Joinville's *Life of Saint Louis,* which has been reprinted by Penguin Classics under the title *Chronicles of the Crusades,* translated by M. R. B. Shaw. Joinville was a life-long friend of Louis IX, and accompanied him on his first crusade. His eyewitness recollections of that experience, although written after the fact, are compelling and immediate, and constitute our best source of material on France and the Egyptian crusade during the reign of Louis and Marguerite. Another French chronicler whose work I also enjoyed, and who substantiated much of what transpired during the first half of Louis's reign, was *The Chronicle of Reims,* written by an unknown minstrel in 1260. This was translated into English in 1937 by Edward Noble Stone.

To add depth and perspective to Joinville's account of the crusade of Louis IX, I turned to the Arab chroniclers of the period. Their work is published and translated in two outstanding books: *The Crusades Through Arab Eyes* by Amin Maalouf, translated by Jon Rothschild (New York: Schocken Books, 1984) and *Arab Historians of the Crusades,* translated from the Arabic by Francesco Gabrieli and from the Italian by E. J. Costello (New York: Dorset Press, 1957). I can recommend both of these compilations as highly informative and enlightening.

For events in Italy and Provence I used the chronicle of Salimbene de Adam, a Franciscan friar and contemporary of Louis, Marguerite, Charles of Anjou, and Beatrice of Provence. Salimbene is as famous as Matthew Paris and his wit is just as delicious. He narrates many salacious anecdotes, which unfortunately I did not have room to quote. They give a flavor for the times that does not often appear in medieval textbooks. In addition to being an eyewitness, Salimbene went out of his way to show both sides of an individual's character, which lends credibility and astuteness to his observations. He does have a habit of quoting the scriptures extensively, however, so it takes a little time to get through his chronicle, but his insights are worth the effort.

The other chronicler I used for Italy and Provence was Giovanni Villani. Villani began his chronicle in 1300, a little after the fact, but it is the source for much of what we know of Raymond Berenger V, the four queens, Charles of Anjou, Manfred, and Conradin, among others. Dante himself relied on Villani's account to provide material for *The Divine Comedy,* and what was good enough for Dante was good enough for me.

Although I have also provided a selected bibliography, I want to highlight a few of my secondary sources as well, just in case someone whose interest I might have piqued with this narrative wants to read a fuller treatment of any particular character or event. Above all, I am indebted to Margaret Howell's authoritative, comprehensive biography *Eleanor of Provence: Queenship in Thirteenth-Century England* (Oxford: Blackwell, 1998). Howell's research was meticulous. She sifted through all of Eleanor's records and there isn't a silver spoon or gold ring that the queen acquired or gave away, no church living or property presented, no legal document, ruling, or royal decree pertaining to her life or those of her varied acquaintance that is not accounted for. Howell made a brilliant catch in dating a letter from Marguerite to Henry as having been written and sent in October 1265, which every other medieval historian had incorrectly dated as October 1235. It is difficult to believe that any future scholar will materially improve on her effort.

The same cannot be said of the only biography of Marguerite that I was able to find: Gérard Sivéry's *Marguerite de Provence: Une reine au temps des Cathédrales* (Librairie Arthème Fyard, 1987). This comes billed as an "interpretative" biography, a term with which I was previously unfamiliar, but which apparently means long on supposition and short on research. Marguerite's life merits a much more studious and rigorously researched investigation. There are no biographies of either Sanchia or Beatrice of Provence extant in any language.

Biographies of the sisters' husbands, although numerous, vary in quality. The most comprehensive (and stirring) account of Henry III's life is the two-volume *King Henry III and the Lord Edward: The Community of the Realm in the Thirteenth Century* by the great Oxford historian F. M. Powicke (Oxford: Clarendon Press, 1947). Similarly, by far the most detailed and objective work on Louis IX is *Saint Louis: Crusader King of France* by Jean Richard. I used the edition edited and abridged by Simon Lloyd and translated into English by Jean Birrell (Cambridge University Press, Editions de la Maison des Sciences de l'Homme, Paris, 1992), now unfortunately out of print. The biographies of both Richard of Cornwall and Charles of Anjou, N. Denholm-Young's *Richard of Cornwall* and Jean Dunbabin's *Charles I of Anjou: Power, Kingship and State-Making in Thirteenth-Century Europe,* respectively, are adequate but no more: there is room for more nuanced, detailed treatments of both men.

Lastly, I must recommend Eugene L. Cox's *The Eagles of Savoy: The House of Savoy in Thirteenth-Century Europe* (Princeton University Press, 1974) as a work of unequaled scholarship. Cox researched the lives of all of the sisters' Savoyard uncles, as well as that of their mother, Beatrice of Savoy, and their grandparents Thomas and Marguerite of Savoy. It was a tremendous effort that brought to light much new and original information. It is a crime that this book is out of print.

SELECTED BIBLIOGRAPHY

Archambault, Paul. *Seven French Chroniclers: Witnesses to History.* Syracuse, NY: Syracuse University Press, 1974.

Axton, Richard, and John Stevens, translators. *Medieval French Plays.* Oxford: Basil Blackwell, 1971.

Baird, Joseph L., Giuseppe Baglivi, and John Robert Kane, editors and translators. *The Chronicle of Salimbene de Adam.* Binghamton, NY: Medieval & Renaissance Texts & Studies, 1986.

Baratier, Édouard, Édouard Privat, editor. *Histoire de la Provence.* Univers de la France: Collection d'histoire régionale, 1969.

Beamish, Tufton. *Battle Royal: A New Account of Simon de Montfort's Struggle Against King Henry III.* London: Frederick Muller Limited, 1965.

Bell, Mary I. M. *A Short History of the Papacy.* New York: Dodd, Mead and Company, 1921.

Bisson, T. N. *The Medieval Crown of Aragon: A Short History.* Oxford: Clarendon Press, 1986.

Bloch, Marc, L. S. Manyon, translator. *Feudal Society.* Chicago: University of Chicago Press, 1961.

Bowers, Richard H., editor. *Seven Studies in Medieval English History and Other Historical Essays.* Jackson: University Press of Mississippi, 1983.

Cantor, Norman F. *The Civilization of the Middle Ages.* New York: HarperPerennial, 1994.

Champollion-Figeac, J. J., editor. *Lettres de Rois, Reines et Autres Personnages des cours de France et d'Angleterre.* Paris: Imprimerie Royale, 1839.

Cox, Eugene L. *The Eagles of Savoy: The House of Savoy in Thirteenth-Century Europe.* Princeton: Princeton University Press, 1974.

Crawford, Anne, editor. *Letters of the Queens of England.* Somerset, UK: Sutton Publishing, 2002.

Denholm-Young, N. *Richard of Cornwall*. New York: William Salloch, 1947.

Duby, Georges, Cynthia Postan, translator. *The Chivalrous Society*. Berkeley: University of California Press, 1977.

Durant, Will. *The Age of Faith: A History of Medieval Civilization—Christian, Islamic, and Judaic—from Constantine to Dante: A.D. 325-1300*. New York: Simon & Schuster, 1950.

Erickson, Carolly. *The Medieval Vision: Essays in History and Perception*. New York: Oxford University Press, 1976.

Erler, Mary, and Maryanne Kowaleski, editors. *Women and Power in the Middle Ages*. Athens, GA: The University of Georgia Press, 1988.

Funck-Brentano, Fr., Elizabeth O'Neill, translator. *The National History of France: The Middle Ages*. New York: AMS Press, Inc., 1967.

Gabrieli, Francesco, editor and translator from the Arabic, E. J. Costello, translator for the Italian. *Arab Historians of the Crusades*. New York: Dorset Press, 1957.

Gies, Frances, and Joseph Gies. *Women in the Middle Ages: The Lives of Real Women in a Vibrant Age of Transition*. New York: Barnes and Noble Books, 1978.

Giles, Rev. J. A., translator. *Matthew Paris's English History from the Year 1235 to 1273*, vols. I–III. London: Henry G. Bohn, 1852.

Goldin, Frederick, translator. *Lyrics of the Troubadours and Trouvères: An Anthology and History*. New York: Anchor Books, 1973.

Gransden, Antonia, editor and translator. *The Chronicle of Bury St Edmunds 1212–1301*. London, Thomas Nelson and Sons Ltd., 1964.

Guant, Simon, and Sarah Kay, editors. *The Troubadours: An Introduction*. Cambridge: Cambridge University Press, 1999.

Hedeman, Anne D. *The Royal Image: Illustrations of the Grandes Chroniques de France 1274–1422*. Berkeley: University of California Press, 1991.

Hilton, R. H. *English and French Towns in Feudal Society: A Comparative Study*. Cambridge: Cambridge University Press, 1992.

Hourani, Albert. *A History of the Arab Peoples*. Cambridge, MA: Belknap Press, 1991.

Howell, Margaret. *Eleanor of Provence: Queenship in Thirteenth-Century England*. Oxford: Blackwell Publishers, 1998.

Humphreys, R. Stephen. *From Saladin to the Mongols: The Ayyūbids of Damascus, 1193–1260*. Albany: State University Press of New York, 1977.

Joinville and Villehardouin, M.R.B. Shaw, translator. *Chronicles of the Crusades*. New York: Penguin Books, 1963.

Kantorowicz, Ernst, E.O. Lorimer, translator. *Frederick the Second, 1194–1250*. New York: Frederick Ungar Publishing, 1957.

Labarge, Margaret Wade. *Saint Louis: The Life of Louis IX of France*. Toronto: Macmillan of Canada, 1968.

———. *Simon de Montfort*. Toronto: Macmillan of Canada, 1962.

Lecoy de la Marche, A. *La France sous Saint Louis et sous Philippe le Hardi*. Paris: Ancieene Maison Quantin, Librairies-Imprimeries Réunies, 1893.

Lindsay, Jack. *The Troubadours and Their World of the Twelfth and Thirteenth Centuries*. London: Grederick Muller Limited, 1976.

Lorris, Guillaume de, and Jean de Meun, Charles Dunn, editor, Harry W. Robbins, translator. *The Romance of the Rose*. New York: E. P. Dutton, 1962.

Maddox, Donald, and Sara Sturm-Maddox, editors. *Literary Aspects of Courtly Culture: Selected Papers from the Seventh Triennial Congress of the International Courtly Literature Society*. Cambridge: D. S. Brewer, 1994.

Muir, Lynette R. *Literature and Society in Medieval France: The Mirror and the Image, 1100–1500*. New York: St. Martin's Press, 1985.

Musa, Mark, editor. *The Portable Dante*. New York: Penguin Books, 2003.

O'Shea, Stephen. *The Perfect Heresy: The Revolutionary Life and Death of the Medieval Cathars*. New York: Walker & Company, 2000.

Paterson, Linda M. *The World of the Troubadours: Medieval Occitan society, c. 1100– c. 1300*. Cambridge: Cambridge University Press, 1993.

Pernoud, Régine, Henry Noel, translator. *Blanche of Castile*. New York: Coward, McCann & Geoghegan, Inc., 1975.

Powicke, F. M. *King Henry III and the Lord Edward: The Community of the Realm in the Thirteenth Century*. Oxford: Clarendon Press, 1947.

Powicke, Sir Maurice. *The Thirteenth Century: 1216–1307*. Oxford: Clarendon Press, 1953.

Quatriglio, Giuseppe, Justin Vitiello, translator. *A Thousand Years in Sicily: From the Arabs to the Bourbons*. Aster Bay, Ottowa, Canada: Legas, 1997.

Richard, Jean, Simon Lloyd, editors, Jean Birrell, translator. *Saint Louis: Crusader King of France*. Cambridge: Cambridge University Press, 1992.

Ricketts, Peter T., editor. *Les Poésies de Guilhem de Montanhagol: Troubadour Provençal du XIII Siècle*. Toronto: Pontifical Institute of Mediaeval Studies, 1964.

Rothwell, W., W. R. J. Barron, David Blamires, and Lewis Thorpe, editors. *Studies in Medieval Literature and Languages: In Memory of Frederick Whitehead*. Manchester, UK: Manchester University Press, 1973.

Runciman, Steven. *The Sicilian Vespers: A History of the Mediterranean World in the Later Thirteenth Century*. Cambridge: Cambridge University Press, 1958.

Saint-Pathus, Guillaume de, M. S. d'Espagne, editor. *La Vie et Les Miracles de Monseigneur Saint-Louis*. Paris: Les Editions du Cèdre, 1971.

Scattergood, V. J., and J. W. Sherbone, editors. *English Court Culture in the Later Middle Ages*. New York: St. Martin's Press, 1983.

Sell, Edward, D. D. *The 'Ayyb and Mamluk Sultans*. London: Church Missionary Society, Diocesan Press, 1929.

Shirley, Walter Waddington, editor. *Royal and Other Historical Letters Illustrative of the Reign of Henry III*. Vaduz: Kraus Reprint LTD, 1965.

Spufford, Peter. *Money and Its Use in Medieval Europe*. Cambridge: Cambridge University Press, 1988.

Stone, Edward Noble, translator. *Three Old French Chronicles of the Crusades*. Seattle: University of Washington Press, 1939.

Treharne, R. E., and I. J. Sanders, editors. *Documents of the Baronial Movement of Reform and Rebellion, 1258–1267*. Oxford: Clarendon Press, 1973.

Walsh, P. G., editor and translator. *Andreas Capellanus on Love*. London: Gerald Duckworth & Co., Ltd., 1993.

Warren, W. L. *King John*. New York: W. W. Norton & Company, 1961.

Weigand, Hermann J. *Three Chapters on Courtly Love in Arthurian France and Germany*. Chapel Hill: University of North Carolina Press, 1956.

Weiss, Daniel H. *Art and Crusade in the Age of Saint Louis*. Cambridge: Cambridge University Press, 1998.

LIST OF ILLUSTRATION CREDITS

ACKNOWLEDGMENTS

I am indebted to a number of people without whose help *Four Queens* would not have been possible. Sue Madeo, the Interlibrary Loan Coordinator at the Westport Public Library, was instrumental in convincing research librarians at other Connecticut facilities to lend me the often rare and expensive volumes of medieval history that I needed to complete my manuscript. David Smith at the New York Public Library helped me comb the off-site listings for obscure material and then took care that the books be available quickly so that I could make the most of my trips into the city. Gill Cannell at the Parker Library at Corpus Christi College in Cambridge was very supportive of this project, and I am deeply grateful to the Parker Library for generously providing the bulk of the illustrations. Rigmore Batsvik at the Bodleian Library at Oxford spent hours searching through slides; Zoubida Zerkane at the Bibliothèque nationale de France and Thierry Dewin of the Bibliothèque royale de Belgique were also of great assistance in locating material. At the British Library, Chris Rawlings, Maz Karim, and Nikki Drydale were so efficient and accommodating that I felt as though I were dealing with my local library and not a prestigious institution several thousand miles across the Atlantic.

I must give a very special thank-you to Nancy Reinertz-Sjöblom in Luxembourg, who helped me with some original translations from the French. Although the troubadour poem she translated did not, in the end, make it into the manuscript, my understanding of the period was much enhanced by knowledge of its contents and she was invaluable in helping me to understand the nuances of some of Marguerite's letters. Also, I am indebted to Wendy Kann, who read the manuscript as carefully as though it were one of her own and whose comments and advice added appreciably to the depth and color of the manuscript.

I would like to thank my agent, Henry Dunow, for his unfailing support of this project and all of the people at Viking who helped, including Jane von Mehren, Caroline White, and Karen Anderson. I am especially grateful to my editor, Carolyn Carlson, who inherited *Four Queens* at a late date but who nonetheless treated it like it was always her own.

Last, there is my family, without whose unconditional support and patience this book would not have been possible. My husband Larry's contribution to *Four Queens* is immeasurable—everything from a painstaking explanation of military strategy using football analogies to a nonsentimental, highly professional reading, which resulted in a tangible improvement in the tone and narrative. Similarly, my daughter Emily's encouragement and enthusiasm—she often gave up her own time to listen to me read aloud from the manuscript—was a gift that I will not soon forget. I love you both.

INDEX